The Wanderers

The Wanderers
Tales of Wandering in the African Bush

by
Hoffman Theron van Zijl

SAFARI PRESS INC.

The trademark Safari Press ® is registered with the U.S. Patent and Trademark Office and with government trademark and patent offices in other countries.

Zijl, Hoffman Theron van

Second edition

Safari Press

2015, Long Beach, California

ISBN 978-1-57157-477-0

Library of Congress Catalog Card Number: 2014947213

10 9 8 7 6 5 4 3 2 1

Printed in China

Readers wishing to see Safari Press's many fine books on big-game hunting, wingshooting, and sporting firearms should visit our Web site at www.safaripress.com

For Gerhard

Table of Contents

Foreword

"There are places you need to see before it's all gone," says Denys Finch Hatton to Karen Blixen in the movie *Out of Africa* as he tries to persuade her to join him on a safari to some remote region in East Africa shortly after the First World War. Generation after generation of hunters and explorers felt the same way as they witnessed the Africa they once loved swept away by the "Winds of Change." The Dark Continent filled with wild animals in pristine wilderness areas far from the madding crowd, where you could wander freely on your own in search of great adventure, is no more.

This is a collection of stories about the wanderings of two lifelong friends who had the courage to live their dreams in some of the last remaining wilderness areas left in southern Africa. As boys, Hoffman and Gerhard's dreams were sparked by the hunting stories of family and friends as well as the writings of South African hunters such as P. J. Schoeman and Sangiro (pen name of A. A. Pienaar), and Englishmen such as Selous, Neumann, Bell, Sutherland, and Taylor. They both lived by Teddy Roosevelt's motto: "Far better it is to dare mighty things, to win glorious triumphs, even though checkered by failure, than to take rank with those poor spirits who neither enjoy much nor suffer much because they live in the gray twilight that knows not victory nor defeat."

In conclusion I would like to thank Hoffman for the homage he paid to my late brother, Gerhard, in this wonderful book.

Dr. Johan Bolt

Introduction

During the early 1970s, two boyhood friends emerged into early manhood, and, sensing their newfound freedom and means, eagerly launched into satisfying the yearnings for adventure that had filled so many hours of their innocent boyhood discussions.

They were both driven by nostalgia for the undiscovered reaches of their fascinating continent, Africa, and for the life lived by the great hunter-explorers of the first part of the twentieth century. Their first expeditions, driven by a youthful fervor for hunting dangerous game, were perhaps overly ambitious and not all that well conceived, sometimes clumsy, even irresponsibly dangerous. These trips were often disappointing, leaving them frustrated that their attempts had yet again fallen short, that their mystic goal, true African adventure, had yet again eluded them, had remained beyond the reach of their as-yet-limited means and experience.

But as they matured, they came to understand that their longing was for the spirit of the distant and untouched African bush, that it was for going "about as far as man can go"* as much as it was for the hunt itself. As their means grew and their companionship deepened, their expeditions became, although ever more ambitious and daring, less feverish and more satisfying, more wholesome. (*Borrowed from a seventies-era cigarette ad, popular with the companions.)

This is their story.

++++++

In writing of our individual and joint experiences, I was driven by a new nostalgia for the times we spent together and by a deep sense of loss and sadness for my late companion, Gerhard Bolt. What you are about to read are the tales of a particular expedition into Mozambique that we took during the late 1980s. Although some names have been changed out of respect for privacy and although memory may have faded somewhat on the exact details here and there, these accounts are essentially factual.

The Journey

I t was around two o'clock in the afternoon. The rains had not yet come, and the Zambezi Valley was dry and dusty and seething with heat and the endless screams of cicadas. Gerhard and I had taken refuge under a clump of bush willow that had enough leaves left to cast a pool of cool shadow. We were slurping the tea we had just brewed, and swatting at the tsetse, each trying to cope with a numbing drowsiness from the heat and the effects of a relentless old male lion that had kept us company for most of last night around our roadside camp.

Running across our front was a bush airstrip, its far western end twisting in the mirage. Looking out over it stirred some old memories, and I felt the adrenaline froth at the base of my chest as I reflected on how it once must have been here—tense with action, filled with the whip of rotor blades, the images of paratroopers running through the dusty haze to their transports, and the stutter of the Dakota's twin engines as it taxied out . . . but now it was deserted and silent and hot. The mopane trees had pushed their branches into the sun-filled space, and here and there tufts of grass had taken root in the unforgiving gravel surface. Few pilots would grant it airstrip status.

We had started out from Pretoria two days earlier. We took the northern highway through the Springbok Flats and the Waterberg hill country, and then through the dry bush land north of Polokwane. We had tea and scones on the terrace of the Clouds End Hotel in the Soutpansberg, enjoying the beautiful panorama of the savanna stretching southward till it hazed into the vast sky. Then we droned on, the Land Cruiser laboring through the steep valleys of the berg, finally stumbling, panting, onto the endless dry northern mopane plains toward the Limpopo.

After jostling our way through a crowded border, we had just a short drive through the Zimbabwe lowveld before we reached the Nuanetsi Valley. We spent the night at the Lion and Elephant Inn on the bank of the Bubi River. It was our usual stopover on trips like these—a basic but pleasant enough hotel (motel), its thatched double rondavels cool in white and green on the lawns under giant acacias. Moreover, the locals that came in for sundowners usually made interesting conversation, and presented the off chance of getting a hunt organized somewhere in the valley.

The next day we climbed up to the grass plains of the Zimbabwe highlands toward Harare, and from there northward toward Mushumbi. At some point the tar gave way to a strip road (only two tracks surfaced), finally giving up altogether and leaving us on a narrow dirt road not much more than a track. By sunset we had dropped into the Zambezi Valley, and, dusty and tired from being rattled and knocked around in the old Land Cruiser, we drove some five hundred yards off the road into the bush and slung our hammocks for the night—oblivious, of course, to the presence of the old lion, which subsequently made it his business to prowl and grunt around the camp, eventually having us resign ourselves, cursing, to make do in the cramped confines of the Land Cruiser cabin.

++++++

Sitting there sleepless and uncomfortable, we were reminded of a similar situation we had been in during an expedition we had made into Botswana in an ancient little Series II Land Rover during the early 1970s. We were heading out to explore the Okavango area, and on the second day of our journey, some way past Gweta on the edge of the Makgadikgadi Pans, the setting sun told us it was time to make camp. The road between Nata and

Maun, now a high-speed tar road, was then just a track that got dragged smooth with old tires strung behind a farm tractor once a month or so, and one couldn't average much more than about twenty-five miles per hour on it. Gweta, now a sizable little town sporting some paved streets, then consisted of just one or two small general-purpose shops and a collection of mud huts on either side of the track.

We had driven away from the road a few hundred yards and found a nice tree under which to make camp. There were no humans for miles, but a lot of sign of game. We gathered a large pile of wood for the night, and once we had everything organized we settled down to grill some meat we had bought in Francistown that morning.

We were busy chatting away unconcernedly when I noticed something moving just beyond the glow of the camp. We promptly got out our Winchester spotlights (the classic 1960s/1970s model with the matte-black belt-mounted battery pack and detachable lamp that could be fastened to the forehead with an elastic band, which we firmly believed to be the only type of spotlight worthy of our type of adventuring) and probed the darkness. But we couldn't see anything, so we went back to our routine. We were little more than boys fresh out of secondary school at the time, and although we had both spent a lot of time in the veld, we were still relatively inexperienced, and we decided that it must have been my imagination.

But soon Gerhard also noticed a vague shape moving, and then there was a deep growl. We hastily moved closer to the fire and trained our spotlights in the general direction. This time we briefly caught at least three pairs of wide-set eyes in the beams. We were now quite certain that there were lions around the camp.

Partly out of ignorance, partly out of misplaced youthful bravado, and partly because we were really excited to be out alone in the wild, and actually (foolishly) thrilled at being surrounded by lions, we convinced each other that the fire would keep them away. We promptly added some wood and continued with our activities, albeit now with considerable unease, and carefully restricting our movements to the area between the fire and the vehicle.

Gerhard had smuggled an old single-barrel bolt-action 12-gauge shotgun across the border, for which we had bought some No. 3 shot for the odd guinea fowl we might come across, and some slugs for when things got really nasty. We placed that handy on the Land Rover's mudguard, loaded with No. 3 shot, which we decided would be sufficient discouragement for a foolishly inquisitive lion.

What we did not understand was that there was regular contact between these lions, living, as it were, on the fringes of human habitation, and the odd human in the area, and that they were quite used to humans and not averse to prey on them when the opportunity presented itself. We also had not yet experienced how the same lions that would run away from a person during the day could become fearlessly predatory when it got dark.

We were constantly aware of them, prowling and occasionally grunting around the camp as we had our meal, sitting with our backs against the vehicle and facing the fire. The occasional probe with a spotlight revealed that there were probably about four or five, which should have been another warning sign to us.

We both expected them to leave after a while, and when they didn't we became more uncertain and scared, but neither was prepared to admit it and suggest that we seek the safety of the cab. So we sat chatting bravely but uneasily for a while, the shotgun now lying across Gerhard's lap.

As the evening progressed the lions seemed to get bolder and noisier, coming closer to the fire so that we frequently could make out the brief suggestion of one in the glow. We were just beginning to wonder if we shouldn't depart for the cab when suddenly one female charged right into the light circle, growling—almost barking—fiercely! We were on our feet, shouting wildly, and Gerhard let her have it with the shotgun!

We don't know how much damage was done, but this unexpected fierce resistance from a normally fearful prey dented the collective self-confidence of the troupe a bit, and they retreated. It was now quiet and restful around our fire, but we had had enough. We were finally ready to admit that it was damn scary to be stalked by a determined pride of lions, and that the cab was clearly the sensible option. Later, when we were more experienced, we knew that we had been nothing but embarrassingly stupid that night.

++++++

Now we were sitting on the edge of this airstrip some miles south of the Zambezi River, close to the point where Zimbabwe, Zambia, and Mozambique meet, waiting for Frank to arrive. We had met Frank in a Sandton pub about eight weeks earlier. Gerhard and I immediately liked him. He looked completely out of place in that pretentious environment—lean and tough and a bit jagged, like a rawhide thong with a bit of hair left on it on display in a fancy fashion shop. He had been introduced by the Johannesburg-based agent of Game Trackers, the safari outfit we were going to hunt with. Frank was a freelance professional hunter who moonlighted for large safari outfits, but sometimes contracted directly with a client and then made a deal with some outfit to hunt with his client in their area.

This time he was flying in an American client for whom he had secured an elephant hunt in the concession of an outfitter named Danny. Danny was operating the concession area inside Mozambique just east of the Zimbabwe border, stretching from the Zambezi southward for some fifty miles. We had to pass through his concession to get to the Game Trackers one, which bordered Danny's to the west, and then ran eastward along the Zambezi for some sixty miles or so, and southward more or less to Zimbabwe's northern border—at least, this was the theory, and it may even have been recorded in some document in a dusty file far, far away in Maputo. But in bush as remote and as vast as this, concession borders were largely irrelevant, as were almost all other rules and laws. All that really counted were the realities of the bush and the honor (or lack thereof) of the men on the ground.

Frank's problems started when his client inquired about the inbound and outbound journeys. Frank had barely been able to convince him that it was OK to fly in with his little Cessna to a bush airstrip that was not on any map, but it was totally beyond his powers of persuasion to get the chap to agree that they would then be going down the Zambezi in a dugout canoe propelled by a mini outboard motor slung on the side. He was met with flat refusal. The client informed Frank that there were hippos and crocs in African rivers, and what was more, hippos were "responsible for most deaths by mauling in the African wilds," and "a canoe was not the proper vessel to go on them infested rivers."

No amount of reassurance or claims to local knowledge that Frank could offer would change his client's mind—and I guess one has to grant (with a smile) that he was not incorrect. Frank was worried he wouldn't be able to fit the rather big chap and all his paraphernalia in the narrow and devilishly unstable dugout anyway.

Roads in the area were nonexistent, and both outfitters operating in the area (Danny and Game Trackers) preferred using dugouts along the Zambezi– it made cutting and maintaining roads unnecessary, and it was a lot quicker than struggling through the bush by vehicle.

So we made a deal with Frank: We would give him and his client a ride to Danny's camp from the airstrip, and in return he would show us how to get there. We had planned to go to Danny's camp (which we thought to be about halfway to where we were going to hunt) to overnight and to confirm our direction. But we were unsure of its exact position, and Frank, having the advantage of the aerial view, and having hunted with Danny before, could be of assistance.

We (Gerhard and I) did not have the canoe option anyway, because the deal with Game Trackers was that we would bring our own safari, so we simply had to drive in. We had often operated like this in the past—bringing our own vehicle, gear, and food, and operating more or less on our own, even when hunting in a concession area. We had come to know a few operators quite well over the years, and we would take some of the game they had left on their license at the end of the season on such a special deal. We actually preferred operating in this fashion, around the fringes of the organized establishment, playing by our own rules.

Gerhard had stumbled across Dave, the South African agent for Game Trackers, by coincidence when the latter came around to buy safari equipment Gerhard was manufacturing in his little factory outside Pretoria. They started talking, and Dave, being rather eager to impress Gerhard with his status as a real bush man, offered lots of details about Game Trackers. Gerhard let him talk, and after a few well-placed questions, he smelled a deal.

Game Trackers was clearly in trouble. This was their first year in operation. It was almost the end of the season, and they had not secured a single hunt. Their American agent (who was also a shareholder, and responsible for filling their hunts) had arrived to shoot several animals in the concession, but had not been able to send them a single client, and with reason: Game Trackers had no proven track record, and American hunters were skeptical and worried about the war situation that they suspected (partly correctly) had not yet been cleared up completely.

At that time the bush war between RENAMO and FRELIMO in Mozambique had fizzled to endless bickering between their leaders at fancy venues while their followers drifted, lawless and frustrated, around the fringes of the tattered society in search of the nice things they thought they were now entitled to.

Game Trackers badly needed to demonstrate that they were able to deliver successful hunts. They needed photographs of hunters posing with their trophies to wave around at the hunting conventions that were soon coming up in the States. So Gerhard called me, and we made a deal with them. We would bring our own safari (vehicle, bush equipment, food, and so on). They would give us the use of their camp (staffed) and a professional hunter for a twenty-day period. We would pay them only the trophy fees for an elephant and a buffalo each, as well as the PH fee. It would not cost them anything more than they were already spending in operating expenses, and hopefully they would get to prove, with some nice photographs, that they had had successful hunts.

++++++

Our wait for Frank was getting a bit long. It reminded me of a similar wait some years earlier on a brooding-hot morning in the southeast of Zimbabwe. We had been hunting elephant in a vast stretch of sand veld to the south of the Gonarezhou Game reserve. There were several good bush tracks running through the area, and we used them to patrol the area for fresh tracks. It was a bit of a game of chance, but if we got lucky it could save us a lot of walking, we reasoned.

But the area was huge, and it took a lot of driving, and after a time we were beginning to run low on petrol. We decided we had to replenish our supply. We had passed a little roadside shop on our way into the area that had, to our surprise and delight, a 1940s-era hand-operated petrol pump with twin glass measuring cylinders—a real classic, still standing tall despite its faded red paint and dented body.

We loaded our forty-four-gallon drum (brought along for extra petrol) and left our camp at dawn, reaching the little shop just before noon. It turned out that they had run out of petrol, but we were given eager assurances by the proprietor, clearly not wanting to forego the opportunity of selling so much petrol in a single transaction, that "the truck it is coming." We decided it was probably worth waiting for a while, and we settled down in our chairs under the only reasonable tree in the area (a wild olive, if I recall correctly) to brew some tea.

Our host, a large, sweaty man with the front of his shirt hanging over his bulging tummy like a tent, sent us each a can of lukewarm Coke "on the house" just to show how generous he was toward his really big customers. The tracker we had brought along was a chap called Nyani. He was not the best tracker I had ever worked with, but he was a very pleasant chap with a brilliant smile and laughing eyes, and, like most Zimbabweans, able to speak good English. He was delighted because he ended up scoring the Cokes.

Once we had settled down with our tea, I had the opportunity to study our surroundings with more attention to detail. It is strange how the average Western mind tends to filter out all but the information directly connected to the mission or task at hand, and how we then often miss a lot of charming detail. Our tree was about sixty or so paces away from the shop, on the opposite side of a dusty track running eastward into the oblivion of the tribal area. The area around us was bare and dust-trodden except for a few defiant gray shrubs and faded mounds of donkey dung deposited by the few rather scrawny-looking specimens (even by donkey standards) that hung around listlessly for reasons unknown, because there certainly was nothing for them to eat.

The little shop was every bit as classic as the petrol pump. It offered anything from agricultural equipment and bicycle spares to warm beer and patent medicine, all safely ensconced behind a counter with a sturdy wire mesh barrier stretching from its countertop right up to the bare corrugated iron sheets of its roof. Its faded sign hanging from one corner, and its cracked front veranda and paint-starved walls with the red bricks showing here and there where the plaster had fallen off, testified that it had not seen any maintenance since being taken over by the present owner. (The previous owner had departed for South Africa or England or such.)

Besides the usual sunglass-sporting loafers posturing self-importantly on the front porch and a noisy group of men playing some game on the cement floor, oiled by generous quantities of beer, there were several resigned-looking people sitting in the narrow strip of shade along one wall. They all had bundles of stuff with them; one had a small wood and wire mesh cage with three chickens in it.

"Nyani, what are those people against the wall doing here?" I asked.

"They are waiting for the bus to come, sir." (Such delightful manners, most of those Zimbabwean chaps.)

"*Ah*, and when is the bus coming?"

"The bus is coming, sir"—a white, matter-of-fact smile.

I looked down the dusty track expectantly, but then realized that his answer didn't mean that arrival was imminent, just that it was expected, possibly this hour, possibly today, possibly tomorrow or the next day—at some time in the future.

"Nyani, the petrol truck—when do you think it is coming?"

"*Ah*, but it is coming, sir." The smile now showed a hint of uncertainty.

I turned to Gerhard and said, "You know what all of this means? It means that bloody truck could be arriving any time between now and next week."

Gerhard hadn't been paying much attention to my and Nyani's discussion, but he paid a lot of attention to my last remark.

"Damn, we'd better make another plan," he said indignantly.

"*Hmm.* Nyani, where else can we get petrol?" I inquired.

"Maybe we can get it at Mwenezi, sir."

"OK. How long will it take to drive there?"

He screwed his face into intense concentration. "*Uh,* maybe it can take three hours, sir."

"*Hmm.* Sounds like about forty to fifty miles," I quickly calculated.

"S---, that's quite a way. Do you think we can make it with the petrol we have in the tank?" Gerhard asked.

"Risky," I said, adding, "and if we got stuck between here and Mwenezi we'd be in real trouble. It could take days before we can get going again. But you know, I'm just thinking of something. Once, when I was a boy, I had to help out my great uncle—my grandfather's brother—on his farm. He farmed next door to us, and he would often send for me to come and help him, actually just to have someone convenient to send around. He had to deliver a load of hay, but his old GMC lorry was too low on petrol to make it to the nearest filling station. So my great uncle simply started it up and let it run warm, and then he added some diesel into the tank—just enough to get to the petrol station. The old truck was stuttering a bit, but as long as one kept the revs up it went."

Gerhard looked at me uncertainly, his eyes narrowed in disbelief. "You sure that wouldn't damage the engine?"

He softened his suspicions when he realized I wouldn't really do anything to jeopardize our vehicle.

"Not really. Of course if there was too much diesel in the petrol, it would simply not run."

"OK. Well, we don't have any diesel," he said, almost with relief.

"No, but maybe they have some at the store."

"OK, let's try!" Gerhard said gamely.

Our generous host took the news that the big petrol deal was off rather badly. He couldn't understand why on earth we were in such a hurry—after all, the truck was about to arrive anyway. He was absolutely convinced it was in our best interests to stay and wait. But we discovered to our (my) delight that the chap actually had a stock of power paraffin "at the pump." He explained that he used it for his pump engine, and he insisted that we accompany him to fetch some and take a look at the installation.

We set off behind his panting hulk along a well-worn footpath. It led to a little pump house that peered out apologetically from among some fiercely growing acacias on the edge of a depression that was treeless because it held water during the rainy season. It was of bricks, but part of one wall had been pushed over by a tree, and some of the roof sheets had been removed to cover something else more important. We couldn't actually get inside because the floor was swamped in a few inches of water from the leaking pump (our host explained that it only leaked "a little bit when it is running").

The engine was probably an ancient Lister, driving a turbine pump of uncertain origin through a single tattered V-belt, augmented by a makeshift strip of rawhide. In several places nuts or bolts were missing, or had been replaced with incorrectly sized ones, some unceremoniously driven in with a hammer, and generous use was made of wire to hold the contraption together. The whole installation was covered in a thick black layer of old oil and caked dust. It was a revelation just to witness (as an engineer) how equipment could somehow be kept functioning under conditions and for periods way beyond what could possibly have been foreseen by the designers. *Some of the industrial and agricultural equipment made by the British during the early part of the century was simply indestructible*, I thought.

Our host insisted that we observe it in operation. He instructed the "operator" that he had commandeered to accompany us to start it, while he remained safely outside on dry land with his guests to enjoy the show. The operator was clearly familiar with the starting drill. He first had to switch from power paraffin to petrol. The old Lister once had a two-way brass valve for this purpose, but that had long since been worn out beyond repair. The switch was now accomplished by simply pulling out and swapping the fuel line from the paraffin tank to the petrol, and plugging the paraffin line with a specially fashioned wooden plug removed from the petrol one.

I had looked around for the starting crank and noticed it lying half-submerged on the floor, battered almost beyond recognition by its various roles as hammer, crowbar, and the like over the years. It didn't look as if it had been used in any other but such secondary roles for a long time. I was right. The operator unceremoniously took a rawhide thong—about three meters long and soft as a piece of cloth from frequent use—off a wire hook on the roof, and proceeded to wind it several times around the large flywheel of the Lister. He then cranked the engine by pulling hard on the thong, showing great skill (no doubt perfected over many, many sweaty hours of trying) at rapidly altering his grip on the thong to keep up the tension on it. The venerable old machine caught and started chugging away gamely, and soon water began to spurt rather forcefully in all directions from the pump, causing the operator to bolt out of the structure to safety behind the wall.

The last bit of the complicated starting procedure was to swap back to paraffin once the old lady was well warmed up. This was again accomplished by the fuel hose-swapping routine, but of course the machine died when its supply of petrol was cut off, so the rawhide thong procedure had to be repeated, now on paraffin—but, having been warmed up, she caught on obligingly.

Our host's attitude was much improved by our astonished remarks and amused chuckling (the motivation for which he might have misunderstood somewhat), and especially by our announcement that we would buy a whole ten liters of power paraffin from him at (his) petrol price. He promptly instructed the drenched and rather dejected-looking operator to measure out the correct quantity and take it to our vehicle. But generosity is relative, and the two cans of Coke also suddenly made their appearance in the transaction.

We got the Land Cruiser going and let it run a bit before adding our power paraffin, plus a liter of methylated spirits and half a liter of sunflower cooking oil we had in the back. And then we took off, Gerhard driving as economically as possible without dropping the revs, and both of us holding our breaths and thumbs and rehearsing our prayers. We actually made it to

Mwenezi, stuttering and lurching a bit, and, to our relief, they had petrol there at the (slightly bigger) little store. We soon headed back, fortified by a Coke each from their fridge. When we drove past our little shop at dusk, the petrol truck had still not arrived.

++++++

Gerhard was just mumbling something about digging out his hammock from the back of the Land Cruiser so that he could sleep in comfort when we heard the drone of Frank's little Cessna above the screams of the cicadas. He had both of us anxiously on our feet as he brought it in, precariously dodging branches, but managing to get it down and stopped by the time he had run out of clearing at the far end, and with only a few ripped-off mopane shoots on the ground marking his path.

We drove up just as they were clambering down. Frank was completely unfazed. The American was putting up a brave front, but he had a funny color and he was trembling so much he had to steady himself with his hands on his knees, and he wasn't much help offloading or pushing the little plane under some large mopane.

I wished I could have been present when Frank introduced his (clearly wealthy and accustomed to a well-facilitated lifestyle) client to their means of transport. It must have taken quite some coaxing to get him onto the plane (Frank called it his Jeep), and somehow I suspected he wasn't going to be leaving the way he had come in. I must admit the "Jeep" looked a bit battered, even by African bush standards. The red and white paintwork was faded and rubbed off in places, the leading edges of the prop were visibly sandblasted, and the tires were smooth as Frank's shaven head. One had to assume that below the outer appearance it was "in excellent flying condition," as Frank assured us while we were hauling their stuff out and piling it onto the Land Cruiser. I quietly wondered if Frank really subjected it to all the required inspections and maintenance procedures, but I didn't ask. It seemed a bit of a sensitive point with Frank.

We headed northeast for the Mozambique border and a place on the map called Kanvemba, rumored to be the border post. Gerhard was driving, with the American next to him and Frank and I sitting on the back on our big food trunk. The track was quite recognizable and made a reasonable pace possible, but the shady spots along it seemed to be the favorite gathering alley for the entire tsetse population south of the Zambezi (and a few visitors from the north). They were giving Frank and me a hard time out in the open.

After a while we came to a fork, the one heading north, and the other turning more east. The north-leading one was clearly the one that would take us to the Zambezi, but taking the east-heading one seemed like the better way for us. However, this soon petered out into only faded signs of an old track here and there, and Frank and I had to get off regularly to search for it, or to chop off a branch or drag a fallen tree out the way. We soldiered on, and at some point we must have crossed the Zimbabwe/Mozambique border. I guess we should have met up with customs officials, but somehow we missed all of it, and we just carried on east.

The afternoon wore on into those special hours in an African bush day when the white-hot sun starts to soften into a friendlier orange, the heat begins to drop, and even the tsetse seem to retire for sundowners. We were traveling through some beautiful wild country. Huge fever berries, Ana trees, sausage trees, mahogany, leadwood, and wild mango stood out in the dense alluvial bush. We came across bushbuck, nyala, warthog, and small herds of waterbuck, and we saw lots of evidence of elephant and buffalo.

We reached Danny's camp after sunset. As often happens in such remote areas, his camp, being the only inhabited establishment for many miles, had become a sort of reference point and way station, and the (very) occasional traveler usually stopped over or even used it as a base for a time. In the fading light I could make out that it was a little shabby and not in a particularly nice spot. There were about eight or so dusty and tired-looking tents scattered around, serving to accommodate guests, clients, and professional hunters. Some thatch structures served as kitchen, store, and dining area. It had been a long and busy season in this remote area for Danny and his crew, and the guys were thinking more about getting back to civilization than keeping the camp neat. As we got to know Danny a little it became clear that a meticulously organized camp wasn't one of his top priorities anyway.

Danny came up to greet us: big and jovial and charming, with a booming voice. We declined his offer to share a tent with two young crocodile hunters operating out of his camp. They were working for an outfit that had a contract to hunt crocodiles on the Zambezi for their skins. Crocodile skins fetched excellent prices in markets in the East, where they got turned into fancy accessories for the rich. The two assured us they would be out on the river for most of the night, but we thought we shouldn't really interfere with the fine balance they had achieved between where they slept and where they stashed their empty bottles and cans, so we slung our hammocks a little out of the way under a clump of bush willow.

When we joined the hunting party at a cheerful fire a little later, we found Danny and his three PHs friendly and hospitable, and we were made to feel completely welcome and at ease. There were two other clients in camp besides our passenger—a Spaniard and another American, and four freelance crocodile hunters that used Danny's camp as a base. The latter worked at night and spent most of the day sleeping. The Spaniard was thin and reserved and proud, and perhaps a bit too serious, but I instinctively liked him. Frank's client was big and hung with big stuff and big talk. The other American chap seemed reasonably likable when one could catch him alone, but in the group he became rather anxious about his image and, especially toward his loud compatriot, took on a superior been-there, done-it-all attitude that was partly amusing and partly embarrassing. The bush guys focused on their jobs and bore it all with polite nods and smiles and just the occasional private grimace.

The conversation started with news for the guys in the bush from South Africa, then news for us from the bush, then hunting stories past and present, each triggering another, and each told and retold and examined in detail. It turned out Danny had had a really good season—several good trophies, including a sixty-pound and an eighty-pound bull elephant. Gerhard and I were relishing our prospects and were casting each other knowing glances. Later in the evening, as the flames flickered lower and men moved closer to the fire and the beer we had bought in Harare started to have more of an effect, the talk became less coherent and a lot louder and started drifting toward women and sport and cheap jokes—good reasons for leaving quietly for one's hammock and a good book.

As usual the hunting camp stirred well before dawn, with hunting vehicles grunting to life in the early morning chill, and PHs and trackers and camp hands scurrying in the glare of headlamps and the flicker of lanterns, and clients stomping around uncertainly, all trussed up in their hunting gear and generally getting in the way and on the nerves of the guys trying to get everything in order for the day's hunting.

Gerhard and I waited on the fringe of the activity until the hunters had left camp, then went to say good-bye to Danny before heading east. "Just keep on going east and don't go too far from the river. Stephan has his camp right on the water on the edge of a large grass plain. You should make it by sunset," Danny had shouted after us, his arms working like a traffic policeman at a busy intersection.

We roughly followed the Zambezi eastward, but moved some distance away from the river to avoid most of the dense riverine forest. The ground was rising to the south and tended to be more gravelly with rocky spots in places, and the bush was not as tall and dense. There were some quite large knob thorns, milkwood, green thorns, brown ivory, mahogany, and mopane, with groves of white seringa and panga panga here and there on the rocky rises. All these mingled with flame thorn, koodooberry, bush willow, mopane shrubbery, raisin bush, buffalo thorn and, of course, the inevitable sicklebush.

It soon turned into another mercilessly hot day, and we had to work quite hard to make reasonable progress. We both understood that the vehicle was a crucial piece of bush equipment, and, as always, we tried to spare it as much as possible, driving carefully, avoiding really bad spots if we could, taking turns with the machete and the bush pick to clear a path ahead where necessary, ramping or filling or bridging the dongas with logs or stones, and all the time doing our best to stay clear of the sicklebush thorns. The vehicle still had to do most of the rough work though, and we both gained new respect for the amount of punishment the Land Cruiser could take without any sign of mechanical degradation.

When we got to the Panhame River we had to turn south for several miles to find a place to cross, but even then the heavily loaded Land Cruiser got stuck in the deep river sand and we had to dig it out and carry some stuff across by hand.

As we finally stood panting on the other side of the river, surveying our deep tracks through the sand, Gerhard said: "Remember that time when we got stuck with the buffalo on the back?"

"*Ja*," I chuckled. "It was quite similar, wasn't it?"

++++++

We were hunting buffalo and elephant in the Nuanetsi Valley in Zimbabwe. It was late November, and some heavy rain had fallen during the previous week, leaving the veld with pans of standing water, and just soggy in some patches.

I had shot a really good buffalo early that morning, and we had it on the back of the Land Cruiser, heading for our camp on the banks of the Nuanetsi. When we loaded the buffalo we had our tracker with us, but we had subsequently sent him off to go and check a leopard bait that Gerhard had set up the day before. We didn't have any special loading gear, and with only the three of us it had been a muscle strain of note to get the buffalo onto the back of the Land Cruiser—we had barely managed, even after splitting the carcass behind the rib cage and loading the two parts separately.

Gerhard and I were picking our way through the bush quite handily when suddenly, without any warning, the ground simply seemed to give way below the vehicle, and we came to an unplanned standstill. We first tried to ignore the obvious; perhaps, by applying the usual tricks like

17

rocking a bit back and then forward, or reversing, we could get out without even getting our feet in the mud, but we were stuck! Investigation confirmed our worst fears: We were down to our axles, about twelve feet into a soft patch some forty yards wide. It looked firm on the surface, but it was rotten-soft underneath. It probably had some impermeable rock below ground that prevented the water from draining away. It was simply slosh in soil disguise!

We had a bush pick, a hand ax, a shovel, and a high-lift jack with us, but no winch. One could use the high-lift jack as a makeshift winch in emergencies, but it is tedious because the available travel along its lifting shaft is limited, which means one has to frequently stop and shorten the anchor chain. We decided it would be best to try to get out backward.

We first tried to jack the rear of the vehicle up with the high-lift so that we could pack some branches under the rear wheels, but the chassis was so deep into the mud that we couldn't get the jack under a suitable lift point at the back. We had to dig a sizable hole half under the vehicle, which required considerable effort in the sticky stuff, and fashion a sort of platform from logs and branches that we had chopped for the jack to stand on. This didn't work, because despite our best efforts we couldn't get the platform stable enough in the yielding material, so the jack kept slipping off it and pressing into the mud instead of lifting the vehicle.

We then decided that we should take the buffalo off the truck to make the vehicle lighter, and perhaps we would then be able to lift it with the jack. It was by then around twelve o'clock, and, as is usually the case after rain, the sun had an especially vicious sting to it. Taking off the buffalo and dragging it away from the back of the vehicle required a strenuous effort in the knee-deep mud, and of course our efforts were soon salted with ever more richly flavored swear words as the heat and the exertion began to take effect. However, our jack-on-platform plan still didn't work—it wasn't the weight that was the problem; it was the softness of the mud.

We then decided that we had a chance to winch it out backward if we tied the top of the jack to the vehicle, and its lift point to an anchor outside the muddy area. Unfortunately the nearest anchor point was too far away to reach with the length of chain we had with us, and the piece of heavy duty cargo webbing we used to extend it had so much stretch in it that all of the (limited) travel on the jack was taken up by stretch, and none by vehicle-moving-out-of-mud.

It was by then getting into the afternoon, and we were highly frustrated and short tempered, which was not good for the friendship. We decided to sit down and rest a bit under a tree. We were victims of the law of diminishing options. With all the struggling around the vehicle the area had become even more slushy, so that getting out was becoming ever more difficult. We probably had one more chance left before our situation would become really desperate. So it had to be a really good plan. We decided we would carefully formulate the options and then decide on the best one.

It seemed we had three options: We could bury the spare wheel to the rear of the vehicle in firm ground, but close enough so that we could hitch it to the jack with just the chain, and then simply jack the vehicle out backward as we had previously attempted unsuccessfully with the webbing. This was feasible, but it would require quite a lot of digging, and there was always the chance that we would not be able to bury the wheel deep enough, and it would just be pulled out of its hole when we applied real force. The second option was digging a large enough hole behind the vehicle to place the wheel in, and then use it as a platform to place the jack on, and execute our original plan of lifting the rear so that we could put material under the wheels. This was feasible, but it would require as much digging as with burying the wheel, but up to the knees in really sticky material, and half underneath the vehicle too. On top of that, the process might have to be repeated if we couldn't get it out in one go. It seemed too ghastly to consider. Our third option was simply for me to run back to camp, get as many people together as I could, and have them come push us out. It was about nine miles to camp, so running was not a problem at all, but we weren't sure that the three people we had in camp would be enough to push the vehicle out—the mud where we would have to find footholds was very soft and slippery by now. All three options had a chance, but none seemed close to certain.

Then, after some staring at the vehicle and scratching of the chins and fed-up sighing, we came up with another option: We would use the spare wheel as a jacking platform, but instead of trying to dig it in deep enough to get the jack under a suitable lifting point beneath the vehicle, we would use the chain to make a sling from the trailer hitch at the back, and put the jack's lifting point into that. It would require a practically achievable amount of digging that could, if necessary, be repeated. It seemed very feasible, but we decided to take out some insurance: After we had jacked up the vehicle and placed enough traction material below and behind the rear wheels, we would use the jack and webbing as an additional pull mechanism as we had attempted before, just to give the vehicle some initial momentum.

This plan still required a fair amount of digging, and a lot of chopping and dragging up of branches, but it worked reasonably well. We had to repeat the jacking procedure only once, when the vehicle slipped sideways off our "traction surface" of branches and leaves. It was close to sunset by the time we finally had the buffalo loaded again, and were on our way to the camp, exhausted, completely covered in mud, and disgusted with allowing ourselves to get stuck.

✦✦✦✦✦✦

We decided we deserved a break after breaching the Panhame—reliving the buffalo episode made us feel even more exhausted. It was our custom, anyway, to indulge in some tea around midmorning and again in the afternoon. We found some nice, deep shadow under the generous canopy of a wild fig, set up our Primus stove and kettle, and sat back in our folding chairs (which long experience had taught us to keep handily stashed for quick deployment at stops), slurping the scalding liquid, munching the cheap, hard rusks we had bought at a little roadside shop in Masvinga, and enjoying the luxury of cooling off and relaxing the strained muscles.

Once we had settled into our chairs we started discussing what a tough and reliable and easily repairable bush vehicle the Land Cruiser really was and what it meant for survival when the chips were down. That made us remember an expedition we had undertaken many years back, when we were fresh out of secondary school.

Gerhard's dad had generously bought him an ancient little short-wheelbase Series II Land Rover. It was hot off the sales floor when Gerhard turned up to show me, proudly announcing that the garage man had assured him that "it was completely done up." Being the aspirant engineer and more mechanically inclined than my pal, I could see that, general reliability of a Land Rover aside, it was actually well past its prime and had been given a "quick and dirty" (in fact the quickest and dirtiest possible) by the garage man, just to get it off his hands before it acquired a bad reputation. Gerhard's dad was even less mechanically savvy than either of us, but he smiled benignly at the enthusiasm and said he thought it was quaint for driving around town and maybe into the near district.

Whatever his intentions might have been with the gift, we immediately started planning grandiose expeditions into deep Africa. Our first trip was to be a modest journey of some eighteen hundred miles through the northern Kalahari Desert of Botswana to the Okavango swamps. This was against the wishes of our parents, and we faced serious protestations from them, with some justification. In the early 1970s that area was still untamed country, with a small track meandering westward between Nata and Maun through vast, wild bush country— it was, in fact, on this expedition that we had our night of amusement with the pride of lions on the edge of the Makgadikgadi. Maun consisted of a collection of mud huts and a few rudimentary brick buildings arranged along a wide sand "street." There were the veterinary offices and the small police station and a little general dealer (those were the brick buildings), and the latter stocked almost anything conceivable, but you had to pump fuel from dented red 44-gallon drums with a hand pump.

We were more than delighted by all of this, and we thought nothing of the fact that we had to remove the bonnet and tie it to the roof rack so that I could sit on the left front mudguard with my feet on the tappet cover for most of the journey, coaxing life into the sputtering little engine. We simply sojourned northeast and then northwest from Maun through virgin bush, crossing over the Selinda Spillway, then doubling back and journeying through Lake Ngami on the southern tip of the swamps and up along the western shores to the Okavango River. Thinking back on it, taking on such an expedition with the little Land Rover was as foolhardy as our over-macho attitude toward the dangers of the African bush, but as the saying goes, "the visions of youth are seldom clouded by something as bewildering as experience."

++++++

After tea we soldiered on, and to our relief came to an area where the bush receded for more than half a mile from the river edge, pushed back by a large floodplain covered with tall elephant grass and some green tree islands here and there in the sea of yellow. We made good progress along the southern edge of the plain, except that we had to watch carefully for deep old elephant tracks in the dried mud, which were about as dangerous as a landmine if driven through at more than a crawl.

We stopped regularly to glass the area north toward the river from the Land Cruiser's roof for the Game Trackers camp, but we didn't mind, because there was a lot of game on the plain and along its edge—mostly buffalo and waterbuck and zebra. Toward late afternoon, as we topped a little rise, we spotted the camp in the distance.

Stephan had set up a really charming camp on a slight rise on the riverbank under some ancient mopane trees. He had no tents, but quaint A-frame thatch structures: a kitchen, a storeroom, a dining/social area, and four sleeping huts, each furnished with a bed and a small table made out of saplings. The place was pleasantly laid out and neat, and we felt instantly at home.

Besides several camp hands, there were the PHs, Stephan and Mack, in the camp, and Vic, a third client we had managed to help Dave secure for them, and whom Stephan had canoed in about an hour before we arrived. Stephan was Game Trackers' "man on the Zambezi," and Mack had come in a day earlier from Zimbabwe, by river, at Stephan's request, to help him with our hunt. Stephan reminded me of the comic character Asterix—small and wiry and intense and a bit dour, with a droopy mustache and a surprisingly deep voice when he spoke, but quite agreeable. Mack was an excellent chap, an experienced PH of good English stock, tough but finely mannered, and full of emotion by English standards, which made his character quite interesting.

We had arrived at a distant and untouched part of the African bush. We were dust-caked and tired and striped with thorn cuts, but the bush spirit had slowly invaded our bodies from the moment we stood on the rim of the valley looking over its smoky expanse a day earlier. It had crept into our veins and awakened something primal in us that sharpened our senses and fired our blood and gave us a primitive kind of resilience. It had also taken possession of our souls, made us feel a close affinity with the bush, and filled us with deep wonderment at its marvels and a longing for its secrets and the adventures that hinted from among the trees.

First Impressions

As the luxurious reds and oranges of the sunset over the wide sweep of the Zambezi slowly faded into softer shades of blue and gray and the day creatures fell silent, we drifted toward the fire: first Mack, Gerhard, Vic, and me, and later Stephan, who mumbled that he still had to do "some things" around the camp.

As darkness deepened, an easy, familiar atmosphere settled around the fire. The smell of wood smoke and canvas, the tinny sounds of utensils and low voices drifting from the cooking fire, and the occasional creaking of a camp chair as someone shifted his position, stood against the background of the murmur and spat of the flames and the sounds of the African night. The flames cast a soft flicker over the faces around the fire—some a little anxious, some tranquil, some eager and animated, some thoughtful.

There was Vic, a doctor and a fine gentleman, we found out. He was a regular hunter of plains game on hunting farms in South Africa, an excellent shot, and an accomplished sportsman. It was his first "African big-game safari," as he called it. He mostly listened quietly, and occasionally asked a question. The conversation unfolding around the fire had brought him to realize that what lay ahead was not like anything he had ever experienced before.

Mack was of British stock, a little past middle age, mellowed by a lifetime of wandering and adventuring across Africa, and now very conscious of the effects of his carefree, nomadic lifestyle on his family, and his prospects for old age. At almost fifty he was a well-respected PH, still in excellent physical condition, highly energized, sharp and alert and bush wise, but he had little else to show on the asset side for his efforts over the years, and it was worrying him. He was one of those rare PHs who was not afraid of his own emotions, and a fine gentleman to boot.

Then there was Gerhard: an adventurer, entrepreneur, and businessman of sorts, made of fine-quality tempered steel. Intense, task-focused, self-assured, and often headstrong, but quite a romantic when he thought no one was looking. To me he was a reliable and tough bush companion and friend. Although we were different in some aspects, Gerhard and I had been companions and soul mates since boyhood. We had wandered across the most remote parts of Africa together on many expeditions, hunting or just exploring. Between us there was a deep understanding and companionship; we shared a restless yearning for the unknown, for the far limits of man's known world. It brought us close and made us resonate.

Stephan, to our surprise, turned out to be the original prototype bureaucrat, the builder and (almost jealous) guardian of the camp and its operations. He immediately told us that he would not be able to leave his camp alone, and besides, he still had paperwork and "things to do," and he had hurt his foot and was not able to walk far. And then he withdrew into a passive and slightly petulant silence.

It was interesting for me to observe the interpersonal dynamics unfolding around the fire. First there was the initial positioning. Stephan was, I suspect, very unsure of himself as a professional hunter who would normally be expected to show leadership and inspire confidence with his clients in the bush. He fell back cantankerously on his familiar turf of making sure the camp was perfect, absolutely avoiding getting involved in any hunting activity or talk, but still leaving a hint that he was actually a formidable bush operator who was just for the moment "otherwise occupied." With Stephan's abdication, Mack had to establish himself as the reliable and experienced hunt leader who would solve all the problems and bring in the trophies. He had a commercial agenda, too, in making sure we were aware of his record and profile for future reference. Vic was tentative, unsure of how far his past hunting experience would support him in these circumstances, intelligent and sensitive enough to suspect that it might not be very far, and careful not to make a fool of himself so early in his trip. Mack immediately adopted a protective, fatherly attitude toward him. I thought this rather nice, because it had to be quite an intimidating situation for Vic, with Stephan distancing himself, Mack's positioning himself as a highly experienced and superior African hunter, and Gerhard and me also doing our bit to get our credentials advertised as guys who have been around in the "real" bush and who were ready and able to operate independently, whatever the circumstances. On top of it, we were probably not going to much trouble to hide our views on those slick urban types who went biltong hunting on farms and boasted of their hunting adventures at fancy cocktail parties and were given to driving around in fancy 4x4 vehicles hung with an array of gimmicky paraphernalia passed off as essential for "survival in the harsh conditions of the African bush," which to them meant rather well-controlled and often luxurious tourist situations.

Mack, Gerhard, and I soon realized that this was to be a rather unusual safari. It turned out that Stephan, despite his official status as the Game Trackers resident PH, knew very little about even the immediate vicinity of the camp, let alone local game populations and patterns. A few well-placed questions raised our suspicions that he did not even have a single good tracker in camp. The area was vast and wild with no roads, none of us knew it, and we had only a rudimentary map that Stephan almost reluctantly agreed to part with.

There was no question of driving out of camp in the morning and returning in the evening in the normal fashion, because there were no roads. We would have to decide on a general area in which we wanted to hunt and then take a day or so to work our way into it with our vehicle loaded with supplies. Once we got to a suitable area, we would have to leave the vehicle in a fly camp and work from there on foot, hunting and exploring the area as we went. If we found it unsuitable after a day or two, we'd have to take another day to move our camp with the vehicle again, and so on.

All of this meant that we had very little time and lots of ground to cover, but none of it really bothered Gerhard and me. As long as there was game around we would enjoy ourselves. In fact, the more we heard, the more gleefully we indulged in the delicious lure of adventure and uncertainty. But I could see that Mack was rather dubious, and getting very uneasy and worried about how it was all going to work out with himself taking sole responsibility for three "clients" (as he saw it) who expected results. He had been asked by Stephan on very short notice to come up from Zimbabwe to help out with the hunt, and had arrived just the day before us. He was an experienced PH and, as are most good ones, a strict disciplinarian with a somewhat Germanic belief that things had to be done in a certain way, and he didn't like what he was hearing. He clearly preferred a more controlled and routine situation, and soon he stepped in to take charge and set things on a sound footing "beyond the camp perimeter," with notes and lists of stuff written on a notepad he fetched from his trunk.

Mozambican hunting laws required that hunters be accompanied by a registered PH. Both Stephan and Mack were registered as PHs in Mozambique, but Stephan's abdication in favour of the camp meant that if we were to stick to the rules, we would have to hunt in a group of five (counting a tracker and Mack), and each hunter would only get an opportunity to shoot every third time we found a suitable target. Gerhard and I didn't say anything then, but we both knew that this wouldn't do. Besides, we were very far beyond the reach of authority and we were both inclining toward a responsible but more liberal interpretation of the rules.

The conversation drifted on into the night, mostly centering on hunting and our options and plans for the next few days, but occasionally drifting off on some half-forgotten bush tale that emerged from someone's memory. Somewhere in the course of the evening, at Stephan's request, we also resolved that we would go out the next morning to shoot something (a young buffalo, preferably) for his considerable camp staff, and for us to have some meat for the first night or two. We would then use the rest of the day to load up the Land Cruiser and head back westward to the Panhame River. There we would turn south and follow the river until we found a suitable spot for our first fly camp, from where we would start working the following day. We weren't sure if this was necessarily a good idea, but it seemed as good as any we could come up with, and there were at least our own tracks to follow—and we did see quite a bit of game on the way in. . . .

The Southern Cross was hanging low on the horizon by the time I pulled the tree-bark thong of the wooden lattice door to my hut tight and lay down in the soft darkness, richly flavored with the smell of fresh thatch and the sounds of the African night.

The next morning we weren't in a particular hurry because our program for the day didn't seem very demanding. Stephan had told us that there was more than one small herd of buffalo (and even a large breeding herd) that frequented the river and the open plain, so it would be fairly easy to fill the pot. After the meat hunt we could set out for the Panhame.

However, Mack's strict program demanded that we do the meat hunt early while Stephan's cook prepared breakfast. We would drive out with the Land Cruiser to try to shoot an animal in open ground as close as possible to the vehicle, so they could "immediately load it and bring it back to camp for skinning while we had breakfast and loaded up," he directed briskly.

We got going quite smartly, driving slowly southwest and then west across the plain, bumping along over the uneven ground, hoping to spot something suitable to bring down. Vic was going to do the shooting (to settle him down), so Gerhard and I sat comfortably in front, while Mack and Vic and the camp hands we had brought along for loading took their chances with the tsetse in the back.

We weren't particularly lucky, and it was only after about an hour that we spotted two old *dagga* boys (old buffalo bulls, no longer able to breed, that tend to stay in a small area and spend most of their time wallowing in their favorite mud hollows) about a quarter-mile away to the west. They were grazing in some shorter grass near a long thin finger of trees that pushed into the open plain, and they didn't seem to notice us. After some debate we decided to try to get one. They weren't the best meat, but they were there and it seemed reasonably easy to get close enough for a shot. It would save us time and allow us an early start on our real business. There was also a nice approach possible along the tree line, and it would be an excellent opportunity for Vic to get his buffalo while also salting him for the big hunt.

Mack thought that it would be best if he and Vic approached them on foot, using the trees and tall elephant grass and the favorable wind direction as cover. Gerhard and I settled down with our binoculars to watch their progress.

They must have covered about two-thirds of the distance when the near bull suddenly threw up his heavy head, stared for a moment, and then swung around and started galloping heavily in the direction of some very tall and dense elephant grass and reeds closer to the river. We weren't sure what had spooked him. From where we were, Mack and Vic seemed well under cover. It might have been a sudden change in wind direction, or perhaps something unrelated.

It was clear to us that they were going to lose the buffalo. They were not even aware of the situation because they could not see the animals. But we could, and we could also see that we were probably heading for a much longer meat hunt than we had planned for.

We decided to try to cut them off. It was going to be a push, because the distance was considerable and the ground was uneven and covered by fairly dense grass, but it was worth a try. We raced off, me at the wheel, bumping and crashing frantically over the rough ground and hoping we did not hit a hidden tree stump or an old elephant track in the dried mud. It was hectic, and getting more so. We were not going to make it before they disappeared into the tall grass. We were still about seventy paces away when it became clear that this was going to be our best chance. I swung the vehicle to the right so that Gerhard could jump out and get a shot.

As the vehicle came to a bumpy and slightly uncontrolled standstill I also jumped (more like fell) out, hoping to get off a supporting shot. I was vaguely aware of the deep boom of Gerhard's .375 Holland & Holland

and his "The rear one!" as I desperately tried to get off a backup shot from behind the Land Cruiser. As the bull broke into the tall grass I squeezed the trigger with the gold front bead of the .404 Westley Richards somewhere below and maybe a little forward of his hip bone. The bull seemed to falter slightly in his gallop, but the next instant they had both disappeared into the tall grass, with only the sound of their crashing and a cloud of dust remaining.

We looked at each other across the Land Cruiser's bonnet through drifting dust and gun smoke as we both eased a fresh round into the chamber.

"I missed the engine room but I think I got him through the lungs," Gerhard said half over his shoulder.

"I went for the spine and I think I saw some dust knocked out of his hide in the general area," I replied.

We stood still for a few minutes, listening intently, but it had suddenly gone dead quiet in the sting of the midmorning sun.

Another exchange of looks and a nod, and we started slowly forward, fingers lightly caressing the triggers, ready for a quick shot. About ten yards into the tall grass we found a large splash of blood on the left side of the spoor, pinkish and foamy. This was strange, as we had both fired into his right side, albeit at an angle from the rear. Some five yards farther there was more pinkish blood, now on both sides, but with more on the left. Several possibilities could now be postulated, but they all meant the same thing. We didn't need a discussion. We knew exactly what we had to do. We turned back to the Land Cruiser and headed for the nearest shade where we could brew some tea. It was looking more and more like a really long meat hunt.

Mack and Vic joined us, puffing and sweating from their trot through the stiff grass and the uneven terrain.

"Well?" Mack inquired when he had regained his breath, and I thought I detected something of "and what good has now come of all these silly pranks?"

"We don't know exactly how, but we seem to have punctured both lungs," I replied, and I could see that this news immediately altered his view on the situation.

"Well, why don't we go after him? We can't leave him. We might lose him!" Vic wheezed breathlessly.

"We will," I replied quietly. "We're waiting for him to calm down. He's only going to go as far as he's going to go," and from the corner of my eye I could see Mack's expression turning to approval and respect.

"But why?"

"Because an excited buffalo that hurts is not good company in the long grass," Gerhard replied matter-of-factly through a cloud of blue smoke from his pipe-lighting ritual.

Vic uttered a barely audible "OK," his expression switching to quiet reflection.

We finished our tea unhurriedly and with deliberate calm. But we knew without saying it that we were facing a very dangerous situation. We had just under a ton of concentrated rage, with enormous strength and endurance and of unknown health status, somewhere out there in the tall grass. And we had to go and get it.

As we entered the grass I firmly told Vic, "You hang back a bit behind me. There's a good chance one of us gets hurt, and then you need to keep him alive." He swallowed audibly and didn't argue.

Visibility in the tall grass varied between eight and fifteen yards. If the bull suddenly charged, he was certain to take out at least one of us. Our hope was that he was either incapacitated, or standing in an open spot where we could see him at a bit of distance, or that he would make a sound so we could pinpoint him.

Despite my and Gerhard's protestations that this was our problem, Mack insisted he would take the center position on the spoor. We moved three abreast, Mack in the center, following the blood spoor and setting the pace and direction, while Gerhard walked to the right and I walked to the left, each about four yards apart. This was a time when one appreciated the presence of more than one experienced gun! We moved dead slowly and as quietly as possible, stopping every ten paces or so to listen, proceeding when we were certain we couldn't hear anything.

Our situation was made worse by the light breeze that eddied and swirled intermittently through the tall grass. The danger was clear to us, but it was as if we were being sucked into a narrowing funnel by a primitive, fatalistic urge that we could not resist. We were inside an insulated capsule in which we had only one choice. It was hair-trigger tense. Every muscle was poised for hyper-quick reaction, drawn quiver-tight by loads of rushing adrenaline. Strangely, I felt calm and at peace, vividly sensing the impressions of each slow second—the sharp sting of the midmorning sun on the right side of my face, the sweet smell and the rustle of the yellow grass, the rhythmic pounding in my chest, the sweat droplets trickling down the insides of my arms and the backs of my calves, the smooth curve of the trigger under my right forefinger. And absolutely nothing else mattered. . . .

It felt like a long time before Gerhard noticed some blood about five paces ahead of him. The bull had clearly turned sharply to the right. Stories of buffalo doubling back on their tracks and ambushing their followers rushed briefly through my mind. But then we saw him as he rose from where he had lain down to ease his wounds and the suffocation welling up in his lungs. He was big and black, with two bright red streaks of blood dripping from his nostrils, and a large frothy swath of crimson on his flank—wary, full of rage, and close. The three big rifles whipped up and boomed as if in a last salute at the graveside of a hero. The bull had already been stiff and sore, and lying down had allowed most of the adrenaline to drain away, and now the three heavy bullets slamming into his right shoulder so close to each other knocked him back and onto his side, and he simply didn't have the strength to get up and face the sudden brutal force that had overwhelmed his world. He kicked a little and died with a last deep grunt.

We were taking no chances. We knocked a fresh round into the chamber, and Mack and I stood motionless, ready, while Gerhard slowly moved round him and put a final bullet into the back of his neck. We stood in silent respect for a few moments for the fallen giant and his great strength before we moved closer to examine the situation.

"Never approach the front of a dead animal," Mack quietly coached the eagerly approaching Vic as he gently nudged him round the side of the bull. "It may just be less dead than you think and able to kill you. And remember the two lessons of today: Never chase after a wounded animal unless you are sure it's going to give you an immediate opportunity for a second shot. Rather let it calm down and then follow it up, and" (ever-so-slightly louder so that Gerhard and I would hear) "never shoot at an animal unless you are reasonably sure you can kill it." We both did our best innocent-looking thing.

An examination of the carcass revealed what had happened in the first encounter. Gerhard's shot had hit fairly far back on the rib cage, punctured the right lung and probably some of the vitals and the front part of the left lung, and lodged somewhere in the left shoulder. Hence the little lung blood through the entry wound on the right side of the spoor. My shot had gone in a little forward of and below the hip bone and traveled clean through the soft intestines, through the left lung and exited quite far forward on the left side, causing a large amount of lung blood to spill out on the left. The three final shots had all hit in a four-inch circle on the left, in line with the right front leg and just above the elbow—deadly.

With a bit of effort we were able to get the Land Cruiser right up to the carcass. We split it in the middle just behind the rib cage and removed the intestines, and although it was then a lot lighter, it took a lot of heaving and grunting and a bit of swearing from the five of us to get it onto the back. Then we finally headed back for camp, feeling limp and drained after the adrenaline highs, each staring silently over the yellow flood plain, which was now twisting and dancing in the late-morning heat.

It was after midday by the time we finally rolled into camp, tired and dangerously hungry. Mack decided (and we coasted along in most exemplary fashion) that it would be better to set out the next day. It would take us at least an hour, probably three, to get everything ready and have something to eat, and by then we would barely be able to reach the Panhame by dusk, he reasoned.

I thought I should just get in a good parting shot, so as I casually slid from the Land Cruiser and reached for my rifle I said quite loudly, "Well, that's that. All's well that ends well, as the Bard said. Oh, and by the way, Vic, here's another bush lesson: Never expect anything in the bush to work out the way you had planned it—or that it will be possible to play by a single rule set."

Getting Started

I woke in the dark to the sounds of clumsy early morning camp activity and the smell of thatch grass and canvas. The darkness, the muffled voices, the thump and clank of camp equipment, the distant moaning of a hyena, the faint odor of wood smoke drifting in from the cooking fire, all blended into a harmony that was an old and familiar part of Africa's history, and I found it comforting to lie quietly, listening and breathing.

Soon I heard the padding of bare feet, and then the splash of water into the canvas basin outside, followed by a muffled clank as the bucket was placed on the ground next to the basin with some warm water left. Mack certainly knew how to suggest to his hunters in a stylish way that it was time to get up.

The morning was moist and still black, but Mack's steaming pot of coffee, generously laced with a rather suspect alcoholic concoction, put a fire in the belly and a sparkle in the eye. While we sipped, Mack was noisily organizing last details, and as the black velvet slowly turned to gray we plunged southwest into the thick early morning fog, featureless, intangible, evasive, its wet fingers caressing one's bare arms and face, and leaving little droplets clinging to one's hair and eyebrows.

We had acquired quite a following thanks to Mack's tireless persistence with a reluctant Stephan, who insisted that he needed all available hands to "do some things around the camp." There was Jerry, who Stephan passed off as a tracker, but seemed rather unsure and quite nervous about his (we suspected quite unfamiliar) status, and three camp hands, one of whom, John, seemed quite intelligent and capable. Gerhard and I thought the labor force somewhat unbalanced because all we really needed were two (preferably three) really good trackers, and we suspected we were now actually saddled with four camp hands and no one even remotely resembling a tracker. But Mack had to go to some lengths to get them, and we knew that there would be heavy work ahead, breaking paths through the bush and skinning and carrying trophies (if we got a bit lucky), and additional hands would mean a generally more comfortable hunt for us.

The first part of our journey over the flood plain was a relatively easy drive, precariously clinging to our tracks of two days ago in a featureless white fog world. But when we reached the Panhame and turned south, we had to start breaking through virgin bush. The early morning mist was now gone and with it the freshness, and a vast heat lived among the trees. But our workforce, with the exception of one, Jimmy, who was clearly suffering from trypanosomiasis (sleeping sickness transmitted by tsetse), rose to the example and the challenge we set them, and applied themselves to the road-making with a will. Despite the rather dense bush, we were making good progress, keeping to the edge of the riverine forest along the Panhame.

When we stopped for the compulsory tea around eleven o'clock in the luxurious coolness of a huge wild fig, I worked up a casual conversation with John and Jerry about tracking and bush skill. Gerhard and I had worked with many African trackers on our various wanderings, and Jerry simply did not look the part. The tracker is the key to a successful hunt. He must of course be able to spot game well, and read and follow spoor, but to be a really good tracker his general knowledge of animals and their habits needs to be of a very high standard—he actually has to get into the psyche of the animal he is following. Having a sharp eye to spot the tracks is only a small part of being able to reliably track under difficult conditions. But skilfull tracking is only part of the role. The hunter, unfamiliar with the area, needs to rely on his tracker for guidance and advice. He needs to have a sound intuition of local animal movements. Animal habits are influenced by local conditions, and differ somewhat from area to area, and from season to season. This means that he must spend almost all of his time physically out in the bush, actively observing the animals. It takes years to build up that kind of experience and "bush intuition," and it shows on the person. The best trackers I have come across tended to be past their late thirties, usually rather demure individuals, gnarled by exposure to the harsh African elements, and with a few old scars from bush mishaps and violent encounters with animals. I usually feel comfortable with such individuals and have developed strong bonds of comradeship with most trackers I had worked with.

A few questions in the course of the conversation with Jerry and John quickly confirmed our suspicions that Jerry was more of a "village man" than a "bush man." The closest he had ever come to tracking was when he worked for a safari outfit in Zimbabwe as a camp hand. He had probably presented himself as a tracker to Stephan to improve his chances of getting a job. The tracker (actually, he should be called a guide) is the most prestigious position in the hunting outfit—even more prestigious than the cook or camp master, and finding a good one is difficult. With Stephan never seriously getting out into the bush, Jerry's skills weren't ever put to a real test. It is to his credit that he realized he was going to be completely out of his depth. Quite early in the conversation he proposed that we find a certain guy named Jo'burg (of all possible names!) that he knew lived close-by, and who was a hunter and tracker of some repute.

This now suggested a slight change of plans—to first go and find the famous Jo'burg. Mack was somewhat reluctant, mumbling that "we would get along," and we "needed to get out there as soon as possible" (without really being able to define where "out there" was) but Gerhard and I insisted. It was simply going to take too long to make this work without good trackers with local knowledge. As it was, Stephan's lack of good wildlife intelligence on the area now had us rather aimlessly working along the Panhame in the hope that we were on the right track, but we might just as well have journeyed along the Zambezi to the east.

Jerry explained that we should carry on a bit farther along the Panhame until we came to a road that would take us to Jo'burg's dwelling.

We reached the "road" after about an hour. It was an age-old elephant path, opened wide and smoothed by the great beasts on their east-west migration through the valley, and now also serving as a main route for both humans and other animals.

The African bush is crisscrossed by paths like this, some made by humans, some by elephants or other game, and used by all. Africans have a preference for using them to get from point to point, despite the fact that it mostly means a strange meandering and indirect route, because none (or very few) were actually planned routes made between two points as Westerners would think of roads. They evolved over time through use by humans and animals under different influences, such as migrations, seasonal imperatives, droughts, travel needs, the presence of water, other environmental conditions and so forth, and they change gradually as immediate local needs dictate. Knowing which combination of paths to use to get to a particular destination is somewhat of an art, informed by personal knowledge of the area. But I had found over many wanderings through the African bush that using these paths usually got one to a destination faster and more rested than trying to move through the bush, where one often encountered obstacles, or had to use a lot of energy breaking through tall grass or shrubs, or was much more likely to encounter danger.

It was decided that Mack and Vic would remain with the vehicle and Gerhard and I would go with Jerry to find Jo'burg. It turned out to be quite a mission: Two hours of walking to get to his dwelling—five tattered mud and palm thatch huts, which seemed to have resigned themselves to gradual deterioration in the dusty clearing, wallowing in the faint sour smell of ripe *mageu* (a thick nutritional drink made from maize, which often build up quite a high alcohol content through fermentation, especially in the summer heat).

As fate would have it, Jo'burg and his brother, Elias, who lived with him, were out in the bush, probably checking their snares. Only three women and a smattering of children were home. The three adults remained seated in the shade on beautifully woven grass mats, talking and keeping themselves seemingly leisurely occupied with small tasks, avoiding looking at us directly. The children retreated and stared (they got gradually less shy and more inquisitive and a noisy nuisance as the afternoon wore on). The eldest woman eventually put down the smooth grinding stone she was using to crush maize in a large hollow rock, and came up to us. She was thin and tall and looked about sixty, but was probably younger in years. Even though she appeared to know Jerry (or at least of him), she stood uncomfortably shifting her bare feet, her eyes averted and head slightly tilted, saying nothing, like someone brought before a strict magistrate to confess a crime. Jerry took the initiative and launched into a lengthy conversation with her. It was largely incomprehensible to me but seemed to relax her a bit because her voice gained some confidence, and she even allowed herself fleeting glimpses at Gerhard and me.

She instructed the youngest woman to bring us something to sit on, and some tree stumps, worn smooth and shiny from years of being moved around and sat on were dragged up for us. The rest of the afternoon was really taken up by waiting. Most Westerners would find this frustrating, but having grown up in Africa and having spent much time in the bush, we knew this was what one had to accept and adjust to with the necessary grace. Already this little sojourn was turning into a major change in our initial plans for the day, but that was another important African bush lesson: Expect things not to work out the way you had planned them, and bend to the situation.

We dragged our tree stumps into the shade of a hut overhang, made ourselves as comfortable as possible with our backs against the anthill-plastered wall, and sat chatting, and I wrote a bit in my diary (which I had slipped into the small rucksack I gave Jerry to carry together with our sleeping bags and hammocks, just in case). We felt fairly confident that our patience would be rewarded. This family was of the kind we had often found in very remote parts. Different from the inhabitants of the more settled village communities one also found scattered in such areas, their kind was usually semi-nomadic, moving from time to time in response to local conditions, shunning larger concentrations of people and to a large extent living off the bush. Occasionally one or more of their number would journey to the settled villages or even more remote towns to trade bush products such as skin, horns, dried meat, mats, etc.

Jo'burg and Elias finally walked into the clearing in the yellow of the afternoon. They were Sena, a tribe dominating the Zambezi Valley. Jo'burg was probably around forty, the younger and the more flamboyant and audacious of the two, with a ready white smile and lively eyes, and he mostly took the lead. He had worked a stint in the mines in South Africa at some point in his illustrious career (hence the name by which he had become known), and could speak a reasonable Fanagalo (a language developed as a lingua franca on the South African mines). This was of course a huge advantage—he even knew a few Afrikaans and English words, and had some understanding of modern white people.

Elias seemed about ten years older, untouched by civilization, and much more demure and introverted, his deeply engraved face and watery eyes leaving the impression of resigned sadness. But I liked him more because while I got the impression that Jo'burg was somewhat opportunistic and would be prone to exchanging honor for pragmatism if the occasion demanded, Elias seemed to me simple but absolutely genuine and honest. More important, I just had an instinctive feeling that while they had clearly both spent most of their lives in the bush (their scuffed bodies showing the imprints thereof), the calm, introspective Elias (pronounced *Ilyas*) had a more profound bush knowledge, a deeper intuitive understanding of the animal habit and mind.

We were fortunate to have both of them agree to join us. Of course it made good sense from their perspective—they would receive food for the duration, some income, and there was a good chance they would have preferential access to lots of meat if we shot something big. This would be good for them and their families and save them days of hard and dangerous work. It was also an adventure for them, exchanging the daily drudge of checking snares and fishing for a sojourn into the bush with these strange white men.

To us it was an unexpected boon, and it made Gerhard and me feel a lot better about our prospects. Even if they were just trapping and not hunting or snaring bigger game (which I suspected they did—at least from time to time), they would have fresh and reliable local knowledge. I have found Africans generally to be extremely active and subtle observers, with memories like elephants.

We left them with the sun already hanging low in the west and their little village mercifully bathed in cooler shadow. They would make the necessary going-away arrangements, and join us early the next morning.

We arrived back at the vehicle at dusk to find that Mack had had the good sense to prepare for staying the night. He was a bit grumpy because we had been away much longer than expected, and muttered something (only partly good-humored) about "never know when the two of you will suddenly decide to set off on elephant spoor." But I suspected he actually felt a bit left out of an important event that would affect the rest of the hunt.

As the professional hunter in charge, he was torn between his sense of correctness and due process, especially given the highly unusual, unstructured, frontier-type situation we were in. On top of this, he was not quite sure what to make of us yet, especially after our unconventional and somewhat controversial behavior with the buffalo.

At that point he probably regarded us as potentially troublesome adult delinquents who did not care too much about conforming to his strict regime, and assumed he would probably have to do a lot of cleaning up after us—such as finding us when we got lost, or following up and killing animals we had wounded. He found Vic much more compliant and took him under his wing. This was an ideal situation for Vic, and although it created a bit of a "them and us" situation, it also suited me and Gerhard well, because it created the psychological space for us to do our own thing.

++++++

Our journey, with its many twists and ramifications, reminded me of the journey of a fellow named Warrick Purdon, whom I had once come across while wandering around the northern part of the Mozambican bush along the Lugenda River. My plan had been to work northeast along the

Lugenda up to the Ruvuma, which forms the northern border of Mozambique with Tanzania. I didn't make it all the way to the Ruvuma on that trip, partly because I ran into Warrick Purdon.

I was driving eastward from the (then) rather dilapidated town of Lichinga along a quite well-used track that, at the time, was the main route to the coastal area, when I noticed a quaint wooden sign nailed to a tree that read "Eagle Farm." I simply *had* to see what that was all about—such a sign, there, in this remote bush, about sixty miles from the town of Lichinga, which was the nearest bit of civilization.

In its previous life, Lichinga had been the provincial capital, a really charming little Portuguese-style colonial town on the edge of a plateau, with white villas facing each other across wide, shady boulevards. When I drove through it on my way east to the Lugenda, it was still the provincial capital, but the streets were potholed and dirty, the villas were a sooty gray and showing bare brick here and there, and almost nothing of the infrastructure was functioning.

I took the Eagle Farm turnoff. The track took me a few miles into the bush to a charming little anthill-and-pole dwelling and a basic but very functional tobacco farming establishment in the making, literally being clawed out of the bush by Keith and Dorothy Purdon, a couple well into middle age. After we had exchanged our stories (theirs much more poignant and impressive than mine), and enjoyed a cup of Dorothy's tea, Keith directed me to his son, Warrick.

Warrick was attempting the same heroic enterprise (but with macadamia nuts) some distance farther to the east and close to the Lugenda. Keith felt that Warrick's place would be ideal to use as a base for my wanderings; I could also pick up a guide and bearers with Warrick's assistance, and I could safely leave my vehicle and extra supplies.

I was warmly received by Warrick and Phen, his petite and very courageous wife. Warrick agreed to give me some assistance (although I almost felt that I ought to be the one giving *them* support), and invited me to stay for the night. The whole encounter with such true pioneers as the

Purdons, taking on almost impossible odds to build something on a grand scale from absolutely nothing was deeply impressive and humbling, and really deserves a more thorough description, but it was Warrick's journey that I was reminded of.

The Purdon family was originally from Zimbabwe. After leaving that country for South Africa, Keith and Warrick had both worked here and there for a number of years, Keith for large farming outfits and Warrick on gardening services and the like, while they saved up and gathered bits of farming equipment. At some point they felt they were ready to launch their dream.

On a reconnaissance trip into the area east of Lichinga they had secured a tentative agreement with the local chief that they could start their enterprises in his area. On the strength of this, and of what they had seen of the area, they decided it was "time." They loaded their farming equipment (which included three John Deere tractors and a small D4-type bulldozer) and their personal goods onto two large trailers, and Warrick set out from the Eastern Cape, the heavily overloaded trailers pulled by two of the John Deere tractors.

He made agonizing progress northeastward through South Africa, uneventful except for having to explain to several bemused, sometimes flabbergasted traffic officials what on earth he was doing on the national roads with such fantastical rigs. They fortunately always let him off after he had explained, just shaking their heads in disbelief as they watched him go. But somewhere north of Pietersburg one of his tractors broke down with major mechanical problems—I seem to recall he mentioned the oil pump.

Unperturbed, Warrick simply took the tractor apart on the side of the road, and went onto Louis Trichardt to get the replacement parts. He managed to find a dealer willing to order them from Johannesburg, and after a few days he was able to reassemble his tractor and continue on his journey.

He worked his way ever farther northward, avoiding the treacherous Wylies Poort by skirting the Soutpansberg on the west side through the Blouberg Gap, then heading for Punda Maria in Kruger Park, and finally crossing into Mozambique at Pafuri. Now he had to turn southeast and follow the Limpopo to a little place called Mapai, where he could drive through the river.

The Mapai crossing of the Limpopo is about five hundred to six hundred yards wide, and commonly used by locals during the dry season, even with two-wheel-drive vehicles (with a bit of assistance), and by South Africans traveling to Vilanculo via Pafuri. But the tractors were not up to hauling the heavy trailers through the lose sand. One got stuck some way into the river. Fortunately the trailer with the D4 on it was still on hard ground, so Warrick built an earth ramp behind it to drive the D4 off the trailer. He then used the D4 to pull the two trailers through the river. On the other side, he built another ramp to reload the dozer, and was finally on his way again.

Warrick could now follow a good stretch of road northeast, heading for Vilanculo, but some ninety miles northeast of Mapai he had to slip off it onto a little track running north to a place called Massangena, where, if one knew where to find it, there was a place where it was possible to drive through the Save River.

The Save crossing was familiar to me and Gerhard, having explored and hunted in the area to the north of the river. It is somewhat wider than the Limpopo crossing, but it has some steep sand banks in places that could be formidable obstacles. Some locals make a bit of money pulling vehicles through with oxen or even (I had heard, but never actually observed) a farm tractor. Nevertheless, Warrick had to repeat the procedure of building a ramp for the D4, offloading, dragging the trailers through the river sand, and building a ramp again on the other side to reload the D4.

He would have liked to travel directly north from the Save crossing to hit the Mutare/Beira main road somewhere near Bandula, but as Gerhard and I had also found on our wanderings, the roads there are problematic. The ones shown on maps don't exist on the ground, and the ones that are on the ground are not shown on maps, and seem to wander aimlessly from little village to little village, without clear direction, making it very difficult to use them to go anywhere in particular. But Warrick soldiered on, trying to work more or less northward, and finally making it to the Mutare/Beira main road east of Bandula at Chimoio.

It now seemed like relatively clear sailing. Reasonably good roads, most of them tar, north to Tete, where he could cross the Zambezi by bridge, and from there through the southern tip of Malawi, with only the last ninety-odd miles to Lichinga a dirt track, and no more backbreaking rivers to cross! But he was just getting settled into a nice momentum along the tar road between Beira and Mutare when his tractor suddenly pulled to the side and nose-dived into the road shoulder, throwing Warrick clear, narrowly missing running over him, and plowing a deep furrow into the earth with its front weights before it finally ran itself to a standstill in a heap of earth. The center pivot pin, around which the front axle swivels, had broken clean off!

It was the day before Christmas. Places would be closed or closing, even back in far-off South Africa. Warrick decided he had had enough. He gathered some stuff together and headed for Beira, then sadly dilapidated and dysfunctional, but at least offering more comfort than the roadside. He took it easy over Christmas in the best bad hotel he could find, and started searching for a place where he could have a center pin made (he had no illusions about being able to buy one). But it quickly became clear to him that there simply wasn't such a capability in Beira.

There was nothing for it but to head back to South Africa, and try to order a new pin at the nearest town of some substance—Phalaborwa. Fortunately, by the time he arrived there, the Christmas lethargy had blown over, but he still had to wait several days for the part to arrive from Johannesburg.

Then he headed all the way back to his stricken tractor. Once there, it was quite a challenge to raise the heavy front of the machine and reposition the axle. But he finally got it right, and had an uneventful but wearisome rest of the journey, finally arriving at his destination many weeks after leaving the Eastern Cape.

++++++

When the morning was just beginning to etch the bush against its blush, our two new companions walked into camp, each carrying a humble bundle wrapped in skin, and a hand ax. Mack had of course been scurrying around for some time like a badger with a serious hunger upon him, coaxing the smoking logs into a thin flame, imposing some fine British military routine on Stephan's rather bewildered staff, and muttering that he would not be surprised if "those characters did not turn up at all," and "we can't wait around all day for them, you know."

Gerhard and I remained in the safety of our hammocks, each with a mug of Mack's coffee, while we discussed the way forward. Mack thought we should carry on a bit farther along the Panhame (he thought that there might be lots of elephants that way). Jo'burg wanted us to follow the elephant path eastward to a place where "we can find many elephants." Gerhard and I trusted Jo'burg's local knowledge more, and he received the vote.

The path was wide enough in places for a vehicle, and we made fair progress. Most of our time was taken up by skirting large dongas and ravines that could easily be crossed by elephant or humans on foot, but not by the Land Cruiser. These often took us more than half a mile off course, and it demanded a stout effort to make a reasonably passable passage that did not risk damage to the vehicle. But we now had a formidable workforce under our command, and the two extra axes meant a lot, especially in such deft hands as those of Elias and Jo'burg.

True bush men could handle their axes (and machetes) with astonishing precision and effectiveness. The axes, as always, intrigued me. They were made from a piece of tough wood with a large knob the size of a cricket ball on one end to give it some weight. Through this was driven a flat piece of iron that was fashioned into an elongated triangle—probably hacked from an old vehicle spring blade because it was hard and tough and did not bend or blunt easily. This gave an ax blade on the one side, usually honed to a fine edge, and a sharp protruding spike on the other that could be used to dig or do other grievous damage.

Although ostensibly crude, hand-fashioned implements, I had never picked one up that was not finely balanced and handled as sweetly as a well-made cricket bat. Each was, of course, a handmade, one-off creation, but the design was remarkably common across large parts of remote Africa, a variant of it having the blade hammered in at a right angle to the handle to be used as a tilling pick.

As the afternoon wore on, the terrain started changing from gentle undulations with occasional shallow ravines and softer sandy soils to more stony ground with steeper slopes and deeper ravines. The mopane, marula, sickle bush, and knobthorn were gradually replaced by more bushwillow species together with wild syringa, wild pear, tree wisteria, baobab, and some buffalo thorn and cork wood here and there. There had been quite a lot of evidence of game all along, including elephant, zebra, waterbuck, kudu, impala, and pigs, but as was to be expected we found fewer signs of buffalo as we got farther into the harder terrain.

By midafternoon we must have been some twelve miles east of the Panhame. When we got back onto the vehicle after a stint of road clearing, Mack, Gerhard, and I had a quick conversation and agreed that the general area we were in was as good as any to use as a base area. When I quizzed Jo'burg on how much farther he intended to take us, I found out that we were, indeed, already in the general area he had in mind. It had been a long day, and we were rather relieved to be able to find a good spot where we could make our base camp. We had left the elephant path around midday, because it had inexplicably (as such paths will), started veering more to the south, and the last two hours had been hard, slow work.

To the east we found quite a nice spot in the sharp elbow of a deep ravine, where a huge jackal berry had established its domain. The southern side of the ravine bed below was in constant shade, and we were able to find enough water there for the camp by digging in the sand. It was also well protected on two sides against predators, and Mack had the camp hands close the open sides a bit with some buffalo thorn branches. This was good; at least one could sleep comfortably and relaxed when in camp.

The next morning Mack had us all (Jo'burg, Elias, Vic, Gerhard, and me) lined up and ready to march out of camp just as it was getting light enough to see the front bead of a rifle sight. It was our first real day of hunting. It had taken us five days of no-nonsense hard work since leaving Pretoria to get to this point. This was the real fruit of our planning and labors: hunting on foot through the African bush. I brought up the rear, and I can still clearly see the picture of the little group trudging out of camp into the dewy gray morning, rifles over shoulders.

Gerhard and I had serious misgivings about the *modus operandi* that Mack had put forward. He wanted us to move as a group, no doubt because he regarded himself as the PH in charge and felt responsible for us—of course, it was also according to the rules and regulations. But we knew (and, I suspected, deep down he knew too) that this was a hopeless way of hunting in the African bush. The group was simply too large. We would create an infernal noise moving along and be easily spotted, and besides, each of us would only have one chance in three for a shot at a good sighting (which we knew was going to be rare). However, we decided to quietly play along for the day. We had insisted the night before on a circular route about three miles out and around our camp. It would give us some idea of the general terrain and game situation.

Gerhard and I constantly kept the pace up through the day. It was hard work in the heat, and Vic, unaccustomed to such hunting conditions, was beginning to show serious strain about midday, but it was to us strictly a reconnaissance outing, with little or no chance of sighting anything, and we wanted to get the best possible picture of our situation so that we could better plan our next moves.

The terrain was more gentle to the west and north, dominated by large mopane with some marula and knobthorn, and huge leadwood, pod mahogany, and Ana trees along the ravines and in the depressions. There was lots of fresh evidence of sable, kudu, zebra, impala, and here and there a lone buffalo bull or a small bull group. We also found elephant sign (spoor, dung, and signs of feeding), but they were breeding herds of six to ten individuals that appeared to wander around and through the area. Water was scarce, but in the dry ravines we came across elephant diggings in the moist spots, which other game also used. It was here that we were also able to establish that this was the territory of a pride of lions—we thought about four adults, and of course, we found the usual sign of hyenas and lesser predators like smaller cats (but no leopard or cheetah), and jackals.

The south and east was more stony, the slopes steeper and the ravines more severe. The vegetation was smaller, defiant against the harsh elements—mostly bush willow species with occasional clumps of wild syringa, some wild pear, tree wisteria, baobab, buffalo thorn, sickle bush, and raisin bush, and a few cork woods. Here there appeared to be little water, but the abundance of sign of kudu, zebra, and elephant indicated that there had to be some water within reasonable distance. The hardness of the terrain made it difficult to pick up predator sign, but there was enough prey for them to be well represented, and the likely concentration of game at the (few) water holes would make their hunting easier.

It was midafternoon when we came to a place where a ravine opened into a larger depression, and there we found a place where the white sand had been churned into moist darkness by the digging of two elephant bulls. The tracks and the tusk marks in the sand hinted with delicious mystery that at least one of them might be a giant carrier of heavy ivory.

Gerhard and I decided to follow the spoor for a bit to see where the wanderings of the companions would take us. Vic was by now bone-tired, and Mack decided to escort him back to camp. Jo'burg and Elias stayed with us and we settled on the spoor leading south along the depression. Within an hour we found a spot where the flattened grass under a leafy marula told the tale of the two bulls having had their siesta over the hottest part of the day.

When they started moving again it was leisurely, feeding as they went. The spoor was now only a few hours old, and meandering from one tasty offering to the next. All this meant that the bulls could not be very far ahead of us—probably only a mile or so, or even closer. It was very tempting to continue till dark, sleep on the spoor, and take it up again at dawn. But we were tired and low on calories. We must have covered eighteen miles or more in the course of the day, and we had only had an early morning rusk, an orange that Mack had fortuitously thrown into his small rucksack, and some wild berries and wild honey that we had been able to find on the way. We had no reserve food or water. We really had little choice but to reluctantly abandon the spoor and head for camp through the fading day.

We walked into the welcome glow of the fire three hours later, half dead on our feet from exhaustion and hunger. Fortunately Mack had been able to bag a reedbuck on their way back, and he had a pot of soup and a grilled reedbuck heart and sweet corn ready.

After about an hour and a bath (I stood on the Land Cruiser floor mat and had John pour mugs full of deliciously cool water over me) we were back in business, and now began the serious issue of deciding how we were going to continue the hunt.

Fortunately Mack had accepted in the course of the day that the one-group idea was not going to work, and he suggested generously that Gerhard and I take Jo'burg and Elias and set off on our own, while he would go with Vic, taking Jerry along. Gerhard hinted that he would like to go southwest to see if he could track down the two bulls, and I, knowing that being together would probably mean only one of us getting a shot, decided to try my luck to the east with Elias. I wanted to roam a bit farther, and I decided to take John along to translate and carry some additional supplies. We agreed that if we did not meet up again at our fly camp within the next four days, whoever was with the vehicle would head back to Stephan's camp and the rest would rendezvous there (it was probably about thirty-five miles or so almost directly north or perhaps slightly northeast).

At this point I moved the kettle onto the coals for some tea, and the conversation settled into a relaxed discussion of our impressions and experiences during the day. But the contributions soon deteriorated into huge yawns and long silences, followed by first Vic, and then the rest of us, slinking off to our various lairs.

Solo

I waited for the others to get going in the uncertain early morning, and watched Gerhard and Jo'burg briskly fading into the gray to the southwest, and a little later a more tentative Mack and Vic and Jerry to the northwest, their calls of "Good luck!" lingering in the still morning air.

Then I set about preparing for my sojourn. I had brought along a sturdy old army backpack, and into this I packed a few essentials for John to carry. These included some dry and tinned food, some of the reedbuck meat they had flame-dried and smoked overnight, a packet of maize meal, a pot we could use for cooking or boiling water, their blankets, two groundsheets, some basic emergency medical stuff, and basic rifle care equipment. In addition, I tied a five-quart plastic bottle onto the back so we could carry along some water if necessary. I gave Elias a small day bag with my personal stuff—hammock, sleeping bag, small flashlight, water bottle, spare batteries, extra bullets, and, of course, my diary and *War and Peace*, which I was reading at the time.

I also handed Elias my favorite canvas water bag. It did not hold much more than about two quarts, but its water was always refreshingly cool, even over the hot part of the day. Elias stuck his ax handle through the rope handles and slung it over his shoulder. He also carried a short fighting knobkerrie (a short sturdy stick, made from a tough wood, and fashioned with a heavy knob on the one end) that he stuck through the rawhide thong tied around his waist. John did not have any tools, so I gave him a panga from our kit, and I carried my rifle, gun belt, hunting knife, binocular, and compass.

Elias led the way into the fresh sun, which silvered the dew-laden grass into a field of pure white crystal, with glints of vivid rainbow reflections here and there. I took a final look back at our minute little circle of civilization around the Land Cruiser, now looking forlorn and abandoned like an explorer's flag planted on a vast arctic plain, and no longer part of my world. I had that deliciously exhilarating feeling of being completely cut loose from all ties, of being totally adrift in a neutral universe, with any direction, any decision, absolutely anything, an equally unknown possibility.

We settled into a steady walk, heading east, stopping occasionally to check some bush sign, looking for evidence of big elephants, and spotting quite a few zebra, impala, warthog, a hyena heading for its lair, and so on. Despite the hard, somewhat stony ground, we found quite a lot of elephant sign, but although it was difficult to tell exactly on this type of ground, I thought they were mostly from breeding herds of six to eight individuals that were not very interesting from a trophy perspective.

We had only covered a few miles when Elias knocked a dew-sogged partridge that had flown up just ahead of him out of the air with a deft throw of his knobkerrie. The two blacks were delighted (me too, quietly). It was going to be really nice eating by tonight, dangling in the hot sun through the day from a bark thong on the back of John's pack.

After two hours I called a halt. I had learned from my days with the Special Forces that it was important to take short rests regularly (actually every hour) in order to sustain a steady pace through the day. I showed John how to brew tea, and when we had all settled down with our mugs, I asked Elias (through John) where he thought we should be heading.

He was sitting on his haunches, elbows resting on his knees, gnarled fingers wrapped around his mug, cupped close to his face, looking a bit like a gargoyle from Notre Dame on the loose. He replied without looking directly at me that there was a water hole (the one skinny arm stabbed vaguely to the southeast) "where we can find many elephants."

"And how long will it take us to get to the water hole?"

It is useless to ask an African like Elias how far something is because they have no concept of distance in miles. If one asked them how far something was, they would reply "far" or "not far," depending on what they thought you most wanted to hear. In this case, Elias simply pointed low on the western horizon, discreetly checking through his squinted eyes if I was pleased. So, it would be by sunset—that is, if we were lucky.

"I see the elephants in this area are mostly cows and their calves. But are there also big bulls, the ones with big *zimpondo* (horns) that walk alone with their *askaris*?" I asked him.

There was a quick sidelong squint at me. "Sometimes you can find them."

Having grown up with Africans, I should have expected this. I settled down to add a few lines to my diary.

We then continued climbing gradually. The bush and the game patterns stayed more or less the same, with perhaps a bit more bush willow. There was quite a breeze blowing from the southeast, which was good, because it cooled one down a bit, and it masked our sound and scent to the front. This enabled us to spot some game as we went along, and to get quite close to a small herd of kudus (usually impossible because of their exceptionally keen senses).

There were four kudu cows, some young ones, and, standing a bit to the side, a truly splendid bull. He was in his prime, neck blue-black and thicker than my chest, magnificent horns grandly spiraling up into their fifth turn. We watched them for a few minutes, and then I clicked my tongue softly. The bull gave a surprised bark, and was gone into the bush in a few effortless bounds, horns thrown back over his haunches, graceful and poetic on his long, slender legs—a ballet dancer.

Around ten we stopped for breakfast. I had some muesli with powdered milk, and Elias and John had reedbuck meat and some cold maize meal porridge that had been left over from last night. When we set out again, the bush was no longer dewy and cool; it was dry, dusty, shimmering in the heat, and filled with the screams of cicadas. We were endlessly tormented by little black bees hovering around our faces and by the tsetse flies.

We soldiered on till around one o'clock, but then it got so unbearably hot that I called a halt in the nearest pool of deep shade. Fortunately the ground was more stony than sandy, so there weren't many tsetse flies. I slung my hammock and read a few chapters from *War and Peace* and dozed off just a bit. My companions built a small fire and smoked and dried the reed-buck meat a bit more.

We set out again two hours later. All through the morning I had had the feeling we were gradually climbing, but toward midafternoon the ground seemed to level off, and the vegetation started changing. The trees appeared taller and more leafy, the foliage wasn't quite so leathery and sun-bleached, and there was more mopane and leadwood. The bush also started getting thicker, but broken by quite frequent swathes of open grassland. It was clear that this area received a bit more rain than the lowlands and the slopes from where we had come. It was beautiful, parklike country, the trees around the fringes of the grasslands rising in galleries from the edges to the tallest trees in subtle hues of greens and browns and grays.

Toward late afternoon, when the sun had softened to a friendlier orange and the shadows cast long swathes of coolness over the veld, we were crossing a fairly large open grass field when Elias suddenly stopped, staring down at his feet. When I reached him I saw what he saw: the tracks of a group of bull elephants. We had come across many sets of footprints through the day, but this was a bull herd, and there was one particular set of imprints. . . .

Without a word, tentatively at first, checking, confirming, then with more assurance, excitement building, we started following it. At some point Elias and I stopped and looked at each other; we both knew that these were the tracks of a big bull, and we had to try to find it. We could not tell for certain (because they had crossed the clearing in single file), but it seemed like a group of between three and five bulls, heading straight for the trees on the other side, with the big bull bringing up the rear.

It was a grand moment. We felt the excitement of the hunt building as we tracked into the low sun, which was splashing the western skies with rich shades of red and etching the tree line ahead of us in beautiful orange-tinged purples and blues and grays. The tracks were fresh, some of the downtrodden grass stems still moist where they had been broken by the great feet, a hint of dust hovering here and there in the still afternoon air.

We reached the tree line. We sensed they were just ahead of us, and the air was suddenly electric with tension and excitement. But we were not in a good situation. The bush was dense, with almost total overhead cover and about five to eight yards of visibility in the dusky light. It was difficult to move quietly through the undergrowth with the crackling of the dead material on the ground, and the wind had died down completely at this hour.

As usual in such situations, the impressions of the moment filled all my consciousness: The glint of the gold front bead over the wide V of the rear sight as I quickly checked if there would be enough light to aim, the smooth slide of the Mauser action as I opened the breech and momentarily glanced down at the dull nickel-and-brass gleam of the 410-grain full-jacket solids, the slow deliberateness of carefully easing one into the chamber and moving the safety catch to half position so that it would block my view of the sights and I wouldn't forget to take it off in the excitement. The tension sat dry and brittle in my mouth and kicked against the inside of my chest; it trickled thinly down my arms despite the pleasant coolness of the musty air against my face.

I motioned John to stay put and we moved forward dead slowly and as quietly as possible, putting our feet down toes first and gradually taking the pressure, Elias in front taking overhanging branches out of the way and holding them for me to take so that they would not snap back or brush against our clothes. The air smelled of herbs and rotting vegetation and elephant, but the bush was quiet, breathless, waiting. And then there was a muffled crack just ahead of us. We froze as if caught in midmovement by a high-speed camera. But the silence washed back over us, blunting our straining senses. But we knew then that they knew we were there.

It was dangerous work. If we got charged here at least one of us was likely to be broken on the musty ground. Elias was bravely leading, but his face was strained and his dark skin was ashen in the dim light. I moved ahead of him. And then, as I looked up from the spoor, I stared straight into the great liquid brown iris of an elephant eye, stark and white-rimmed with tension and fear. It was absolutely all I could see of him through the foliage, so close that I could make out the little red veins in the white. For a vivid moment that hung completely suspended in time, disconnected from all before and all after in its all-consuming intensity, we stared at each other, and then, with barely a rustle, he was gone.

I stood frozen, straining to see through the foliage in the dim light. *Where was he? Where were the others? Was one of them suddenly going to crash through the thick vegetation wall at point blank range and simply obliterate me?* I thought briefly that the .404 would not be worth much more than a peashooter in these circumstances. I looked back at Elias for reassurance. His normally slitted eyes were wide and white with fear, but he came forward. Together we strained to fathom the silent wall. I dropped to my haunches to try to see below the undergrowth, but there was nothing, only a spicy smell on the cool silent air. We stood for a few minutes, senses probing frantically.

Then I nodded at Elias and we started moving forward slowly. But we found only a few deep marks in the soft soil where he had swung round, and a whiff of dust. He had gone. They were all gone. Silently and effortlessly the great beasts had disappeared, like wisps of smoke on the breeze.

We took up the spoor. The bulls were now moving separately, and the spoor was difficult to follow on the thick leaf mat in the poor light. When the trees finally started thinning out and we could see across the grassland, there was still no sign of them. We knew we had lost them. The light was failing fast, and they were now surely moving much faster than we could track them. We turned back into the trees to find a good spot for a camp, our bodies still trembling and our speech broken with tension.

It was almost dark and we hurried to drag in as much firewood as possible for the night and to get the fire going for some light. Then Elias and John set about clearing an area of grass and growth and John, who had since started adopting me as his personal responsibility, made a mat of grass underneath my hammock so my feet wouldn't get dirty when I got off it.

That's not to say my feet were clean after the day's walking wearing sandals. I had found that a pair of sturdy sandals worked the best for me in the bush. One has to be extra careful of stepping on a puff adder but they are cool, they do not accumulate burrs or grass seeds, and they dry out very quickly if one has to wade through water or dew-laden grass.

We finally came to rest in an easy camp pattern. We had very little water, but I carefully wet an old T-shirt (that I always carried along as a general-purpose rag) from my water bottle, and wiped my face and arms and finally my legs and feet. I settled down in my hammock (which I had slung in such a way that I could also use it as an easy chair), with my little Cadac gas lamp and my diary. John had made me a splendid cup of tea, the evening air was pleasantly cool, and I felt the heat stress of the day slowly draining from my body.

The two black men were fiddling around the fire, endlessly re-living the events of the afternoon in ever-richer narrative, and preparing the food. John was the more animated of the two, more the man of the world, and was doing most of the talking. Elias sat on his haunches, his face drawn into a million wrinkles against the burn of the smoke, fiddling in the coals with a stick and giving an occasional grunt of recognition.

I watched them idly in between writing, and occasionally interrupted John's jabbering with a question or a remark about the food or the day's experiences as I re-lived them in the writing.

The behavior of the elephants puzzled me. They seemed uncharacteristically nervous and wary, even scared. Even before I got the feeling that they were suspecting our presence there was none of the usual feeding and tummy noises, nor flapping of ears, nothing. And the fear I saw in that eye . . .

"John, ask Elias if there are people hunting the elephants in this area."

Some conversation then ensued. Elias sat sideways from me, but he did not turn toward me at the question. He simply answered John, who relayed: "He says there are people."

"Are they many?"

"Sometimes they are many."

This did not mean much. "Where do they come from?"

"They come from other places"—emphasized with an outstretched arm gesturing toward the east.

"How do they kill them?"

"*Da-da-da-da!*" Elias's body convulsed graphically as he animated firing with an automatic weapon, and now he turned his head and when the watery eyes focused on me they bore a look of stern forbidding.

I brought the wrong rifle, I thought briefly. I was not expecting this complication. As Julius Caesar had learned at the dawn of our era, Africa always has something totally unexpected in the works for you. But in a sense it was not so surprising.

Less than two hundred miles to the east, on the banks of the Zambezi, lay the town of Tete, where there was one of only two bridge crossings over the mighty Zambezi in Mozambique at the time, the rest being ferries of dubious reliability. I had driven through the town a few times on my way to the northern reaches of Mozambique, and I knew it to be a sprawling settled area stretching for miles around the dilapidated town center, with various other settled areas sprouting out from it as far as ninety miles away. These hunters probably came from such settlements to the west of Tete, although they would still have had to travel more than sixty miles to get into the area where we now were.

The bull I had looked in the eye did not necessarily see me, even though he was so close. They have excellent hearing and smell, but poor eyesight, and I was moving very slowly in the dim light. One thing was for certain, though. They were not relaxed, and when they became aware of us they moved away with deliberate silence and speed—something that is amazing about elephants, the complete silence and speed with which they can move if they want to.

"How long will it take us to get to the water hole? Will it be early in the morning or around midday?" I asked.

"It will be early," Elias replied

"Will it be before midday?" I asked.

"Yes," he replied.

"Is there other water in this place?" I asked.

"There is other water, but it is far," Elias said.

"How long will it take us to get there?" I asked.

"Maybe it can take us two days."

This could mean the river, I thought.

"Which side is it?" I asked.

Elias gestured to the southeast without answering.

I thought he was getting a little bored or impatient (I wasn't sure which) with all the questions, but it was important for me to orient myself in the situation, so I pressed on. This meant that the other water hole was closer and perhaps more convenient for the machine-gun hunters coming in from the east.

"At this other water hole, are there elephants there?"

Slowly stirring in the coals with a stick, he said, "They can be there, but not so many."

"Why are they shooting the elephant? What do they want?" I asked.

"They want the meat and the horns of the elephant," Elias responded.

"Do they kill other game too?" I asked.

"They kill them if they can find them," he said.

John had by then finished preparing the food. We rinsed our hands and gathered around the common bowl—a few strips of partridge meat boiled from the bone and plenty of maize porridge.

When we had settled down, I asked: "These men, when they are walking in the bush, do they walk alone, or do they walk together?"

"Sometimes you can find one, sometimes you can find many," the translator informed me.

"Has Elias ever spoken to any of them?" I asked.

"He has spoken to them, but he does not like to speak to them."

"Why not?" I asked.

"*Ah*, because they are not good," the translator responded.

My worst fears were beginning to come true. I wondered what the situation to the north would be like.

"How long can we take to get to the river, the Zambezi?" I asked

"Maybe we can take three days," the translator responded.

"Does Elias know the area toward the river?" I asked.

"He knows it a little bit" was the reply.

I wasn't sure what that meant. "Does he know if there are elephants and other game in that area toward the river? And the hunters, are they also there?" I asked.

"You can find them," Elias said through the translator.

"Are they more there"—I gestured to the north—"or more here?"

"He does not know. Maybe they can be more there," said the translator.

They would probably use their dugouts to move up the river to hunt—makes sense, I thought. I wondered briefly if our good Stephan, focused on his camp, was aware of the presence of these hunters. I doubted it.

"Is there other water before we get to the river?" I asked.

"You can find it," I was told.

This probably meant if you dug in the right places in dry ravine beds.

"And lion, are there lions here?" I asked out of pure curiosity.

"*Ah*, sometimes they are many" was the reply.

"And the buffalo, are they here or are they closer to the river?" I asked.

The response was simple: "They are."

This scene is the stuff of an art film, I thought: The warm colors of the flames dancing over the background vegetation, nuancing the three bodies in the little circle into many aspects through the drifting smoke; the background sounds of insects and night birds and small animals in the vegetation; the occasional distant lament of a hyena or jackal; the simple meal from the common bowl with the low drone of voices slowly piecing together a picture of people and game and bush, with just a hint of evil in it. . . .

"How is Elias thinking—should we try to follow the bulls, or should we go to the water hole?" I asked.

"Maybe we can go to the water hole, or we can follow the bulls if you like."

Hmm. I was clearly on my own on this one.

There was some merit in following the bulls. We already knew there was a big bull among them (although we didn't know the size of its tusks). Although they had probably been moving at a speed of between six and nine miles per hour, we still had a chance to track them down if they did not take too long before relaxing again. (Our tracking speed could be as slow as half a mile an hour once they started grazing and not moving in a specific direction and as fast as 2.5 to 4.5 miles an hour if they were moving, especially if one or more were trailing each other and we could follow at a trot.) But it was a gamble.

Now that we had spooked them, they might carry on moving fast for quite some time into the night, which meant we could start with a distance of eighteen miles or more between them and us, and that would mean at least four hours of tracking just to wipe out the overnight distance. They almost certainly were not moving in single file, so tracking them would be more difficult. On the other hand, they could have calmed down quickly and could now be grazing peacefully just a short distance from us. I thought this unlikely, however. They were simply too nervous and scared.

"I think maybe we should go to the water hole," I said.

When John explained, Elias allowed a brief flicker of agreement at me. If I had said that we should follow the bulls he would most probably not have objected, but he understood from experience that it would most likely be a futile enterprise, and the fact that I also came to that conclusion gave me some bush-knowledge points. We were slowly developing a mutual respect.

I wondered briefly about the psychology of respect. One had to see respect in context here. John had apparently almost frivolously accepted that I represented something modern and progressive and wonderful and he wanted to learn by serving me with abandon in any way he could. I respected him for his simple but genuine efforts to do his best.

With Elias it was a bit more complicated. From my perspective it was something mostly rational and only slightly emotional. Something he earned and had to accumulate through his display of bush knowledge and his dignified behavior. His apparent aloofness did not bother me. For me, it was not part of the equation of respect in this situation. Besides, I half-assumed that his behavior was at least partly due to uncertainty, a sort of defense against something he might be struggling to place in context.

I wondered how he perceived me. If my assumption was correct and he had had very little or no contact with Westerners before, he was probably uncertain. He was a dignified man in a simple way, and quietly proud, used to being his own man, answerable to no one, and this was a very different situation. Did he perceive me as someone much less accomplished in the bush, and therefore to be viewed with some disdain, to be borne with the best possible fortitude until payday, or was there perhaps an element of admiration of someone clearly very different from himself? Did he even perceive or consider the difference? Did he also, as I suspected John did, see some symbol of hope, of change, in me, albeit in a more reserved way?

My discussing the elephant behavior, asking questions and advice, and showing fear and tension there, facing the elephant, probably removed some of the uncertainty of what kind of human he was dealing with—at least one who felt uncertain and fearful at times, but then again at other times so much more self-assured and commanding. I thought I would like to get to a more companionable, even follower-teacher relationship with him. But it seemed difficult to get through to him.

The evening had progressed past the hour of nine surprisingly quickly, and it was clear that rest was needed all round. I set the watch turns: Elias first, John in the middle, and myself taking the last stretch before dawn, and settled into my hammock.

Breaking a Bullet

CHAPTER 5

S itting the last watch starting at three o'clock, I watched the gray subtly seep in through the trees around four o'clock, building slowly in
delicate hues of pink and orange and red behind the black-etched
trees, finally spilling over the eastern horizon, brazen, triumphant, unstop-
pably engulfing the night. The sounds of night creatures lingered tentatively,
punctuated by the distant moans of a hyena, and, splendidly, the roll of a lion's roar on the wind from far to the southeast, then were gradually hushed
by the first few stirrings of day bird chirps here and there, and then the
abrupt burst of a bushveld pheasant's call, all building into a rich gallery of
different calls and wing flaps and rustles.

I decided that the best of the dawn was past, and I called my companions
from their night lairs. John had his introduction to making proper coffee,
and after each gnawing through one or two of our notorious hard rusks we
struck out through the dew-crystalled grass.

We had had an uneventful night, and we were rested and fresh and
eager for our first sighting of the water hole. *The allure of open water to
humans is a fascinating thing*, I thought. The light wind had built a bit, still
from the southeast, and Elias had us skirt around to the north so as to approach upwind.

The sun was still young and pleasantly warm on our dew-soaked bodies
when we came upon the hole, an oval of water lying in a strangely gray, dust-
trodden depression of some three hundred yards in diameter, bare except for
a few giant leadwoods and Ana trees. It looked to me like the ancient crater

of a meteorite strike. The rim was slightly raised, and the gray dust slid gently downward into the water at the center. It was evident from the water marks that the whole depression filled up in the rainy season, but now the pool had shrunk to not much more than thirty yards across. There wasn't any game, but it was clear why Elias, wily old hunter that he was, brought us to this place—here we would find the tracks of any animal in the area.

The water was like thick pea soup. I had John scoop it up with a mug and pour it into our containers through a shirt. It wasn't very pleasant, but it could save a life. Meanwhile Elias and I eagerly skirted the pan's edge, checking for tracks. There were so many in all directions that it was difficult to look at a particular set. But spotting elephant tracks wasn't a problem. I found two fresh sets from the night before, both belonging to breeding herds, with cows and young, and some bull spoor, partly obscured and about a day old—I suspected made by the bull herd we had come across. This was a bit disappointing, because we had nothing immediate to go on, but I was very optimistic that we had a very good chance. It was a question of patience.

Now that we knew the situation, I had us move away a bit downwind from the water hole, to where one could just see over the rim if one stood up. We settled down to have breakfast and make our plans.

"John, ask Elias if he had seen any spoor of big bulls," I ventured when the moment seemed opportune.

"No, but they are here," he volunteered uncharacteristically without being asked, clearly pleased with himself and quite convinced that I was going to be too.

"Yes, now if we come tomorrow, maybe we can find the spoor of a very big bull here?"

"Ehè!"—from deep in his belly and accompanied by a vigorous nod of head and hands.

"Hmm, now how would it be if today we walked around"—I demonstrated a clockwise circle around the water hole—"and tonight we sleep perhaps over there"—I gestured to the north—"but not too close, and tomorrow we come and take a look?"

"It is right."

I wanted to know what it looked like to the east and the south, but the wind was not in our favor for walking south, so I pointed Elias eastward, and we set off, more relaxed and focused on our environment because we were not really going anywhere in particular. Much as I had enjoyed walking to the water hole, this was the ultimate experience, being able to pay attention to small details of the bush, and piecing together the stories around what one saw with the help of someone of Elias's experience: a pile of millipede skeletons where a civet had made his latrine, the tracks of a troop of striped mongooses across a soft patch of sand, the scuff marks on a raisin bush where a sable bull had sparred with it, the pug marks of a male leopard on a tree trunk, the brown, smelly markings of hyena on the grass, a martial eagle nest high up in a leadwood, the tracks of a huge puff adder across the soft sand, and the birds and trees . . .

After about two hours of walking, the ground started getting more stony, and sloped gently away to the east. We appeared to have been on a smallish plateau where the water hole was, with different soil and vegetation patterns from the area around it. We continued along the northern edge of a shallow, eastward-running ravine. It was getting deeper and steeper as we progressed, and the vegetation inside it and along its banks had become quite dense.

Suddenly Elias stopped dead in his tracks ahead of me and dropped to his haunches. I immediately did the same and inched forward to him. I looked along the gnarled black finger pointing straight ahead. The ravine curved slightly to the north, and on its far bank in a small clearing were two elephant bulls. They were plucking tufts of dry but still tasty buffalo grass from a lush stand that had flourished there in the clearing where it received just enough light, but had some protection from the sun. The bulls were both in their prime, but the nearest one had the bigger tusks. I estimated them at about fifty pounds a side—not particularly exciting, but not to be sneezed at, either.

This was a difficult situation. The bull was not really trophy material, but it was entirely possible that for this area he was a good bull, even one of the better ones. I had simply not been here long enough to know. His tusks seemed bigger than the biggest bull I had shot up till then. If I did not take the shot I might be forgoing a good opportunity. If I took it, I might be forgoing an even better one, or not? If I could only ask Elias how the bull compared. I looked back at John, but he was crouching some way back. I was going to be on my own on this one.

The shot was a bit farther than I would have preferred—about sixty yards, but not too far and not difficult. The wind was light from our left, taking our scent across their front, and I did not want to risk moving closer along the ravine edge, although there was ample cover. The wind might just eddy a little, and if they smelled me they could be instantly gone. The alternative was to cross the ravine and approach them from the upwind side, but it was very deep and steep at that place. If I was going to take a shot, this was it. I decided it was worth it.

I had slid a round in the chamber when we left the camp that morning and moved the safety to half position, as was my habit. The bull was standing half-facing me, presenting his left shoulder. I had to stand up to fire over the low shrub behind which Elias and I were sitting. I laid flat the safety catch and placed the gold front bead in the center of the big front leg bone in line with where the heart was. *If I hit the bone, the .404 will break it and I will have another chance. If I miss it to the left, I'll hit the heart or at least some of the arteries; if I miss to the right I'll hit the lung—both deadly shots*, I reasoned as I waited for the front bead to drift over the spot, and touched the trigger.

The sudden brutal explosion of the shot into our careful silence and the recoil knocked me back a bit, so I didn't see where the bullet went, but as I was knocking a second round into the chamber, I saw the bull stagger back against his companion, which steadied him, and then they both wheeled around and were gone. I lowered the rifle. No chance for a second shot. As a startled silence washed over the crashing panic of their flight I quietly chewed on a curse for not having had a double in my hands. It was at moments like this when one understood that doubles weren't invented just because they are so damn beautiful!

I motioned John forward. He was standing with shoulders drawn up, open palms held forward, all white teeth and white eyes, looking like someone expecting to hear that he had won the lottery. "Ask him where I hit him," I said. (Not quite the lottery-ticket news.)

Elias pushed his shoulder forward and with a loud "*taow!*" demonstrated how the bullet knocked the dust out of the elephant's hide when it hit, and animated how the bull staggered backward, bumping his back against his companion. At least that gave me some comfort. The shot appeared to have gone where I had aimed.

We had to move back up the ravine for quite a way to find a place to cross. When we got to the clearing, the deep gashes in the ground where they had turned and thrown themselves into flight were clear, but there was no blood. We searched around and then started following the spoor, but still no blood. All I could see was that the bull was dragging his left front foot a little. I showed Elias, animating with limp left hand, and he nodded an acknowledgment, but he was clearly puzzled and a little worried. It wasn't looking good.

We settled onto the spoor. It was easy to follow because the bulls had moved fast, scuffing the hard earth, knocking over tree stumps, kicking away rocks, crushing vegetation. I eventually found a little blood smeared on the leaves of a shrub at about the height of my shoulder. The spoor was running downwind—due south. We stuck to it, moving as fast as we could, often at a trot, leaving poor John with his pack far behind. After about an hour the bulls seemed to have settled into a brisk walk. They were moving separately, and the spoor became more difficult to follow on the hard ground. We lost it once and had to circle to find it.

By one o'clock it was unbearably hot. With the sun almost directly overhead, tracking had become difficult. I called a halt. We had moved fast for about three hours, and must have covered at least nine miles or more, with no sign of the bulls slowing down. We lowered ourselves gratefully to the ground in the cool shade of a marula. John and Elias immediately went for the water, but I stopped them, trying to explain that it was much more effective if one waited until one had cooled down and had stopped sweating before one drank, and that we had to conserve our water. The total incredulity with which they looked at me showed that they did not share my views. *Why not drink water when you are thirsty? The white man has lost it in the heat!* I assumed they were thinking. But I stuck to my guns. It was unclear where we would end up and when we would find water again. We might have to survive on what we had for quite some time, murky as it was.

We sat out the worst of the heat, my companions dozing off or engaging in low, murmured conversation, me with my back against the marula trunk, unable to untangle from the bull and the shot, how he had staggered back against his companion, how they wheeled and crashed away, and Elias slapping his left shoulder —*"taow!"*—throwing out his arms to show the dust exploding from the bull's hide, and then the dragging left front foot and the small smear of blood high up . . . it was haunting me, and soon I chased them out of the shade and into the panting heat. They did not complain, simply leaned into the task, settling into the routine.

We stuck to it grimly for another three hours or so, each occupied with his own fatigue and pain, our world one of reddish, sun-baked earth, with here and there a faint mark, or a crushed leaf, or a downtrodden grass stem, each part of a bigger puzzle, each having to be verified as belonging to the bulls and consistent with their direction and likely behavior. Elias was a master, but tracking was now becoming very difficult and slow on the hard ground, and although the sun had spent most its white fury and it was a bit cooler, we were very tired. We must have covered twenty-five miles or more in the course of the day, some of it at a trot. As we came up to a clump of trees that offered us a reasonable campsite, I called a halt. The sun was hemorrhaging the last of its strength across the skies to our right, and the far trees were already beginning to blend into a uniform grayness. It was becoming impossible to track anyway, and I wasn't even sure that we were still positively on the spoor.

This was a remote and lonely area, without water, with sparse tough grass and smallish leathery trees. We had seen few tracks—small antelope only—on the hard stony earth. The trees under which we made camp were pleasant enough, but our camp was detached and sad, almost as if it had its mind elsewhere. Not even the fire flickering its warm glow against the tree trunks could change it, and outside its glow the bush was silent, stirring uneasily in a slow, warm wind. We were bone-tired and I sought my hammock early, but the events of the day and their agony were endlessly writhing through my mind, and finally I gave up on sleep, just lay on my back, my senses filled with the talking wind and the mosaic of black-etched leaves moving against the stars.

Somewhere in the course of the night the complicated maze of thoughts that milled through my mind got stuck on the strange interplay between conscious action and the universe. The latter is supposedly neutral, yet seemed to contain vast prearranged arrays of cause-and-effect-connected sequences that we could trigger with our actions. If we do, we get launched down a particular chain of events that seems more or less inevitable, predetermined. Yet the sequence that follows has (so it seems to us) unique challenges and choices at each component event, opening up yet more cause-and-effect chains. And even though we may seem to control our destiny through these choices at any point, they are really influenced (even determined) by the circumstances prevailing at the component events, which are in turn not independent of preceding events all the way back to the original trigger event. And the kinds of choices we make at the trigger point and all along the way may be influenced by who we are, and what our inclinations are. But that again is a product of a similar series of events farther back in our personal history, and at a meta scale we may really, then, have very little control over our destiny, and what we believe to be control may just be insignificant variations we can affect through our choices.

And in that sense, the Universe is not neutral. It actually controls us through its immutable rules—rules at macro level, rules at meta level, rules at micro level, right down to the very basic rules that govern the interaction between two atoms in a chemical reaction. But then there are the accidents of life, the extraordinary events, out of pattern, that happen and change this predetermination, like a mutation breaking the steady pattern of a DNA regime. In some lives there aren't any, in others several—in some countries, hemispheres, there aren't any, in others they occur more often. And behind all this, there is God, I believe, so remote, so completely incomprehensible behind billions upon billions of years and billions upon billions of laws, and billions upon billions of galaxies, yet so close, around us, caressing our minds, inside us, perhaps. . . .

At this point a grateful calm finally settled over me. Still, the slow return of the grayness, and with it the obligation of action, was welcome. I had my two companions moving early, the sun still not clearing the horizon, providing just enough light to track in the difficult terrain. I was by now almost totally convinced that trying to track down the bulls was fruitless, but I had to be sure.

After about two hours of relentlessly difficult tracking, we came into a sandy clearing where the bulls had crossed. We could read the spoor very clearly here. They were now quite far ahead of us, I suspected, but for the last hour of their flight their track showed that they had slowed to a walk, and had started meandering a bit, and now we could see that my bull wasn't dragging his left front foot anymore. Elias and I looked at each other and we both shook our heads, and then we stopped. It was clearly no use following any farther. The bull showed no sign of distress or impairment, there was no blood, and they were beginning to relax and even pluck at the odd clump of leaves again. This was not an animal that was going to suffer a slow death.

My suspicions were confirmed. The bullet must have broken up on the heavy front leg bone, making a relatively minor flesh wound and causing some initial pain and discomfort. I then remembered Taylor saying in his book *African Hunting Rifles and Cartridges* that, although he had used a .404 extensively and had never experienced the phenomenon himself, he had heard of an experienced hunter in Tanzania using a .404 relating instances where the 410-grain solid bullet had broken up and failed to penetrate. This was actually quite surprising, because it was very heavily jacketed (Taylor even commented on it). Sometime later, when I told the story to a professional hunter, he immediately said that the .404 ammunition (especially the particular brand I was using) had a reputation for sometimes breaking up on heavy bone.

"John, ask Elias if he knows of any water closer than the water hole of yesterday."

"He says he does not know the water in this area, sir."

"OK, so how will it be if we turn back toward the water hole and walk till the sun is there, and then we make camp?" I pointed low in the west.

"It will be right."

"OK, John—which direction do you think we should go?" I had roughly kept track of our direction through the day by regularly checking my compass, which I always carried on a thong around my neck and tucked into my shirt pocket, and I thought that the water hole had to be somewhere to the northwest, but I was interested to see if Elias would agree and if John would also be able to tell the direction.

John simply smiled a shy smile and shook his head. "I don't know, sir." Elias turned around without hesitation and led us northwest. I was again amazed at the natural sense of direction of good bush men like him. He just knew, with the same instinctive certainty that I would have about the direction to the airport from anywhere in Johannesburg or Pretoria, even though I might not be sure of the specific streets I would have to follow. I did find, however, that people like Elias sometimes became uncertain when they were in an area that they had never been in before—it was as if they got to "know" the bush that they had worked before.

We walked hurriedly, almost grimly leaning into the rising heat, not noticing much of our surroundings, as if we had to escape from our experience in this barren stretch of bush. I now insisted on a strict discipline. We rested every hour in as cool a spot as we could find. And I controlled the water. There was not much left, and if we didn't find any on the way, which was likely to be the case, we would barely make it back to the water hole with what we had.

By our midday rest I had only allowed a mouthful to each at the stops, and there was only one more small drink left for each. I thought that we had to be about another four to six hours away from the water hole—too far to make it before dark. I asked Elias through John what he thought. He said "Maybe tomorrow," and I knew this was going to be grim.

"Now, if we had finished all the water yesterday, what would we do now?" I asked, looking at them quizzically. They both looked down and didn't answer, but I sensed a certain admiration. "Ask Elias if he knows of any other place that is not too far where we can find water."

"It is only the water hole."

"I think we must wait here until the sun is not so hot (I pointed at the lower third of the western horizon), then we must walk, and tomorrow we must start early and walk far before the sun is hot, because I am scared if the sun is very hot like now we will get very thirsty and maybe we will not reach the water hole," I tried to explain as simply as possible. They realized that the situation was dangerous, and they felt comfortable with me deciding.

It was around four o'clock when we broke from the shade and started walking into the angular sun. We carried on until dusk, and I estimated that we were almost on top of the plateau. We had been gradually climbing all afternoon, but the slope seemed gentler now, and for the last half-hour the terrain had become softer, I thought. I still felt strong, but I knew that I was already half dehydrated. My mouth and throat were dry and sticky. I felt a little dizzy at times, and I had developed a slight headache.

We made camp hurriedly in the half light. Elias disappeared into the dark, and after a while he walked into the fire glow, holding a few pieces of thick root. I discovered the next morning that he chopped them from a white syringa tree that he had spotted some distance from camp. He hung them over a pot, and we watched eagerly as water slowly dripped from them. I forbade them to have any of the smoked meat because it would take more moisture to digest. We ate some of the tinned food, from which I had them carefully pour off the liquid and add it to the water from the syringa roots. Before we retired for the night we shared the moisture—only a few small mouthfuls each, but wonderful.

We decided we had to keep watch. We were not very far from the water hole, and we could very well receive visitors. I took the first watch. The night was pleasantly cool, and I felt a calmness settle over me after the intense walk of the day. I was feeling a lot better from the food and the small drink, and less worried that we wouldn't make it. We would probably reach the water hole by early morning before the sun was too hot, and then we would be fine. I had my little Coleman lamp going and I wrote up my diary and read a little and thought.

I wondered how Gerhard was doing. Had he shot anything yet? Was he in camp with Vic and Mack, or was he sitting alone in the veld around a fire with Jo'burg? And Vic—had he gotten anything yet? How was it working out for him with Mack and Jerry? When I finally shook Elias awake I was feeling calm, and I drifted off to a pleasant sleep despite the thirst.

A Dangerous Encounter

We got going with the remains of the night still lurking in the denser groves. Walking through the dew-damp grass in the dawn coolness made the thirst almost bearable, but soon the sun lifted relentlessly above the treetops, towering over us, white-hot and merciless, sucking the moisture from our bodies and pulling the knot tighter around our throats until the thirst filled our minds like an evil demon shouting incessantly in an empty room.

We walked fast, as fast as we could. We took turns with John's pack, barely noticing our surroundings, just aching for the sight of the water. It reminded me of some desperate days I had known during my time with the Special Forces, force-marching over long distances through hostile territory, heavily loaded with equipment and ammunition. We finally broke over the rim of the water hole after ten with great relief, and half-stumbled down to its edge. I didn't even bother to take off my clothes or sandals or try to drink. I simply waded in and lay down in the thick green liquid, letting it run into the cavities of my body, soaking it up, feeling the mud ooze up against my sides and waiting for my mind to slowly regain its perspective.

We must have spent an hour at the water hole before we were ready to put together some breakfast. While John got a fire going some way off, Elias and I scouted for tracks in the dust and mud. As before there were many, but only one set was of interest. They were made by a breeding herd, either very early in the morning or possibly late in the night. But there seemed to be two sets of bull tracks with them, and one of the two seemed really big. I thought it a bit unusual to see two sets of mature bull tracks with a breeding herd, because mature bulls usually join breeding herds when they are in musth and there is a cow in the herd that is ready to mate. Could this be two bulls in musth with the same herd?

During breakfast I thought about what we had observed of the elephants at the water hole the two times we were there. We hadn't seen tracks of the same herd two days in a row. In fact, there seemed to be different herds visiting on different days. One could not be sure, but it appeared that with all the grazing closer to the water hole used up, they had to move far out to find enough to feed their great bodies. So they would come in probably every second or third day, covering the distance in the cool of the night, and then heading out again to the east and south.

Elephants heading somewhere specific would move a lot faster than we could walk, let alone track them. It would only be once they started grazing that they would slow down a bit. But if they had a head start on us as this herd did, the chances of catching up with them were slim. Our only hope was to do our best at the tracking and catch up with them while they were resting over the midday heat. We could not risk following them much farther because, as was so starkly demonstrated over the past two days, we could not move away from the water by more than a day, maybe another half-day if we were not pushing ourselves too hard, unless we were sure of finding new water along the way, which seemed unlikely. So, if we hadn't caught them before they moved on after their midday rest on the first day of leaving the water hole, we would most probably have lost them.

We were in a rather challenging situation. It would not make much sense to stay at the water hole and ambush them as they came in, either. Apart from the fact that I didn't like the idea at all, it probably wouldn't work, because they mostly came at night. Our food situation was also becoming an issue. Almost all of the dried meat was gone, and the rest was at rock bottom. This situation was made worse by the probability that my companions at the vehicle might pack up and go—we were already into our fourth day, and it was a bit more than a day's walk back to the vehicle. It was very possible that they would leave today as we had discussed, and that would mean that we would have to live on game and veld fruits only, and would have to walk all the way back to the river camp. Finding enough food in the bush to survive on could take a lot of time—it would not leave much for focused hunting.

I decided to take the chance of dispatching John back to the vehicle to fetch some supplies. There was a real risk that he would not make it before they left, but it was worth a try. It would make the hunt a bit more pleasurable if I had just a few additional basics like tea and some maize meal and dried milk and cereal for breakfast and so on, and perhaps even some red wine to slowly roll over the palate during those beautiful sunsets.

I was not altogether comfortable about John going. He might not find the vehicle (although he assured me he would), and it would be a problem communicating with Elias in his absence. But Elias and I were beginning to develop a mutual understanding that required very little talking. I thought fleetingly: *It's a bit like Gerhard and me.*

I briefed John as well as our limited mutual mastery of Zulu and Fana-galo allowed. He was to carry the few supplies and camp utensils we had left back to the campsite where we spent the night before we reached the water hole. There, he had to stash all but just enough food for himself to get to the vehicle and back, and then carry on as fast as possible with an empty pack to try to catch the others before they left. We would meet him at the camping spot. I gave him a short note to Gerhard with a list of supplies on a page I tore from my diary:

To: The Esteemed Hunters-in-Temporary-Residence
From: A Wanderer through the Bush

  Greetings, and may your hearts be pure and your aim true, and may the Goddess place before you, and keep stationary until you have delivered a true shot, the bearers of great ivory.

May it please the Great Hunters to receive my humble envoy with kindness, for he has traveled far at great speed and endured many dangers to bring to you this dispatch from the Wanderer.

Let it be known to the Great Hunters that no bearers of great ivory have yet been slain, but that the earth bears witness to their presence in this place.

Let it further be known that the Wanderer has run out of supplies and needs you lot to send back the following stuff with John:

+ 1 packet of muesli
+ 500 gr. of maize meal or rice
+ 1 bottle of the best red wine you have left
+ 1 sachet of tea bags
+ 200 gr. of sugar
+ 1 packet of powdered milk
+ Assorted snacks to chew on
+ Some rusks

Good hunting. Write me a note so I can know what the hell you are up to.

The One Who Wanders

Then I hurried my companions through the breakfast. They were unaccustomed to the relatively high-intensity type of situation we had been experiencing over the past days, hurrying to achieve an objective and working against a deadline, however critical to survival or otherwise important it might be. I could see that they were uncomfortable and a bit bewildered. I made a mental note that I would have to slow down.

It was past twelve before we finally set off on our separate ways—Elias and me taking up the spoor to the northeast, and John heading west. I hoped he would be OK as I watched him heading off, his round head bobbing above the half-empty backpack. We had seen quite a bit of lion spoor around the water hole, but I had thought it best not to tell him about it. It was unlikely that they would bother him anyway. This area was extremely remote, and lions were likely to be unaccustomed to humans and naturally afraid of them—at least that's what I assured myself as I swung the .404 onto my shoulder and turned to follow Elias's tall frame through the trees.

The spoor was easy to follow. The herd was moving quite fast, making a big track in single file, steadily heading almost directly northeast.

We moved abreast ten or so paces apart, both tracking, so that we would reduce the risk of losing the spoor. I loved watching Elias track. He had an amazing instinct for the animal mind, and he would constantly be mimicking their behavior as he read the signs—plucking at some leaves with hand held like the snout of an elephant trunk and bending it to his mouth in typical action, even dropping the few shreds that lay scattered still green and soft on the ground, or acting with limp curled fingers how one had allowed its trunk to draw the short drag mark in a sandy spot, or how the matriarch in front had stopped suddenly, lifted her trunk and tested the air, one arm cocked for the great ears, the other searching through the scents and sounds on the slight breeze from the west. It was at that point that the matriarch had abruptly swung more north, and quickened her pace, for a reason yet unknown to us.

By early afternoon I was beginning to lose faith in the spoor. We had been tracking fast for about two hours, and must have covered around six miles. Although the spoor was still relatively easy to follow, it seemed to me that we had not managed to catch up with the herd at all—it was still several hours old, and since the sharp northward turn they had kept moving at a pace. I stopped, and as Elias looked across inquiringly, I pointed to the spoor and mimicked running with my fingers. He nodded resignedly, looking sadly down at the spoor and swatting absently at the torment of the tsetse. It was clear that he also did not think this had much of a chance of success.

I looked around for a leafy tree. *Might as well do my thinking sitting down and out of this bloody sun*, I thought. It was then that I suddenly noticed an unusual mark on a tree trunk. I called Elias over and we went to investigate. It was a fresh chop mark made by an ax or a machete. There weren't any tracks at or around the base of the tree, but it was unmistakably human made. The brown globules of gum that had seeped out from the white wood were still soft on the inside, so it was probably made a few days or possibly a week ago. It was typical of someone wanting to mark a route or a position, perhaps to a snare or a beehive or a kill. But who on earth would be wandering around here?

Now communication was a problem. Elias might have had some idea of who had made this mark in this remote spot and why. But how to ask him? Could it be someone from another semi-nomadic family living in distant isolation? I looked around, and, sure, there was another mark on a tree some two hundred yards away. I pointed it out to Elias. He nodded but seemed strangely averse or disinterested; I couldn't quite place his reaction. I was intrigued by the marks, wondering who had made them and where they led to, and I started following them. They were easy to follow and I moved quite fast, Elias tagging along unenthusiastically and looking a bit miserable.

After about an hour I found some human footprints made by someone wearing sandals made from old car tires, and then more footprints along a fairly well-worn path. Elias was now getting inexplicably uncooperative, lagging behind and shaking his head every time I looked back at him.

At some point I caught a whiff of wood smoke and the hint of fried meat. This was really interesting! We were both ravenously hungry, and I was painfully aware of our precarious food situation. Could we perhaps scrounge off some bush dwellers?

Then, suddenly, we came upon a huge baobab tree around which the vegetation had been cleared for about fifteen paces. There were three men there, sitting on their haunches around a lazily smoking fire, eating meat from a lattice made out of saplings tied together with bark. They jumped up as they saw us, their faces ashen with fright. One hinted at running away, but restrained himself, and as we stood uncertainly staring at each other and they gradually got over their surprise, their attitude turned more surly. I looked around warily. The area around the tree was trodden to powder and untidily strewn with waste and camp equipment: sleeping mats, some spread, some rolled up, a few earthen pots of various sizes, items of clothing, animal skins, some spread out, some hanging, and lots of meat, mostly cut into long thin strands, and at various stages of drying, hanging from sapling frames. Leaning against the baobab trunk stood a muzzleloading gun, homemade, with a water pipe for a barrel —crude, but probably deadly at close quarters.

It suddenly became clear to me: It was a hunters' camp. Some would call it a poachers' camp, because this was an official hunting concession area (or at least I assumed we were still in the Game Trackers area), and no hunting other than by the concession holders was supposed to take place in it—in fact, every operator winning a hunting concession would have as one of the conditions of his tenure that he must control poaching in the area.

We greeted the men but their response was hesitant, and I sensed a guardedness on their part, and an unease on the part of Elias. They started a conversation with him and I had an opportunity to look them over more closely. The "wanted to run" character was the youngest, and still seemed as if he was a bit homesick, but anxious to live down his almost-ran reaction. *Those types are usually the most unpredictable*, I thought briefly. Of the two others, one seemed like an affable, harmless sort when by himself or in different company, but the other one, very dark in complexion with heavy eyelids, was staring at me somewhat insolently and, I noticed, taking the lead in being quite assertive in his manner. He also showed a special interest in my rifle.

In my experience interactions with Africans are usually friendly and relaxed, but the atmosphere here was nervous, even a bit hostile, and I suddenly realized why Elias was so reluctant to follow the spoor. We were in a very remote place, where there were no laws but the honor of men, and right then we were in the company of men who lived by a harsh code and regarded my high-powered hunting rifle as probably the greatest possible prize they could win in their entire life—the means to a much easier hunting life and a source of great status. I suddenly realized that both Elias's and my life weren't worth much more than the risk of injury to them, and that they knew we would be almost completely untraceable if we should simply disappear here.

Their attitude and reaction was quite understandable. They had lived off the land for generations. The laws now preventing them from hunting and snaring were alien to them, made by some unknown entity very far away from their little bush village in a place called Maputo, of which they were only vaguely aware. They probably did not understand those laws, did not agree with them, and resented them and all things associated with them.

From the signs around us it seemed as if the camp was being used by at least fifteen people, and thinking back on Elias's graphic demonstration of how these hunters killed their prey, some would be armed, most likely with an automatic weapon or two that had spilled over from the war situation. All of this flashed through my mind, together with an acute awareness from long years in Africa that for all their friendliness and spontaneity, Africans could be totally cold-blooded and ruthless in a conflict situation if they sensed that he had the upper hand. A familiar cold tightness in my chest threatened to press my breath up into the top of my lungs, but then the Fatalist lurched forward carelessly from the shadows, twisting the corners of my mouth into a smile and brazenly shouting "What the hell!" in my mind, and Fear slinked away and lurked uncertainly in the background.

I had to keep my poise. I fixed a cold stare on Heavy Eyelids and casually but deliberately swung the .404 from my shoulder and slipped off the safety, at the same time discreetly retreating with my back toward the tree and the muzzleloader. We were lucky to have found only the three at home. Elias was talking to them, and I noticed him gesturing vaguely to the west. By this time I had moved back so that I had some distance between myself and the men, and my back against the baobab. I casually sat down on my haunches, rifle resting across my legs. I was heartened to see that my unyielding attitude seemed to have caused some uncertainty in them, and especially in Heavy Eyelids, who had now averted his gaze.

I felt we could actually afford to be a bit brazen while I was holding the cards, and I wished I could get Elias to ask them if they had permission to hunt in the area and to tell them that they had to leave immediately and that I would be back to check, but there was simply no way I could get such complex communication over to him. But I knew that the situation could turn against us very quickly if some of their armed colleagues came back, so when Elias looked back at me I gestured with my head that we should leave, putting on an air of bored irritation. I wanted to exploit their temporary uncertainty to make a clean breakaway, and leave them sufficiently unsure to not consider following us, even if some of their companions returned after we left. I immediately started out purposefully, heading west and keeping an eye on the three. Just before we disappeared into the trees I looked back at them. They still stood as we had left them, and I stopped momentarily and gave them a hard parting look, hoping to drive home the advantage we had gained. Mr. Friendly made as if he was going to wave, but then he noticed that his companions were not, and he quickly sneaked his hand back to where it belonged.

I could not discuss their behavior with Elias, but they certainly had a motive for trying to eliminate us and gain access to my rifle, or at least prevent knowledge of their presence spreading. The chances were good that they had the right attitude for it, but their type was usually cowardly (or, perhaps, sensible), and they were unlikely to take on something they were not convinced they had a good chance of overpowering without too much resistance. But I remained concerned about them trying to follow us as soon as their numbers and firepower gave them sufficient confidence. They would certainly have the tracking capability to do it. I was hoping that the three would paint a fairly ferocious picture of us to their companions, and that they would be further discouraged by the uncertainty of whether we had any companions, and how far away they might be.

When I thought we were out of their sight I quickened the pace, keeping west. After about thirty minutes, we got to a rocky area where it would be extremely difficult to follow our spoor. I crossed over it, keeping west, but then, after about half a mile, doubled back in a wide loop, coaxing Elias into leaving as little sign as possible. When we got back to the rocky area I stopped and explained to Elias in sign language that he should move back some distance to see if someone wasn't trying to follow us. He understood immediately, and cleverly took a route some way off our path. When he got back, shaking his head at my inquiring glance, I swung sharply south, seeking out the hard ground for some distance before I gestured to Elias to take the lead back to our campsite. I was applying classic anti-tracking measures. If they were reasonably good trackers they would pick up our tracks on the western edge of the rocky area and continue west with them, and hopefully when they disappeared where we doubled back they would give up. If they had a real master tracker he might still be able to figure it out, especially if he knew something of anti-tracking, but we could now only hope for the best.

It felt a bit silly taking all those precautions, but on the other hand, it could be an extremely unpleasant situation if the poachers paid us a visit. I also resolved that we would no longer hunt to the northeast. It was clear anyway that the game was aware of the presence of the hunters in the area— it was no doubt the reason for the sudden change in direction of the elephant matriarch we had followed.

We had a good four hours of walking back, because we had to go via the pan to collect water. A brisk breeze had sprung up from the southeast, chasing pink clouds across the gray-blue sky and mercifully cooling us down as we strode through the late afternoon. When we reached our old campsite the dusk had already invaded it, blending shapes into each other, and making us stumble clumsily, cursing, over dead branches and brush as we tried to collect enough wood to last the night.

Our camp that night was without the low drone of voices, but with a soft companionship between us in the glow of the fire. Each kept busy with his own thing, exchanging only a glance or a sign now and again. Elias sat on his haunches beside the fire, staring into the smoke with slitted eyes, fiddling in the coals and tending the porridge. I was scraping together something to have with the porridge from the tattered remains of our food, wondering what on earth he could be thinking. It was quite late when we had finished feeding ourselves and doing all the camp chores and could finally surrender to our fatigue. We gratefully sank down beside the fire, too tired to even bother about watch turns, and succumbed to a light sleep that kept a constant vigil for any unusual sound, each of us waking from time to time to lie listening and throw on a piece of wood.

A Sad Elephant Hunt

CHAPTER 7

W
e woke as the morning stirred among the trees, and reluctantly fumbled into readiness. We were feeling a bit fuzzy and inclined to sleep on, but we knew without speaking that we had to pick up elephant tracks early if we wanted to have even a slight chance of catching up with them in the course of the day. We bundled the last few scraps of food we had left, plus sleeping bag, hammock, groundsheet, and blanket into the small pack, and then, with eyes meeting in fleeting agreement, we set out for the water hole.

We approached upwind in the glow of the young light, and there was a herd of sable drinking, unaware of our presence—six cows and some young, and a splendid bull. He stood regally aloof, satin black over the white of his belly and face, magnificent horns arching back grandly over his withers. He saw us first, and with a sharp snort sent his herd bursting away in a cloud of dust and spray. But he didn't immediately run away—he tossed his head at us defiantly before he swung around and pranced away, peering back at us with a white eye as he went, head held high and neck arched in pride. It left me breathless! To this day the image is etched in my mind: him standing there, alone for a moment in the drifting dust of his disappearing herd, the low sun making his black coat gleam like brushed velvet, facing us defiantly, like the last Spartan warrior standing on the field.

I dutifully joined Elias in searching for tracks around the edge of the pan, but now I felt like a clerk of the court guiltily delivering a letter of summons to a noble gentleman. We found some promising tracks leaving the pan toward the southeast, roughly the same direction we had gone a few days ago when I took the shot at the bull. They were made by a group of three bulls, two big ones and a younger one. They were fresh, not more than three or four hours old, and I nodded to Elias to follow them.

They were following a well-trodden elephant path with several other sets of tracks on it, and the challenge was to keep following the right set. This was where my tracking abilities fell short, and I had to rely on Elias's bush sense. He walked leaning forward slightly, hands clasped behind his back, his knobkerrie dangling loosely from between two fingers, appearing to seldom look directly at the spoor, but rather a bit ahead and around, muttering under his breath in a low drone, mimicking the bulls as he went.

We were making slow progress, but I enjoyed watching Elias completely absorbed in his tracking, his mumbling blending in with the murmur of the leaves in the wind and buzz of the flies and the bird calls, which always seemed to me to grow more melancholy as it got hotter. After an hour I was beginning to worry that we were wasting our time. But then Elias suddenly veered off the track to the south, and walked back at a slight angle to the elephant path. I could see that he was not following any tracks, and could only hope that he knew what he was doing. Fifteen minutes later he triumphantly pointed out the tracks to me, leading off to the south. The bulls had evidently left the path some way back, probably in an area where the ground was very hard and it was difficult to be sure, but Elias had clearly noticed something, had suspected that they had veered off, and had noted their general direction, but had carried on for a bit along the path to make sure before he went back. Once he was sure, he cut across to intersect them rather than going back to the turn-off point, and he was able to know that the tracks we were now staring down at were those made by the very same bulls. I was in the hands of a true master! What a delight, a privilege, to watch him at work, noticing every minute detail, getting deeper into the mind of the animal, almost becoming the animal at that point in the past! I spontaneously shook his hand, and I

85

could see that the fact that I understood and appreciated what he was do-ing and how fine it was gave him satisfaction.

++++++

He reminded me of Ruben, who I met when I was taking the very first nibbles at the adventuring that would punctuate the rest of my life with so many memorable experiences. Ruben was as tall as Elias (maybe taller, although he was bent into a permanent stoop with a hump, probably from polio or some childhood injury). He had precariously thin legs that protruded from oversized shorts like stilts, and long, spindly arms that always hung limply down his sides, palms held backward like two grotesquely shaped garden tools. He lived on a stretch of land once owned by a rich distant cousin of mine who had made his money (far too much of it) from property speculation. The farm was vast, even by the standards of that remote area in the northeastern part of South Africa—something like 37,000 acres or so. Ruben (I later found out) had been born on the farm and had lived there all of his life, so the farm came with Ruben.

I ended up there because my rich cousin, at some family gathering where he wanted to impress everyone within earshot, had generously offered that I could go and hunt kudu there, and boomed (although I later realized he regarded the farm purely as a transaction and had never been on it), "There are thousands of kudu there, man, and let me tell you, I have seen some really big bulls there." He let the last bit of his sentence trail off into a conspiratorial whisper—for effect, I now suspect.

I was still at school and highly impressionable, and I eagerly accepted, not even noticing (or not wanting to notice) the knowing smirks on the faces of some of the older members of the family. It was the first time I was to be alone in the veld in such a relatively remote place, and I was a bit apprehen-sive, but I nevertheless set out some weeks later in my father's reluctantly loaned blue Isuzu pickup, armed with a wonderful Anglo-Boer War vintage 7x57mm Mauser carbine that I had inherited from my great grandfather, some rudimentary camping gear, and an abundance of youthful determination and naiveté.

There were the remnants of a house on the property, but it had been invaded by bats and birds and other creatures and it was so dilapidated and dirty that I decided (with some trepidation), to make myself a camp on the veld. Traveling along the half-overgrown tracks in search of a campsite, I came upon a lone windmill in a small depression. Although gap-wheeled and twisted by angry winds, it still towered tenaciously over a little brick-and-mortar dam into which it managed to deliver the occasional spurt of brackish water. This fiercely defiant relic of long-past attempts at taming the vagaries of the elements gave me some comfort, and I decided to make my camp there. I would have water close-by and moreover, the lushly growing acacias around it, smug with moisture stolen from the rusting pipes, would provide cool shade during the hot days, and they seemed comforting in themselves.

I was young and fit and eager to pour my seemingly limitless strength into whatever effort it took to get one of the enormous bulls Cousin Piet had told me about. I set out the next morning at dawn, Mauser slung over my shoulder and a banana and an orange in the small shoulder bag that my mother had insisted I take along despite my protests. That day and the next and the next I roamed the faded jeep tracks (I stuck to them, scared of getting lost) covering many miles.

By the end of the third day I hadn't seen as much as a hint of kudu—or any game, for that matter, let alone a giant bull. There was the (very) occasional set of tracks in the red sandy soil that I chose to believe was made by a giant bull, but in truth, at that stage I knew too little of tracks or the bush to be sure. I half-limped back to my camp with blisters on my feet and an acute realization of how big 37,000 acres was if you wanted to cover it all in three days—and a better understanding of the limits of my own strength when pitted against the fierceness of the sun and the endless patience of the loose red sand.

At first I did not see him where he sat motionless in a spindly tangle against the black trunk of an acacia. It was only when the tall frame unfolded itself into a standing position and said *"Middag Kleinbaas"* (Afternoon, Young Master) that I noticed him.

I was a bit alarmed, but he seemed good-natured enough, and I replied in Afrikaans (which was all he spoke besides his native Tswana), "Good afternoon, and who are you?" not quite managing to keep the guarded tone from my voice.

"I am Ruben, Young Master. I live here."

He said it with such matter-of-fact finality that it simply was beyond questioning. But Cousin Piet had said. . . .

"But Ruben, I don't understand. Master Piet told me that there was no one living here."

"Master Piet, I don't know him. But I have lived here all my life. My father, too. He was the tractor driver for Master Andries. And I, I looked after Master Andries's cattle."

His tone was mildly bemused as if he found it incomprehensible that anybody could not know these facts.

Andries was probably the name of some previous owner, I surmised on the trot. "Where is Master Andries now?" I asked without really knowing why, because I didn't know Andries and I didn't care where he was.

"Ah, Young Master, he died."

"He died? When?"

"Ah, Young Master, I can't remember, but it is a few years now."

I suddenly thought with a hint of sadness how innocently unaware Ruben (and many more like him, in such circumstances) carried on with their lives, unable to even imagine the fantastical deals concocted far away in plush offices between opportunistic speculators and unscrupulous executors, and how it then came to affect their lives.

"Every day I see the Young Master walking so fast all along the tracks," he said expectantly.

Every day? How the hell could be watching me every day without me knowing it? I wondered uneasily. I said, "Yes, I am looking for a big kudu bull. Master

Piet . . ." but then I stopped, suddenly realizing that Cousin Piet's opinions were really irrelevant.

"Young Master, the kudu they are scarce, and the big bulls they are here, but they are very scarce and they are very *skelm*"—the Afrikaans word *skelm* in this context, means something like resourceful and secretive.

"Really, Ruben? Have you seen any? Where should I look?" I now asked eagerly.

"*Eisch*, Young Master, they walk everywhere. Sometimes I can see them."

Hmmm. I was beginning to wonder if Ruben might not be of some assistance to me.

"But tell me, Ruben, what are you doing here on the farm now that Master Andries is dead?"

"At this time I look after my goats."

"Your goats? Have you got many goats?" I asked, wondering embarrassedly about all the tracks I had thought were made by kudu.

"No, Young Master, they are not so many because the tiger is eating them."

"The tiger!? What tiger?" I exclaimed, astonished. "But Ruben, there are no . . . !" I started admonishing just as I realized he meant leopard—tiger being a common name used for leopard by simple bushveld folk. He probably heard it from Andries. "Oh, you mean a leopard?" I corrected.

"Yes, Young Master. Today he caught a young one," he said, the watery eyes flashing with indignation. I felt a chill run down my back. How many times might I have been contemplated by this clearly audacious leopard?

"Really, Ruben? Where?" I asked, half out of curiosity, half out of uneasiness.

"It's not far, Young Master. I can go and show the Young Master."

I thought about my blistered feet and the tea I was going to make for myself, but I was curious. "OK, let's go and take a look."

Ruben's "not far" turned out to be a good two hours away. His young billy goat was safely wedged in a fork high up in a marula tree. A little distance away he showed me the cat's silent, upwind approach, the quick acceleration in its stalk, and the claw marks where it had launched into its final charge. He pointed out how the leopard had held the goat by its throat, lying down with little exertion, the goat struggling briefly in the iron grip on its throat, then how the cat had dragged its prey to the marula, and how the hind feet had brushed the ground here and there. As the cat had climbed up with the goat in its mouth, the blood had trickled down the trunk. Finally, I saw where the cat had come down and had landed when it jumped from the lowest fork, and had slunk off "to go and drink the water."

I was completely fascinated by the primal saga, reconstructed in such rich detail by Ruben from faint and seemingly disconnected marks—no, not even marks, mere suggestions of disturbances of a twig, crushing of a leaf, bending of a grass stalk . . . I remember thinking how much I'd like to be able to read the bush like he did.

Then he said, "If the Young Master waited there behind that bush"—he pointed to a low-growing thicket —"then the tiger will come again to eat, and the Young Master can shoot him."

His voice sounded hopeful, imploring, and it suddenly dawned on me why I had been honored with the visit. He was hoping he could coax me into killing the leopard that was slowly destroying all his earthly wealth.

I had never hunted leopard, but I had lived in the Kruger Park as a boy, and I had seen many and listened to many tales from men who should know of how fierce they are and how much killing they took and how dangerous they were when wounded. I knew that the standard practice was a somewhat heavier bullet than the 120-grain 7mms I had (although at the time I took much pride in the fact that Karamojo Bell was reputed to have shot many of his elephant with a 7x57), and a 12-gauge shotgun with heavy shot if it had to be followed up, and that following up a wounded leopard really was a two-man job.

I had always abhorred the idea of shooting animals on bait, but this was not really bait, and I found myself weighing my chances. At the time the Mauser was not scoped, but I was still a deadly shot with it, and the bush that Ruben had pointed out was a mere sixty yards or so away. I was sure I could drop it out of the tree with a deadly shot, especially if I was sitting down and resting the rifle over a branch. The excitement was suddenly dry and sticky in my mouth and pounding against my chest, and I decided I was going to do it!

It was late afternoon, and we crawled into the bush and made ready for the wait. We sat until the light was too poor to shoot accurately, and then mercifully abandoned the project. I was relieved. I had felt uncomfortable with the idea all along, and it was excruciating for me to sit so still for so long. I decided then that this style of hunting did not suit me and I would never again allow myself to be lured into it.

The next morning at dawn Ruben was sitting patiently against the tree trunk waiting for me to emerge from my little tent. He wanted us to go and see if we could not track the leopard down. I realized how much more difficult the shooting was likely to be under those conditions, and that the risk was high that I might wound the leopard and that I would then be in serious trouble—but the lure of dangerous adventure was irresistible.

When we got to the tree it was clear that the leopard had returned during the night and had eaten almost all of the remaining meat. "He will not come again," Ruben said as we stood contemplating the now bare and blackened skeleton.

"Is it a male or a female?" I asked.

"No, he is the big man," he said half-absently as he studied the faint marks hidden among the grass and fallen leaves.

We started tracking him from the tree. Ruben held the tracks for two hours with unerring intuition for the animal's instinct, his circumstances, even his state of mind, it seemed, and an astonishing ability to notice the smallest detail. He walked with his tall frame leaning forward, the long arms dangling in front of him and the hands gesticulating, constantly murmuring to himself in a throaty whisper, completely absorbed in a world of his own. Actually, it was the world of the male leopard strolling through his territory, confident in his strength and the knowledge that very few could challenge him, his hunger satisfied, inclined to having a drink and then make his leisurely way to his daytime lair.

Ruben showed me where the leopard had left a few hairs on a low-hanging branch when he had lazily turned to rub himself, and the place where he had slaked his thirst in a marshy area, leaning far forward on his front paws to keep his feet from getting muddy, his twitching tail lightly caressing the fine sand as he drank, and where he had lain down to sun himself in a clear spot at dawn and how he had licked himself and rolled over playfully and stretched, and then marked his territory with urine and left his nail marks on a tree as he went.

Although at the time I realized that what I was witnessing was far, far beyond the abilities of myself or anyone else I knew or even knew of, I could not fully appreciate the subtle mixture of insight and knowledge and skill and attitude Ruben had slowly developed over time, living in the bush behind his goat herd, and before that behind the cattle herds, and before that with his father. It was only later when I had seen many trackers at work and had tried it myself and had learned some of the art—enough to at least appreciate a true master—that I was able to recognize a real master at work.

The tracks finally led to a granite outcrop and into a smallish crevice. We both knew that it would be absolutely foolhardy to try to crawl in after him.

"If we wait outside, won't he come out?" I asked hopefully.

Ruben shook his head. There was a bitter resignation on his face and an unquestionable finality in his voice when he said, "Young Master, he will not come out. He knows that we are here to kill him. We will not kill him today or tomorrow. Maybe some other day."

And so the leopard had completely outplayed us, always retaining the initiative, always remaining one step ahead, and seemingly without even exerting itself. In the end, it would be Ruben who would execute the sentence passed on the leopard in his last words, "Maybe some other day."

++++++

The bulls were now alone, heading purposefully south-southeast, and the sun was at an ideal angle for tracking, although there were some clouds drifting in front of it occasionally. The morning's wind had kept blowing

92

steadily from the southeast, and was slowly building a white bank of cloud low in the northwest. We made quick progress, shifting into a shuffling trot wherever we could.

Then, after about two hours, the tracks mixed with quite a large breeding herd. The elephants appeared to have milled around when they met up, and it took us some time and a few false starts to work out which directions they took when they got going again. The tracking was now easier with the big herd, and the rather brisk wind was still in our favor, albeit diagonally across our front.

Soon, however, the tracks entered a fairly dense patch of bush and started spreading out—clearly the herd had started feeding. This was very difficult tracking because they were moving in all directions over a large area, and it was extremely difficult to determine in what direction the herd was actually drifting. Then, suddenly, we heard them ahead of us—the breaking branches, the shuffling, the deep drone of the intestines. It was around ten o'clock, and they were feeding noisily.

We moved closer carefully, not yet able to see them in the bush willow thicket, but awash in their sounds and their pungent odor. I had gathered up a clump of dry elephant dung and had set a small spot on it alight, which was now smoldering slowly and emitting a thin wisp of smoke to help mask our smell and show the direction of the wind.

Suddenly I noticed a movement on my left. It was an elephant cow in the shadows about sixty paces away, and another just ahead of her. We were already inside the herd, but luckily on the downwind fringes, it seemed! We tried to move forward a bit so that we could see all of the elephants. There must have been fifteen to twenty animals of various sexes and ages in the herd, and they were spread over a large area. We actually had to move from group to group.

It was a strange experience, walking around unseen in the company of those noisily feeding giants that were many times our size and strength and bound to be hostile when they found us out. I felt as naked as a rookie cop trying to crash a mafia don's birthday party, dressed all wrong and with his badge forgotten on his belt.

Several times I felt like succumbing to the cold tightness in my chest, but the Fatalist was there, nonchalantly mouthing, "What the hell!" through a twisted smile, and Fear was once more relegated to petulant nagging in the background. Fortunately the wind was steady and we kept it on the side of our faces as we moved forward, hoping that none of the giants we had passed would move far enough across our rear to pick up our scent.

I constantly glassed the bush around us, trying to make out as many as I could, but there was no sign of the three bulls, or of any mature bull, for that matter. Elias was also straining to make sense out of the situation, but after a while we looked at each other and shook our heads. Our bulls were not in this herd.

I motioned to him that we should retreat. We tested the wind and turned around, but we had only gone a few careful paces when a cow about eighty paces behind us and to our right suddenly trumpeted and started running almost directly at us. She was flanked by a young calf about eight months old, and a teenage bull, probably a calf from a previous year.

I grabbed Elias's hand to steady him. She seemed to be simply running in panic, not charging us, or even knowing of our presence. If she kept her course she would pass about twenty yards in front of us, I quickly calculated as I eased the safety over. If we kept still the chances were that she would rush past without even seeing us.

But the teenage calf kept ramming against her shoulder, knocking her off course, and pointing her more and more in our direction. As I stared at her, rapidly weighing the options of run, shoot, or stay perfectly still, I was vaguely aware of the rest of the herd getting into motion with an infernal amount of screaming and breaking of branches. I fleetingly hoped that no other elephants were heading in our direction in the confusion, but I dared not take my eyes off the charging cow to check. I certainly did not want to shoot her, and running would just ensure that she would charge.

We were now victims of the Law of Diminishing Options. She was looming frighteningly huge, frighteningly quickly. The ground was trembling under our feet, and I thought: *Just one more small bump from that damn youngster, and she is going to run us into pulp anyway.* And then they were past us, the power of their rush fanning our faces and making our guts quiver and spraying debris over us. We stood trembling for a good few minutes, the adrenaline roaring through our veins, listening to the fading sound of the stampeding herd, me discovering that I still held tightly onto Elias's wrist.

I went and sat down with my back against a tree trunk to calm down and think the situation through. The few seconds she had taken to cover the eighty-odd yards had been one of those experiences where things seemed to get sticky and slow, calculated thinking turned into alarm and an over-whelming desire to run away, and then to a calm acceptance of the slow advance of fate. Miraculously, Elias had also kept his cool through all of this, my grip biting into his arm, partly out of terror!

I now felt sure that the bulls had just met up with the herd and had not joined them, and that we would be able to find their tracks at the meeting place. It was a mistake for which I wanted to kick myself to have assumed so easily that they had joined the herd. But it was still early enough for us to have a chance of catching them if we could find their tracks quickly again, especially given the fact that this breeding herd had not gone much farther from the meeting place before they had slowed down to "feed speed." But how to communicate all of that to Elias? I managed to make him understand with sign language that I wanted us to go back.

We found the meeting place easily enough by backtracking. I thought it reasonable to assume that the bulls would keep to their course of earlier, so I had us skirt widely around the southeast side, and we were lucky. After about fifteen minutes we picked up the bulls' tracks, heading steadily south-southeast. It was about eleven-thirty, and I remember thinking that if we did not find them within three hours, we would have lost them.

The wind had by now built the bank of cloud in the northwest to fill a third of the sky, with a dark band at its base. As we approached noon, its cooling breath had subsided a bit, and now the heat was thick and heavy and

95

the sun had a humid sting on our faces. We went as fast as we could, tracking abreast, often breaking into a trot. After about an hour the tracks became very difficult to follow. The ground wasn't hard, but the bulls had started feeding in some thick, shady bush and were walking around randomly. The directly overhead sun with cloud drifting over it wasn't helping.

It was here that Elias again proved himself a master tracker, patiently mimicking his way through their minds, working out what they had been up to. I tried my best to help, marking the last confirmed sign every time I saw that he had lost the track, checking ahead when he was moving, but the going was slow. I was convinced that they would be resting now, but once the sun moved permanently behind the clouds, it would quickly cool off enough for them to start moving again. I fretted quietly.

We were topping a low rise, moving along painstakingly. The tracks were now very fresh. I had stopped looking at the spoor, and started concentrating on the bush ahead and to our flanks. It was about two-thirty. The sun had dipped behind the cool white plume of the clouds, but down here the land was still twisting in the smoldering heat. Our steady wind had deteriorated into occasional uncertain gusts, unfaithful, deceitful.

Then Elias froze, gripping my arm. We heard it faintly as the wind wafted mockingly in our direction for the briefest fraction: A sound like the sails of a tall ship flapping in the wind, rising briefly above the screams of the cicadas—the elephants slapping their ears against their bodies as they fanned themselves. We looked at each other knowingly, and then we started creeping forward, me breathless, trembling a bit, nervously testing the wind with pinches of dust thrown into the air.

We found two of them standing in the shade of a huge baobab, facing the trunk, the younger bull closest to us, masking one of the big bulls behind him. A little to the side under a knobthorn was the third bull, and he was huge, but tuskless.

I remember thinking briefly of the lore that tuskless elephant bulls were especially aggressive and dangerous. I strained to see what size the other big bull's tusks were, but he was standing with his head behind the shoulder of the younger bull, and there was too much vegetation in the way for me to see. I had to move closer and a little to their front to get a clear view of him.

I motioned to Elias to stay put, and I crept forward carefully, wary of the treachery lurking in the wind. When I was about twenty to thirty paces away I could see one of the bigger bull's tusks. I was not an experienced judge of ivory, but I thought they had to be about sixty pounds. They weren't very long, but they were thick as the top of my leg at the base.

At least ten pounds heavier than the bull I lost. It is the second bull we have found in the category of between fifty and sixty pounds—maybe that's the average size in the area, and it's going to be very hard to find anything much bigger. This is as good as it gets, I thought.

I decided I had to try to take him, but I had no clear shot from where I was standing. His vital areas were still obscured by the younger bull, and there was almost no cover I could use to get to a better position. Also, moving more toward their front would take me right under the nose of the nasty tuskless bull, which was now about forty paces to my left front. One of the three was almost certain to see me if I moved much more.

I was still wondering what to do when I felt the backs of my sweat-bathed legs suddenly go cool, and I knew I was being betrayed by the wind. It was a matter of only seconds now before the bulls would pick up my scent. I braced myself for a quick shot in case he offered an opportunity as they broke.

He suddenly lifted his trunk, searching the eddies, then nervously lifted his head—clear above the shoulder line of his younger companion, the sleepy eyes now wide and alert to danger. I had one very brief chance for a side brain shot at a bit of an angle—difficult, but probably the only one I was going to get, and no time to wonder. I swung the .404 up and as the gold front bead caressed the spot that I had hastily nominated, I touched the trigger.

The shot exploded the bush out of its panting torpor. In an instant all was crashing, screaming pandemonium. I had a recoil- and gun smoke-hazed impression of the bull going down and the young one wheeling away, and then, as I feverishly rammed another round into the chamber, I tore my eyes away to see what the tuskless one was doing: He was running.

97

When I looked back, my bull was up and running diagonally away from me across my front. My throat was choking with a sensation of hopeless failure as I fired again, half desperately, aiming at his right flank, a little back from the shoulder and about a third up, hoping to hit the lung, and should the bullet would go far enough, the big arteries forward. He seemed to stumble a little at the shot, but then he was gone, and there was just the dust and the sudden silence, thick and humid and hot.

I looked around for Elias as I opened the breech to replace the two spent bullets in the magazine. He came trotting up with a rare wide smile on his face, clearly well pleased with the situation. I was incredulous, and he must have seen it in my face, for now he poked his thumb into his ribs under his right arm and mimicked the elephant going down. This made me feel a lot better, for Elias was no beginner and certainly not given to frivolous emotional displays.

We went forward to check for blood, and sure enough, within fifteen yards we found some—lots, in fact, frothy and bright pink. I had definitely hit the lung and hit it well! I now allowed myself some optimism that I would not have another lost bull.

Although I would normally have preferred to give the animal time to settle down before following up, a previous experience with a lung-shot elephant taught me that they died very quickly, so I felt it was OK to go forward slowly. Following up wounded game is dangerous, and so, with our emotions held tautly in check, we went forward carefully, abreast. Elias tracked while I scanned the bush ahead. I was especially watching out for any sign of the tuskless one—elephants often stay behind or return to assist a sick or wounded one.

My heart was hammering hard against my ribs, and every nerve was drawn bowstring-tight. My senses seemed acutely aware of those slow seconds, distilled from the great universe of time and space to contain only the sharpest essence of the moment: The sun, briefly emerging through the great white cloud-plumes in the northwest, stinging against the right side of my face and arm, the bright pink-red spatter of the blood on the ground, gravelly, with little loose stones, making our shoes go *crunch, crunch,* the cicadas' macabre shrilling in the background, almost drowning out Elias's low muttering, the occasional cool lick of the breeze, the reassuring feel of the .404's stock in the palms of my hands, the trees and shrubs and grass shifting as we moved, revealing ever more, yet nothing.

Then we spotted him. He was lying on his side, the bush broken and churned around him, a large pool of pink-red spreading like a fallen banner from the tip of his outstretched trunk, his mouth gaping pale crimson in a silent scream. He was dead, and I could see, now, that he had been a bull in his prime, not the old warrior in his last days that I was subconsciously hoping to save from an infamous death.

Elias inspected the carcass with uncharacteristic overt delight. I tried to feel the elation of success, but I felt only sadness, standing there, looking at him among the mangled vegetation and broken soil where he had spent the last of his desperate rage.

I sat down with my back against the sole of one huge front foot and wondered what to do next. We had to at least get the tusks out and try to find some use for the meat, but it was already late, and the light would soon start fading. There was a storm building in the northwest, although still far off. The best plan would be to make camp there and continue the next morning, but we had little water left and no food. There was no way I could discuss all of this sensibly with Elias.

I now really needed John. I was tempted to return to camp and come back the next morning. *John should be back in camp, and with food,* I hoped. But it was at least a four-hour walk, and it would take quite a bit longer in the dark. I decided it was best to stay for the night and go to the camp the next morning. At least it was easy to get Elias to understand that we would be spending the night. It was clearly what he thought, too.

We set about finding a suitable spot and making ourselves as comfortable as possible, gathering wood, building a makeshift shelter from saplings with a leaf bed under it that would keep us reasonably comfortable and dry if it rained, and I slung my hammock in case it did not rain. Elias cut himself some meat from the elephant, but I decided I was not that desperate and I stuck with the few scraps of food we had left.

By the time we had finished our chores, a soft darkness, full of little sounds, had settled around us. It had been a long, hard day with high adrenaline and very little food, and I was grateful to be able to finally sit back on the edge of the fire's glow and ponder the events and emotions of the day. My thoughts inevitably drifted to the deep sadness, even disillusionment, I had felt when I finally stood there next to the dead elephant, Samsonian amid the destruction he had caused in his last moments.

The fascinating thing was that I had suspected, even known, deep down, that the sadness, the self-reproach, would be inevitable. Yet I was irresistibly drawn into the primal challenge of the hunt, enormous in its physical and emotional dimensions, adrenaline-driven, disaster-courting. I knew, however, that it was more than the hunt itself. For me it was also in the lure of the truly wild African bush, with its fascinating mix of breathtaking beauty, extreme physical challenges, and yes, mortal danger. There was also a deep tranquility and spirituality that is elusive, sometimes unnoticed when too close to it, but intensely longed for when far from it.

I remembered the words of Sir Edwin Landseer, nineteenth-century painter of the famous *Monarch of the Glen*: "There is something in the toil and trouble, the wild weather and scenery that make butchers of us all. Who does not glory in the death of a fine stag?"

Yes, somehow the tragedy of death, and the stark recognition that it could be your own, combines into an irresistible allure, akin to the magic of the tragic sagas sung by the bards around herdsmen's fires in the rugged hills of ancient Greece.

I sat there, the wild African night lapping around me, watching the silent dance of the flames on the surrounding bush, and Elias absently stirring the coals with his stick, and I tried to think of anywhere else that I would be able to experience this total sensual and emotional fulfilment. I knew that for me, there was no other such place and that Africa was bred deep into the marrow of every nerve.

It did not rain during the night, but there was an occasional flicker of lightning and a muffled rumble far to the northwest, and the morning broke hot and sullen, wearing a dark band of cloud on its brow. I had slept uneasily, partly due to the hyenas' activity at the carcass, and I got Elias going as soon as there was enough light to work. I had decided we would take out the tusks and take them with us to the camp. There they would be safe, and with John's translation services we would be able to make plans to utilize the meat.

I explained to Elias using signs what I was thinking. I could see that he didn't like the idea at all, and he launched into an animated sign explanation of his own, which I eventually understood to mean roughly that he wanted to go east where there was either a village or some other group of people living in the bush, possibly another nomadic group like his own, which he wanted to alert to come and fetch the meat.

I did not like the idea too much because we had very little water left and if I didn't go along I would effectively be stranded at the carcass until he got back—I was not sure that I would be able to find the temporary camp all by myself. I had to admit, however, that his plan did make some sense.

It would take us at least a day of hard walking to carry the tusks to our temporary camp and get back to the carcass. Over this time the carcass would be at the mercy of scavengers, especially hyenas, which had already started feeding and were gathering in numbers, and, of course, it would be decaying in the heat. I also had sympathy for the fact that he and the local people were clearly desperate for meat, which was probably one of the reasons he joined us in the first place.

On the other hand, I was not particularly keen on going with Elias to fetch the people. I had been to many of those seminomadic little dwellings in the past, and I much preferred spending some quiet time with my book and my thoughts. If I did not go along with him, I would have to head back to the water hole for water.

The problem was that I was not sure I would be able to find it on my own. I knew that it was roughly north-northwest of us, so theoretically all

I had to do was to head north for about seven to nine miles and as soon as I then hit a major game path it should lead me to the pan because it was the only water in the area. That was the theory. The African bush has a way of disabusing even those wise in the ways of bushcraft—after all, it is not a city with streets and maps.

After another bout of sign language and mimicking, I was satisfied that Elias understood what my intentions were, and I had the expectation that I might see him back as soon as that evening. Before we parted, we cut open the elephant's stomach. We did not have time for the gigantic task of removing the intestines to prevent bloating and slow decay, but the scavengers would be doing that for us.

A vast, humid heat was building among the trees as I headed back to the water hole, but I enjoyed the walk. The wind was at my back, so the chances of seeing any game were remote, but I barred haste from my mind and tuned my senses to the air and the ground and the plants, taking time to explore their rich language of signs and smells and sounds: the bird calls, some excited and urgent, some petulant, spiteful, some melancholic, some with a forlorn yearning; and the insects, some unremitting, insistent, some whirring by tersely, some lingering, vexing.

The smell of the grass and the ancient dust bore in it a subtle mixture of life and decay, and the soil held the imprint of eons of ebb and flow, of turbulence and tranquility. Where it was soft, the transient signs of the wandering of beetles and centipedes and snakes and birds and a porcupine and a badger and a steenbok were visible. I was lucky to spot the tiny telltale mud spout of the little black bees' nest in a dead tree stump. I broke open the decaying wood with my hunting knife and feasted on the delicious dark honey and powdery bees' bread, said to cause serious tummy ache if too much is eaten, but I was too hungry to care, and mercifully I was spared the ache.

At one point I noticed something black and shiny lying under a tree some sixty paces away. For a moment I thought it was a discarded truck tire, but of course, that was impossible, and besides, it was too shiny. As I came closer I saw that it was a gigantic rock python, lying in heavy coils on a mound of loose earth that an aardvark had dug out from beneath an anthill. He was enormous.

At his thickest part his body seemed thicker than my upper leg and almost thicker, it seemed, than my 32-inch waist size. He did not look as if he was busy digesting something he had recently swallowed—he was just that big! He lay motionless even as I approached, just his black tongue lazily lapping out from time to time, and his gray eyes staring coldly, without expression, like a dead fish.

I very much wanted to get an idea of his length, so I picked up a stick and went closer to poke him, hoping that he would move off. He merely lunged at me sideways, almost disdainfully, as if to say, "Bugger off, you little twit, before I crush you like a cupcake." He was big and formidable enough to insist.

When I arrived at the water hole, I found it deserted, lying mirror-smooth in its bed of gray dust. After I had laboriously filtered some water into my canvas bag through my shirt, and had had enough to drink of the brackish, organic-tasting fluid, I selected a large, leafy leadwood on the downwind side and climbed into it, settling in its broad fork from where I could sit comfortably and would have a good view of game approaching.

I had barely made myself comfortable when I noticed a strange movement among the trees on the west side. It was Gerhard and John! I watched them as they scouted around for tracks, pointing and talking, and on the eastern side excitedly gathering around a sign and having an animated discussion.

Suddenly it occurred to me that they were looking for our tracks! I whistled thin and high so that Gerhard would know it, and I saw him whip his head round, listen for a moment, incredulous, then shrug and carry on with the discussion. It was only after the third whistle that he silenced John and stood listening intently. I guided them to the tree with my whistles, and then, as they were about to walk past, I said quietly, "Mr. Bolt, I presume. Is there any way that I might be of service, sir?"

The reunion was rather jubilant with much backslapping for such normally reserved individuals as Gerhard and myself. We were both delighted, not least because we had both been a bit unsure and worried about the other's disposition. My first concern was food (the second and third, too). Gerhard had had John carry a good stock because he was unsure of how long it would take him to find his "lost" companion. We moved away from the pan a bit and settled under a nice leafy pod mahogany to eat and share the latest news.

We each related our experiences over the past days in poetic detail, actual and improvised, salted with appropriate comments and asides, and washed down with endless mugs of tea that poor John had to brew, although he did not seem to mind because he apparently was feeling quite pleased that we were still around and had actually shot a big elephant.

Gerhard had not been successful in his initial quest for the big bull. It had simply been too far ahead of them. But they did find encouraging signs of elephant to the southwest as they went, and two days later he got a good bull, about sixty pounds plus per side, he thought.

Over this period, Vic and Mack had been less successful. Vic was by then quite despondent, and the next day Gerhard offered to accompany them with Jo'burg. They worked northwest from the camp, and actually walked into a large breeding herd, but there were no suitable bulls in it. Late in the afternoon on the way back they found very fresh tracks of a bull herd. They followed these, and within thirty minutes they found them.

The biggest bull carried about forty-five pounds, but Vic was quite keen to shoot him, having already had more than a week of hunting without firing a single shot. The light was failing, and Vic's shot was good but did not drop him in his tracks. Both Mack and Gerhard got off good back-up shots, but they had to leave him because of the light. They found him quickly the next morning—he had only gone about two hundred yards. They spent the rest of the day getting the tusks into camp and putting out word on the meat.

When they got back to camp, my special emissary was waiting for them. Mack and Vic favored returning to Stephan's camp because their elephant hunt had been completed and there were very few buffaloes in the area. Gerhard decided to give Jo'burg to them to improve their chances; he would then join me in the east. He took an additional bearer (one of

Stephan's unfortunate press-ganged camp hands), stocked up well on food (because we would have to walk back to Stephan's camp), and set out with John. Mack and Vic took the vehicle back to Stephan's camp—with strict instructions to drive carefully and look after it like a baby!

They got to our temporary camp by late afternoon. They could see from the ash heap that Elias and I had been there, but they could not make out how long ago and how often, because a light shower had fallen in the area and all but wiped out our signs.

When we did not return that evening, Gerhard was convinced that something had gone wrong. In the morning he set out with John to try to find us, leaving the extra bearer behind to look after the camp and make some improvements to keep him busy, like cut some grass to walk on and fashion a rudimentary table to work on.

And now the familiar companionship had settled around us like a favorite old jacket on a chilly evening. Between us there was a strange combination of comfort and challenge and good cheer all at the same time, and at its base lay a solid mutual respect and understanding, built over years of wandering the dangerous paths together, as we would again do now.

We moved closer to the pan where Elias would be able to find us, and waited out the afternoon, talking endlessly and watching the clouds making another assault on the dry valley air from the northwest, pushing ahead their fantastical advance guard, billowing out boldly in brilliant white to meet the sun at its zenith, while the assembled main strike forces hovered darkly on the horizon, surly and shuddering with pent-up energy.

Elias finally walked into the fire's circle around nine, hungry and gray with fatigue and dust. *He must have done quite a bit of trotting to have made it*, I thought. He had reached the bush village (about fifteen people, according to John) and they were on their way to the carcass. I got him to sit down while John made him a decent meal, and we set about preparing shelters against the rain for the night.

The evening was angry, filled with a noisy, unfriendly wind and white flashes stabbing into the clouds in the far northwest. There was little talk, except a brief discussion about going to the elephant to supervise taking out the tusks, and how we would carry them back. Elias seemed doubtful if the men at the carcass would be willing to help because of the meat they had to get to their village. We would have to make do to another little bush village about a day and half's walk away (and he gestured quite a bit more west than where I thought Stephan's camp had to be), where we should be able to find men to help carry the tusks.

It was becoming clear that getting back to Stephan's camp wasn't going to be a simple straight-line walk, but rather more of a circuitous odyssey—not that the prospect was unattractive. "I just hope your camp hand hasn't buggered off in despair by the time we get back," I remarked to Gerhard, referring to Stephan's hapless erstwhile staff member left behind to look after the temporary camp.

This set me wondering about Elias's and John's share of the elephant meat, and when I asked John about it he replied that the village people would keep some for them and they would fetch it later. It would mean a journey of at least three to five days from the area where they lived to the little village, and a bit longer back. *A bit different from visiting the butcher round the corner for a quick purchase of meat for tonight's braai*, I thought.

We agreed on watch turns and each withdrew into his own little defense against the elements.

A Deliberate Coincidence

CHAPTER 8

It had been a blustery night, with the wind noisily worrying through the trees and throwing spark-showers from the flames, but thankfully again without rain. Toward dawn it calmed, and the morning broke bright and pregnant with the promise of rain. But as it got warmer the wind started, and got stronger, relentlessly tousling the trees, driving herds of grass galloping over the open spaces, and chasing up eddies of dust where the earth was bare.

We arrived at the elephant carcass around eleven o'clock. About eight people—men, women draped in beautiful bright fabrics, and a smattering of noisy children—had already arrived from the village and were excitedly inspecting the carcass, which was still in a remarkably good state.

Elias and John took charge and marshaled them away with lots of shouting and arm-waving and the occasional glance in our direction to see if we still approved—we, of course, did not have much of an opinion on the issue, except that I thought there was enough noise for all game within ten miles to be suffering from a nervous condition.

We took some obligatory photos, and then Elias and John went to work to get the tusks out, submissively watched by the villagers, who were occasionally granted the great honor of being summoned to help hold or carry. Elias clearly knew exactly what he was doing, no doubt from his own occasional ivory-poaching activities, we surmised.

Gerhard and I stood around for a while, awkwardly conscious of the kingly status we had been accorded, and then we decided we would best serve our royal image by gracefully departing for the water hole and waiting for John and Elias there. We took our leave with appropriate dignity, waving and nodding as we went, Gerhard furiously puffing at his pipe.

The walk back to the water hole was pleasant, and turned out to be quite exciting, too. The wind was at our backs, but so strong and noisy that we came quite close to game on our flanks. At one point I noticed a strange shape under a dense clump of sickle bush. We went to inspect, and found a freshly killed zebra, dragged deep underneath the tangle of branches.

Deciphering the signs on the ground led us to conclude that the killer was a single male lion, and a large one at that. He was nowhere to be seen. He had either gone off to drink, or had heard us approaching and had departed quietly. He had made the kill during the night or the early hours of that morning, about fifty meters from the spot where the carcass was lying, and then he had dragged it under the bush.

What was particularly interesting was the seemingly calculated way in which he had gone about preserving the carcass: The bush under which he had dragged it was the densest in the vicinity, and low-hanging, so that the carcass would be invisible to the sharp-eyed vultures, and difficult to spot in general . . . but he had done much more. He had torn out the intestines and buried them about twenty paces from the carcass by scraping earth over them. He had also kicked dirt over all the areas where the skin had been broken—where he had torn out the intestines, and where he had fed on the hindquarters.

It was as if he realized that he could potentially feed on the kill for several days but that he had to do something to protect it against scavengers. The actions he took were not only the best under the circumstances but they were calculated to produce the optimum results.

A brisk straight-line walk to the water hole took about four hours, but our almost-stroll brought us there well into the afternoon. The bank of clouds in the northwest had by then again built itself into a towering white mass that hued gradually grayer to a dark blue fester on the western horizon. We were hoping to make it to our temporary camp by that evening, but now we could not do much more than wait for Elias and John to turn up with the tusks.

We decided to brave the vicious sting of the afternoon sun and browse through the tracks around the pan. It was on the southeast side of the pan that we found the fresh lion spoor. We studied it a bit and agreed, in hushed tones, that there was a mature male, about three or four females, two or three young and about as many cubs in the pride.

"They are probably resident. This is their territory," I remarked. "There is no other water for miles. I think this is where they ambush game coming to drink. They are probably not far away."

We stood for a moment, staring at the spoor and contemplating the surrounding bush. Although we had often come across lions in the bush, we had never actually hunted them. But the ashes of many campfires bore witness to us telling each other how we would one day want to. But not on bait, and not from behind a blind as is commonly done, but like this, to track them down and find them . . .

We did not say anything, but our eyes met, and suddenly the Hunt had slipped cunningly from among the trees where it always seemed to hover mysteriously, and it came into our midst and entered our veins like a thin ether. It made our blood race, bewitched the tendrils of our nerves, pricked our senses until they were sharp and precise as surgical needles, and lured us into the ever-narrowing funnel of the chase until there was no way we could escape. Yet we hesitated, testing the wind, pushing a cartridge into the chamber, checking the safety catch as we explored tentatively, then started sensing the direction of the spoor, drifting half-deliberately along it, one on either side . . .

I was a bit doubtful that we would be able to follow the spoor for any substantial distance at all. Following lion spoor in the fine gray dust was one thing, but once they got to harder ground and entered the bush . . . We carried on a bit, uncertainly hovering between experiment and the real thing. The sun had now disappeared behind the clouds, and the dispersed, shadowless light made tracking even more difficult. But the Hunt had drawn us far into its mysterious lure of fear and excitement, and we carried on, like Odysseus, who would have been fatally doomed to follow the sweet Siren voices on the wind had he not tied himself to the mast.

Even the playful white cloud tips were now becoming ominously dirty gray, flashing and breathing hoarsely in the distance, and the wind was blustery, grabbing angrily at the bushes, chasing up brown dust swirls across our front and adamantly tugging at our bodies.

The ground in the vicinity of the pan was powdered from many thousands of game visits and relatively easy to track in, but the pride had spread out in their leisurely stroll from the coolness of the water that morning, leaving single tracks that were difficult to follow. We quickly settled into our familiar *pas de deux* when tracking dangerous game: the one with a positive sign tracking as fast as possible, while the other ranged ahead, looking for the animal and trying to find spoor, or arc-searching if the spoor was lost, and then taking over the tracking role as soon as he positively identified it.

I was about ten yards behind Gerhard, tracking, when suddenly the boom of his .450/400 exploded over us! I ran up to him.

"He was there," he said, breathlessly pointing to a clump of shrubs about sixty yards ahead of us. "When I looked up, he was there. The others had seen me and sprang up, and I thought, *They're going to run.* That's when I shot him. He fell, but then he jumped up again and ran in that direction," he said, pointing to our left, his voice quivering with emotion and excitement.

"Was it the male?"

"Yes."

"OK, well, that's that. Let's go and see," I whispered, my heart knocking so hard against my chest that I thought the wounded lion must be able to hear it.

We moved slowly forward, caught again in that time-arrested capsule of hair-trigger-tuned nerves and the acute awareness of only that which was there in that moment. Nothing else existed. It was as if we were in a dream. I was not expecting to find the pride, or for this to happen so suddenly. Thinking back on it, it was almost as if we were playing with the idea, exploring, just to see, never really intending to seriously hunt them. Of course it happened, almost out of our control, like those inevitable sequences one gets launched into and over which one has little control no matter what one thinks.

It had become darker. Wisps of red dust were angrily racing past us from behind, blurring the spoor and the bushes ahead. The thunder was rising, now rolling deeply around us, and the first pregnant drops were ominously slapping into the ground, pasting the red earth around us with large dark spots. We came to the place where the lion had stood when Gerhard fired. There were marks under the shrubs where the pride had rested, and the deep fresh gashes where their claws had dug into the earth as they tore away. And, some ten paces further, fresh blood, bright red, browning slowly as it seeped into the earth.

We both knew without saying that it was wrong, very wrong, to take up the spoor immediately, but the storm was only minutes away, and once it broke there would be absolutely no chance of finding him. I took the spoor; Gerhard, with his double, walked some five yards to my right, concentrating on the bushes ahead. The lion had run downwind, so he would smell us as we came closer. I could see from the track that it was dragging its right rear foot. *That might be our saving grace,* I thought briefly, prophetically.

We moved forward grimly, eyes screwed against the dust, straining to see and hear through the raging elements . . . and then we heard its growl: long, deep, primal, again, and again. It was there, just ahead of us, somewhere under a bush, or behind a tuft of grass, low and close, so close that I could hear the gargle in the back of its throat as it growled. We could not see it, and it was then that I understood what real fear was, cold and brutal and irrational.

We stood transfixed, rifles half raised, fingers trembling at the triggers, struggling to see, to pierce the very earth. Desperate minutes dragged by, feeling like hours. At that point the storm broke, hurtling itself at us in crashing, driving fury. I desperately stepped a little to the side to get a different angle, and then, in a sudden flash, like an image flitting past a car window at high speed, the lion burst from the ground some thirty yards away, its short roar rising above the noise of the storm and crashing over us like a powerful wave.

It came hurtling at us through the sheets of rain, a small dark-yellow blur of rage, low and incredibly quick. Briefly our shots boomed above the rumbling thunder. We saw the lion falter and then stumble. Gerhard let loose his second barrel (oh, sweet, sweet double!). It staggered desperately, its great mouth strained open to engulf its enemies. I fired again, at less than ten yards, feverishly blessing the flawless slide of the Mauser action, and the lion fell, sliding on its left shoulder until it came to rest about five yards from us. It dragged its legs under it and lifted its great head, and I fired again, this time at point-blank range.

For a few breathless moments we stood in the driving waves of rain, overcome by the moment, and then we went closer, moving round it and approaching from behind. The lion was dead. It lay on its side, the rain washing away the slow ooze of blood from its wounds. Gerhard knelt down at the great head and lifted its lip. It was past its prime, its great incisors blunted and yellowed. It was probably lucky to have survived as the pride male for so long. It was only a matter of time. Gerhard's first shot had missed the chest and had hit him on the left flank, then apparently passed through the lung and intestines to break the right thighbone.

"You know, if both its hind legs were working we probably wouldn't have stopped it before it got one of us," I said thickly.

Gerhard nodded. "We were lucky," he growled simply as he looked up at me, rain running down his face like tears.

After the hot excitement of the hunt, our situation had suddenly turned very miserable. We now had a dead lion on our hands in the driving rain. It was a bit like a serious hangover after a night of indiscretion. There wasn't much else to do but wait out the storm. We settled down on the leeward side of a thick marula trunk where we were at least a little shielded.

When the storm had finally dwindled to muffled rumblings far to the southeast and whispered dripping around us, we settled down to skin the lion. It was a slow and laborious task, having to take off the skin without damaging it, and free of any flesh or membranes. We did not even attempt to skin out the head and feet. With our inexpert and rain-numbed fingers it would simply have taken far too long. We simply cut them off, leaving them on the skin, hoping that we would find time later.

We finished close to sunset and set off westward, the fantastic hues of red and pink and purple of the dying sun through the breaking clouds towering over us. We took turns with the wet skin and got to the water hole at dusk, where John and Elias were waiting for us with the tusks. It was too late to try to make it to our camp. We had to stay for the night.

It was a relief to finally sit down beside the fire with its flames sizzling and sputtering on the wet wood, reasonably clean after a shower from many mugs of green water. It had been a day of wholly unexpected developments, and a lot to talk about. Gerhard and I were taking turns trying to skin out the feet and head of the lion in the firelight, but without much success despite each subjecting the other to lots of advice and criticism, most of it unhelpful.

Elias eventually called our attention by timidly asking John something about the lion in a way that we could clearly understand to be a question really directed at us (although we could not understand the substance thereof). I looked at Gerhard and we winked. They were both apparently dying to hear what had happened.

"Now, this lion . . ." I began, not doing too well with my poor prosaic powers in Fanagalo, and having to add a lot of demonstration and animation. Of course Gerhard added quite a bit of his own, but John and Elias were transfixed by the story.

Then Elias rose to his feet and started the story of the elephant hunt from the point where we found the spoor at the water hole. Although he told it to John in the local Sena, Gerhard and I could follow almost all of it because he animated it masterfully, almost dancelike, right down to our emotions, the sounds and actions of the animals, the boom of the gun, the thud of the bullet . . . It was wonderfully entertaining, and we followed him rapturously, John completely forgetting about the porridge he was cooking, and burning it (for which Elias took time off the story to scold him).

The memory of that night stayed with me as one of my finest to this day. Elias, his tattered shirt flapping around his black torso above the impala loincloth, the flames casting rich, orange nuances over his face, intensely alive in animation, the long, thin arms gesturing wildly, then subtly, the deep voice droning soothingly, then stabbing like a gunshot, the gnarled feet plastering the damp earth around the fire to a smooth shine, and us three staring in total enthrallment. When he had finished, I couldn't resist standing up and giving him, master bard of the African bush, an ovation, and Gerhard and John joined in.

When we had eaten and the mood around the fire settled down a bit, I said, "What about the skin? Do you think it will be OK if we finish skinning it out tomorrow morning? It has fortunately not been hot."

"I think so, but we don't have nearly enough salt to preserve it properly," replied Gerhard. "We can skin it out, but I'm not sure if—in fact, I don't think we'd be able to get it to Stephan's camp in a good enough state to save it."

++++++

Our situation brought home to us how preciously scarce certain commodities that one would simply take for granted in civilization are in the remote bush. It reminded me of a scene we had come across once while exploring the bush in the area north of the Save River in Mozambique. We were looking for signs of elephant in some fairly dense savanna bushveld when we suddenly happened upon a large, open area about the size of two football fields, almost completely bare of vegetation except for a few scrawny shrubs here and there. The bare earth there had a dark brown, if slightly reddish color, but it had streaks of gray-white in it, almost like marble.

As we were standing, wondering what to make of this unexpected phenomenon, we heard human voices, and we noticed a group of people, one or two older men, but mainly women and teenage children, among the trees on the other side of the open swath. This was even more surprising, because we had seen almost no people in the general area in about eight days, and according to our estimates the closest meaningful habitation was a good three days' walk to the north. The group was busily working away at something, and chatting loudly in the usual African way. I asked our guide and tracker, a guy named Mazenya, what on earth they might be doing there, and he quite matter-of-factly replied that they were gathering salt.

We decided we simply had to see what this was all about. Of course, meeting African people in the bush is hardly ever a brief and to-the-point affair, especially in remote areas such as that, where meeting anyone at all is an event in itself. There is usually an extended period of social formalities involved, which is often tedious to the Western, task-oriented mind, but I have come to appreciate the socially and personally wholesome practice. In this case it was even more extensive because of Mazenya, who was something of a showman and who could simply not resist any opportunity to give anyone he met a performance by impressing on them his illustrious background. However, once this was all politely worked through, we started looking around and inquiring.

It turned out the soil over the whole open area contained a very high concentration of salt—that was the gray-white patches we saw. The people were chopping up the earth, using their typical hand-fashioned hoes (such as I described earlier), and dissolving it thoroughly in water. Next, they would filter out the soil particles through pieces of cloth they had brought along, and then they would pour the solution into flat-bottomed containers of various types—several well-worn tin vessels of assorted shapes and sizes, and one or two interesting contraptions made of animal skin loosely stretched over a circular wooden frame to form a shallow bowl. They would leave the containers in the sun for the water to evaporate, and this would leave them with a minute quantity of dirty-brown salt in the container, which they then carefully added to their carrying containers. It was a painfully slow and laborious process, yielding very meager rewards of salt, but if you had no other way . . .

It was an age-old practice, and people would walk for days from far and wide to this ancient salt patch (and no doubt others like it) to gather the precious commodity during the dry season. They would carry all they needed and spend days, even weeks, at the salt patch.

But the one thing that intrigued me was where they got water from toward the end of the dry season, as we were in then. We had really been

battling to find water, and it was a good nine miles to the Save River—
certainly not practical to carry water from there, I thought. And they would
need considerable quantities, because they would also need to eat and drink.
Then I noticed a deeply rutted southward-heading track. To the side there
were also several crude sleds in various states of wear.

They had been fashioned in the usual African way, by chopping off a
large tree just below a reasonably even fork, and then severing the branches
that formed the two legs of the fork about one and a half yards from the
split. Through the unforked end, a hole would somehow be drilled and a
leather thong or chain would be run through it to drag the fork along, lying
flat. Between the two legs they would then fix some cross slats with wooden
nails to serve as a carrying platform. The fork would simply be dragged
along by the narrow end as a sled.

They would clearly come with some oxen or donkeys, which would then
be used to both carry their equipment and spoils, and to haul water from
the river once whatever they could find from digging seepage hollows in
nearby dry ravines had dried out.

They would bring some food, but would mostly live off the land because
of the extended period they had to spend there. In fact, while we were there,
a lean, brown hunter, naked except for an impala loin skin, carrying a bow
and arrows and a machete, came in to enthusiastic ululating from the diggers
with a porcupine and a snake he had managed to kill.

✦✦✦✦✦✦

These were pleasant reminiscences, but digging for salt wasn't an option
for us in the circumstances.

"*Hmm,* I think you are right," I said. "But it's a hell of a thing. There
must be some way . . . what if we dried it out in the sun?"

"No, pal, it would take days."

"OK, OK, but there must be a way. These Africans have been preparing
skins for hundreds of years."

"Well, of course, they spread it out and let it dry and then they work it soft, so we're back to drying it."

"OK. But first, before we go to too much trouble about preserving it, what if we could? How do we go from there? If we take it to Stephan's camp, well, as we know, we weren't really supposed to shoot a lion. In fact, I don't even know if Stephan has one on his license."

"Hmm," said Gerhard. "Well, if they do have one on license, I can't see that they wouldn't be prepared to include it in the deal—of course, for a fee," he ventured.

"Sure, but that means we first have to find out before we declare it, and if they don't . . ."

Before Gerhard could answer, the methodical engineer in me took over. "Look, here's what I think," I said. "We can make a frame from wood that we tie together with bark, and then we can stretch the skin over it and let it dry while we move. So that's that. Now they"— I glanced in the direction of Elias and John, chatting among themselves, blissfully unaware of our devious plotting—"suggested that we make a day and a half detour to this other dwelling, where we pick up more people to help carry the tusks. But actually, if your camp hand is still there, the poor lost soul, we could manage to carry the tusks to Stephan's camp between the five of us."

"Ja, OK, taking turns with two carrying the tusks at a time. But not the tusks and the frame," Gerhard interrupted.

"Exactly. It would be a hard push with the skin on a frame and the tusks. So with the skin we have to go via the village. It will probably be a day or a day and a half of hard slog, which is not too bad. Then we leave the skin there. We carry on to Stephan's camp without it and with an extra helper to carry the tusks, just for convenience. If I have to guess from the direction they said the dwellings are, it would probably take us about another two to three days to camp. If we find that Game Trackers doesn't have a license for a lion, we leave the skin there and we make a deal with Elias that he will fetch it to his home and tan it for us—the African way—and keep it until we can come and get it some other time. If they do have a license, we simply send Elias and John back to fetch it for us." I looked at Gerhard expectantly. He looked dubious, but I could see that I had stirred the gambler in him.

"Or, you know what," he said, "We could probably make a quiet deal with Danny to work it past all the legal issues of getting it out of Zim and into South Africa."

"Maybe, and I think it is reasonably safe to assume that Danny is going to be operating around here for a few years, because he seems to have had a fairly good season, and one good season is the basis for another good season in his business. I don't think I'd put the same odds on Game Trackers from what I see of their operation with Stephan. But anyway, that would mean Danny would have to have a lion on his license that he has not taken, and that's unlikely. Remember, by the time Elias has finished with the skin it will be as soft as a wet chamois, and we would be able to fold it into a neat, small bundle. I was thinking of simply smuggling it across."

Gerhard looked at me with those narrowed eyes that were so typical of him when he sensed a chance of pulling a fast one, so to speak. He chuckled delightedly past the stem of his pipe and said, "Pal, I'm in. But how do we make sure Elias actually does go and get the skin and tan it and keep it for us? I guess we could tell him that we pay him for his trouble at the point where he hands over the skin?"

"Yes. We have to trust him to an extent, of course, but I think it's worth a try. The one thing we need to be a little careful of is letting this whole episode of the lion go wider than you and me and Elias and John and the bush."

"I agree. Let's promise that we don't talk about it unless we both concur beforehand."

I then swore Elias and John to silence until I said they could talk about it, and so a pact of secrecy about the lion was sealed.

Our sleeping gear was still wet, but we slung our hammocks close to the fire against the sudden night chill, and after arranging for watch turns, we settled in for the night. I had the last watch from four o'clock. The night had been uneventful despite the wet skin and fresh tusks in camp, probably thanks to the rain and the abundance of standing pools in the veld, which made it unnecessary for scavengers to journey to the water hole. Although there was still the muffled sigh of thunder far to the southeast, most of the clouds had cleared away, and the stars shone exuberantly through the rain-washed atmosphere.

I had scarcely settled myself against the tree trunk next to the fire with my mug of coffee when the first light started creeping in from east and slowly stood up among the trees, bright and sharp and delicately laced with bird voices. The morning sang with that special joie de vivre that follows a night shower after a dry spell. Sitting with my mug of coffee, enjoying this cheer, I followed through on the plan that I had devised to save the lion skin.

I got Elias and John to construct a square frame a bit smaller than the body of the skin out of strong, light poles, held together with bark. Then I had them fold the wet skin flat over the frame with the hair on the outside, and stretch it tight with strips of bark through holes I made along its edge. Now it could dry while we carried it. I got Elias to mix all the salt we could spare with ash from the fire, and rub the mixture thoroughly into both the flesh side and the hair side. They were all quite skeptical about the idea, but they agreed it was worth a try, and certainly better than throwing the skin away.

We finally set off through the rain-fresh morning, heading west toward our temporary camp. Carrying the frame proved a bit of a challenge. It was quickly clear that it was quite difficult for one man because of its dimensions. I then got John and Elias to grip it in the front and rear and walk in tandem, and that was a huge improvement. Gerhard then suggested that we should carry the tusks lying flat on the stretched skin so that two of us at a time could walk relatively unencumbered and rest. This proved to help a lot, too. While watching Elias and John carry the lot, I came up with the idea of adding two longitudinal carrying poles that stuck out from the front and the rear of the frame, and tying bark loops to them so that we could suspend the frame from our shoulders. The design was so perfect in fact that we began wondering where we would be able to apply for patent rights!

It took us a good hour longer to get to the camp than we had estimated. Although all of our innovations worked quite well, as the sun started steaming the moisture from the earth, the intense heat and humidity began to take its toll on our bodies, and carrying our load through the bush became hard work. I suspect it was worse for Gerhard and me (of course we never let it show) because although we had both been provincial-level sportsmen at university and had stayed quite fit, we were less accustomed to the heat, and neither of us had a daily routine of carrying heavy loads around for extended periods. It was made a bit worse by the fact that there weren't really any pathways we could use apart from the odd bit of game path here and there. Our path took us all through the veld, and the frame frequently caught on vegetation and threw us off balance, so it was almost like dragging the thing through the bush.

We arrived around twelve, and fortunately found everything in place, including a deeply worried Lost Soul, as Gerhard and I had dubbed Stephan's erstwhile camp hand, patiently awaiting salvation. The camp was in a rather pleasant, cool spot, and we were hot and hadn't eaten yet, so we decided to make ourselves a good meal, wait out the worst heat, and then go as far as we could in the cooler part of the afternoon.

We spent the midday hours resting, repacking so that our loads would be well distributed, and making some adjustment to our frame system. Even adding Lost Soul to our carrying enterprise, it was going to be hard work to get to the dwellings. It would take us that afternoon, all of the next day, and half the day after, we thought.

Among the four of us we had used quite a bit of the water we had brought from the water hole in our few containers. What with the hot work of moving and using water for cooking and cleaning utensils, our supply was already a bit low. Our biggest problem would be finding water by that evening or definitely not later than midday on the next day. If we didn't, we could be in serious trouble. I asked John to ask Elias about water. He did not seem to be worried. Gerhard and I were also quite relaxed. From what we understood, we would be passing a little south of where we had left the vehicle in the fly camp, and we remembered finding water quite frequently in dry ravine beds in that general area.

Hunting in Tete province, Mozambique, 1989.

The Land Cruiser packed and ready for an expedition.

Adventures with the little Series II in the Kalahari Desert, Botswana, 1983.

Stuck in the mud after the buffalo hunt in the Nuanetsi Valley, Zimbabwe, 1984.

Great excitement surrounds the arrival of a vehicle and a white man. This was during our trip

Negotiating for hunting rights in the trustlands north of Gonarezhou, Zimbabwe, 1984.

It was hard work to cut a path for the vehicle, and the result was a lot of swearing.

With no roads, a lot of work with hand tools was required to get the Land Cruiser through the bush.

It wasn't easy getting the vehicle across the ravines in Tete province, Mozambique, 1989.

Building crossings between the Chinizua River and the Zambezi Delta in Mozambique, 1988.

Taking a break from clearing bush in an area north of the Save River, Mozambique, 1985.

Natural land mines! Elephant tracks in the dried mud.

Gerhard and the author in the fly camp before they parted ways.

We found these really huge elephant tracks in Tete province, Mozambique, 1989.

The author and John during an overnight stop on the hunt.

A tea break during the hunt.

Our efforts to find water paid off!

A warthog for the pot.

The warthog being smoke-dried.

Using smoke to dry reedbuck meat.

Locals ready to leave with warthog meat.

It takes patience to wait for meat to dry enough so that we can continue.

Breakfast during the hunt.

Back in the temporary camp.

Buffalo from the Nuanetsi Valley, Zimbabwe, 1984.

Gerhard with a buffalo shot for meat in Tete province, Mozambique, 1989.

Gerhard (left) and the author at the end of the sad elephant hunt.

The author, a tracker, and Techu (right) with the author's elephant, Naivasha, southeastern Zimbabwe, 1984.

Gerhard with an elephant taken in Naivasha, 1984.

The author on the open plains close to the Indian
Ocean and south of the Zambezi Delta, 1988.

Gerard's elephant from Tete, Mozambique, 1989.

The chefe struts his official stuff with seminomadic villagers. The night we were in this village, there was a torrential storm. The structures did little to keep out the rain.

The author in front of a nomadic bush house.

Bush dwellers inside their cooking structure.

The sangoma' conducts a prayer session to the north of the Save River, Mozambique, 1985.

The author's hunting party with Jacqui the tracker on the right, northeast of Gorongosa, 1987.

The surgeon at work in his bush theater removing a large thorn from the author's foot. From left, the author, Vic, and Mack.

Stealing honey from the little black bees.

Gathering bush information from a local hunting party.

Roadside night stopover on one of the author's expeditions.

Settling in for the night during a stopover in the bush.

Preparing a meal in fly camp.

Gerhard with elephant tusks from Tete province, Mozambique, 1989.

The author with elephant tusks from Tete province, Mozambique, 1989.

The Wanderers—Gerhard (left) and Hoffman—at a soirée on the author's estate in Elandsfontein, South Africa.

Lion Skin, Tusks, and an Evil Buffalo

CHAPTER 9

We struck out slightly northwest, heading for the little bush village. It was already late afternoon but the heat was still fierce, and we did little better than slog on, taking turns with the loads, scarcely aware of our surroundings, barely surviving between resting places, each next one acquiring the status of ultimate deliverance. I had to constantly remind myself of the logic for taking this two-day detour: *We have to go all the way to the dwellings because we have to leave the skin there in case Game Trackers does not have a lion on license. That way Elias can collect it from there later and tan it and keep it for us at his bush dwelling until we can come to fetch it.*

Gerhard apparently had the same thoughts because at one point during the afternoon he said, "Damn, I never thought a lion hunt could be such hard work and last so long. Are you sure we're not getting some of it wrong here?"

I merely smiled ironically.

The sun was almost touching the treetops when we reached a dry ravine that showed promise of subsurface water, and we gratefully decided to call it a day. We got everything set for the night on the edge of the steep bank, and then took time to have a long-overdue wash, pouring generous volumes of cool, sand-filtered water over each other. Our three companions also went off shyly around the bend for a wash.

Gerhard and I settled down in the orange luxury of the late afternoon, each with a mug of our precious red, and enjoyed the slow evaporation of the heat from the panting earth and the coolness of night spreading among the trees. It had been backbreaking labor, and tomorrow we would have to do more of it, but we accepted and enjoyed it as part of the package. When our companions returned, and we settled into the routine camp activities, there was a new understanding, an easy, deeper camaraderie in the talk and in the silence around the fire.

"Listen, pal," I said at one point. "I suppose I need to get these tusks back to camp, but they really are not your problem. I'd be quite happy if once we get to the dwellings and are able to get additional carriers that you take Elias and make a bit of a hunt out of going back. We can meet up at Stephan's camp later."

"*Hmm*, maybe. Let's see how we feel when we get there," Gerhard answered.

"Sure, just so long as you know how I feel. Carrying the stuff back is not going to be wildly exciting or interesting."

"*Ja*, thanks. I'm not sure I really feel like taking a long detour on my own. Besides, it might be a better idea to send a carrying party straight to camp—maybe the camp hand and one more. That way, you and I and John and Elias can take a slightly different route back?"

"Now that's a bloody excellent idea. Maybe a bit north, and then swinging back northeast?"

"Yep, could be nice. Thing is, we still need to shoot a buffalo each," Gerhard stated.

"*Ja*, precisely."

Fatigue thinned out the talk and stopped it early, and with Gerhard taking the first watch, we sought our lairs. It was never going to be a quiet night with the scent of the skin and the tusks having been spread in a long trail across the veld all day. Through the early evening we had been aware of some jackal cries and the foghorn hoots of hyenas that seemed closer than usual.

As the evening wore on, however, we caught the fleeting image of a jackal at the far fringes of the fire's glow, and another, and another, all of which could be heartily ignored. But then there was the hulking shadow of a hyena, and soon another, at first quietly lurking around the edge, but getting noisier as the evening wore on and the numbers grew to four or five, sniggering and bickering among themselves and edging closer. It was as if the bush was angrily pushing back the feeble glow of our fire, reaching out to claw back what we had taken from it.

++++++

"Collecting" the hyenas like that reminded us of an occasion years back when we had descended into the depths of setting bait for lions and had gotten hyenas instead. At the time we were barely twenty, inexperienced, dangerously naïve, and unhealthily hungry for the hunt. Neither the state of our finances nor the strength of our connections gave us much hope of fixing the front bead of a rifle on anything much bigger than a kudu. However, through some rather dubious sources, it had come to our ears that lion and elephant sometimes strayed from the Gonarezhou Game Reserve in Zimbabwe into the vast adjacent tribal trust areas to the west of it, attracted by the farm animals and maize there. Once they did, there was, for all practical purposes, an open season on them—if the local small farmers had the means to hunt them, which they seldom did.

We were aware that the accuracy of our information was questionable, but such trivialities were not considered important in our arguments toward embarking on an expedition into the area with the intention of styling ourselves as protectors of the beleaguered communities against the marauders.

In the trust areas individual farmers appeared to hold some rights over an allocated piece of land where they cultivated a bit of maize and kept some animals—a few head of cattle, some goats, and quite a few donkeys, which seemed to be the only element in the local farming industry really prospering (at least as far as their numbers were concerned). The whole area was rather depressing. The land was over-farmed and worn out to its bare bones, with the few meager patches of maize eking out a spindly yellow existence, and the animals desperately clinging to life in varying states of emaciation.

It took some negotiation and a bit of monetary largesse to find a reasonable spot where we could make our base camp, conducted through the person of one Graham, a rather, shall we say, opportunistic character whom

163

we had recruited at a small tribal village called Chikombedzi to be our guide and go-between. On the ground we found most of the local farmers friendly to our overtures, even if probably less interested in our (free) crop and animal protection services than in the possibility of actually extracting a monetary reward from us.

We spent a few frustrating days piteously scavenging around the area, getting no closer to any indication of the big invasion of marauders than the odd mongoose or rabbit, usually spotted at a distance, frantically diving for cover. All the while though, we were encouraged by tales (enthusiastically but most likely inaccurately retold by Graham) of bands of lions, elephants, and even buffaloes frequently roaming through the area, leaving devastation in their wake. After about a week of not seeing even a single track made by a wild animal larger than a rabbit, we began to suspect that we might be facing a hopeless situation, both from a hunting and a protection-service perspective. Moreover, the community appeared to be disconcertingly relaxed in the face of an imminent marauder invasion.

We were by then quite frustrated and more than a little peeved at having been taken for such a ride, and we decided that if we were to salvage anything from this desperate situation we would have to apply some natural external intervention—to see if we could not make the mountain more attractive to Mohammed, so to speak. We proceeded to buy a donkey from one of the local farmers. (By that point, their plans were actually coming together nicely, and the money was beginning to flow.) We shot it, and dragged parts of the carcass over a vast area behind the Land Cruiser, right up the border of the Gonarezhou. Then we hung what was left of it from trees in spots we thought lions might wander through.

The next two days were spent carefully checking our baits—yes, baits. We had actually set baits, although we preferred to think of the initiative in a more holistic way: We had really launched an effort to attract the vanguard of the marauders from the Gonarezhou into the area so that we could exterminate them before they would (inevitably, of course!) become a nuisance. It was no less than a comprehensive preemptive maneuver.

On the morning of the second day we found some hyena spoor at one spot. This we considered very encouraging. Our plan was clearly beginning to show results. More hyenas would come, followed in short order by lions, we assured ourselves. We even started contemplating expanding our operation with more donkeys in more areas. In truth, however, the whole experience was quite unpleasant to us although we chatted ourselves into a positive view. Despite our best efforts at rationalizing our actions, we still felt uncomfortable, for we knew deep down that we were actually pathetically scraping the bottom of a hopeless situation. There was, of course, no game in the area, so there was no question of any hunting, and we spent most of our time idle, getting more and more frustrated and short-tempered. It was depressing, even humiliating, and we had an uneasy realization that this was not what we had anticipated or really wanted to be involved in.

On the morning of the third day upon our return from our bait-checking rounds (where we found nothing except more hyena spoor), we received a visit from our "landlord" and two other local farmers. They appeared upset—in fact, they suddenly seemed much more like people having to bear the brunt of a major marauder invasion. After the usual polite (but now much briefer) small talk, they informed us that a calf of theirs had been caught by hyenas during the night. We were at once excited and delighted that the invasion seemed to have started at last, but disappointed that the despicable slaying of the defenseless infant had not actually been done by lions.

Our hosts, however, surprised us with the attitude they chose to adopt in the circumstances. They stated that we had "called" the hyenas, and were therefore responsible for the loss, and the owner of the calf wanted compensation. Their financial exploitation of our presence was progressing very satisfactorily indeed, I noted. Our situation had now turned from unpleasant to appalling. We briefly mumbled that this kind of exploitation bloody well justified leaving straight away, but what little feeling of honor we had left did not really allow us to simply pack up and leave—it would probably not have been a good idea anyway.

We avoided discussing what type of compensation might be expected, and solemnly denied that we could have had anything to do with the loss of the calf—but, as the protectors, we would of course immediately go and investigate the situation; they should please not disturb the scene, as that might spoil our chances of exterminating the dreadful vermin. Our accusers eventually left, clearly not happy with the view we took of the situation, and especially not with the apparent slow movement of hard cash, but placated to some extent by copious solicitations by Graham (which I suspected might have included some exorbitant promises made on our behalf). I remember remarking to Gerhard that I dared not even think what he had offered them, and that we could expect them to come back within a day or two.

Whatever the possible future scenarios, we knew that we had to act quickly to contain the situation. Our scheme was beginning to show serious fraying at the edges. Although some hyenas must have been frequenting the area to scavenge the odd farm animal that had succumbed to the ravages of existence in those bare circumstances, we may have caused them to concentrate, with potentially bad consequences for the local inhabitants. We concluded that we should remove our baits so that they would assume their natural distribution again.

We first went to see the carcass. It was a calf of about nine months old. It was lying on its back in a narrow ditch, and it was clear to us that the most likely cause of its death was falling in (probably in an advanced state of weakness), and then not being able to right itself again—cattle will die from an accumulation of gas in their digestive tract if they are kept lying on their backs or sides for long. Even if it had not died as we suspected, it would have been an obvious target for an opportunistic hyena in its poor state, and it might have fallen into the ditch during a chase.

Whatever the precise reason for its unfortunate (but I suspected imminently inevitable) demise, blaming it on our activities offered the enterprising owner a fortuitous opportunity for some monetary gain from an otherwise dead-loss situation. However, simply informing him of our suspicions would not really have contributed much to our image as community protectors, so that was not an option we could adopt under the circumstances. This was really more a case of "guilty irrespective of how proven." What was more, although there were two threadbare dogs feeding on the carcass as we arrived, there certainly was some hyena spoor around.

Quite a bit of meat remained on the carcass despite the efforts of the dogs, so there could not have been more than two hyenas feeding during the night. This meant that they were likely to return after dark. We decided that our best approach to try to improve our situation would be to ambush and kill them. This would also place us in a better position to mitigate against the claim for compensation.

We left Graham at the carcass with instructions on how to build a blind and how to keep the dogs at bay, while we went off to go and remove our other baits. These we burned, and we were back at the carcass by sunset, just in time to set ourselves up for the night. Graham had done a fairly good job on the blind, so we drove the Land Cruiser away about half a mile or so, and moved in on foot, Gerhard and me with our rifles and water bottles, Graham with the spotlight and Land Cruiser battery.

Graham received a quick course on how to shine the spotlight, and then we settled in for the wait. Sitting dead-quiet, listening to the dogs having a feast at the carcass, feeling the mosquitoes boring away at us, and unable to do anything about either—in fact, unable to do anything other than just wait while it got gradually more uncomfortable and cold, was an unpleasant and frustrating experience.

The Southern Cross was already leaning low by the time we finally thought we heard the dogs being chased off by the hyenas. We waited for a few minutes, and then had Graham switch on the light. Of course, he didn't shine it anywhere near the way he had been instructed, and in the few brief seconds that followed we were barely able to make out that there was just one hyena at the carcass. I felt like using my rifle on Graham for possibly spoiling a chance at a shot after such a long and uncomfortable wait.

I grabbed the light from him to shine it properly, hoping to give Gerhard at least one decent shot. He hit the hapless scavenger well enough, and the heavy bullet sent the beast spinning away with a pitiful series of yelps. I kept the light on him as he tried to drag himself away, and Gerhard was able to finish him, grumbling afterward about the two expensive bullets spent on the damn hyena.

When we got to our complainant's dwelling the next morning he was mercifully not there. Through Graham we explained to his teenage son that we thought the calf may have died from an unfortunate accident, but that we had killed the hyena anyway, just in case it bothered him. Then we vacated the area—in fact, we abandoned the whole endeavor as fast as was possible without creating the impression that we might actually be in a hurry to get away.

◆◆◆◆◆◆

We didn't get much sleep during the night. At one point during his watch John nervously hurled a burning log at a hyena that came too close for his comfort. Of course we then had to insist that he retrieve it in case it set the bush on fire, which he was too scared to do alone, and Gerhard finally took pity on him and got out of his hammock with his rifle to go with him. It was simply too hectic to get any sleep, and we ended up drinking coffee and chatting most of the night except for the odd snatch of uneasy sleep here and there.

We set out the next morning feeling heavy and numb, and the day was an endless slog in the pitiless heat, punctuated by grateful rests in cool shade sanctuaries with mugs of tea, but very little else.

Mercifully we found water again by late afternoon, and with the prospect of being able to wash off the sweat and the caked dust and relaxing with a few sips of wine in the cool evening, our outlook on the situation became much more positive. Our companions (notably Lost Soul and John—Elias seemed relatively unfazed) were decidedly nervous about the prospect of another night of scavenger-fending. John said he was scared some lions might come, and he wanted us to put the skin and the tusks some distance away from the camp so that the scavengers would be attracted away from us. I could see they were both really scared.

I have to admit that I felt I could do with some decent sleep too, so I suggested that we drag up a large pile of wood so that we could make three fires and sleep between them. Gerhard and I would have to give up our hammocks because there wouldn't be room for them between the fires, but we were not unaccustomed to sleeping on the ground—in fact, a hammock is comfortable but cold, so we often took to the ground when it got really chilly—it was less comfortable but certainly better than lying awake shivering all night. The three-fire solution calmed them down, but clearly not to the point of complacency, because they brought up a pile of wood sufficient to stoke the ovens of Babylon!

++++++

The situation reminded me of a similar one I had been in once. I was wandering around with three companions—two bearers and a tracker called Camisu, in an area a bit south of the Zambezi Delta, not very far from the Indian Ocean. We were heading in a northeasterly direction but not going anywhere in particular, so when we came upon one of those ubiquitous footpaths I agreed that we could follow it for a bit (Camisu had a particular preference for such footpaths, for good reason).

It was clearly a well-used path, mainly frequented by humans. Camisu, who spoke Fanagalo, explained that it "led" to quite a large village some three days away on the Zambezi and that it was the main path between there and villages on the road some five days to the southwest. (Of course, "led" is a bit of a misnomer; "aimlessly meander" would probably be a more appropriate description.)

We soon met up with a small group of people moving southward—two men and four women. It was, as always, a special occasion to meet people in such a remote place, and the customary drawn-out social exchange was inevitable. The men, both in their forties (I guessed) wore somewhat tattered Western clothes. The women had beautifully colored sarilike garments wrapped around them. Two of them were older, about the same age as the men, and there were two younger girls, one about thirteen and the other a preadolescent.

I couldn't participate in the social exchanges and I stood around, a bit impatiently, because I still wanted to put some distance between us and last night's camp. When we were finally on our way again, I noticed that my companions were unusually talkative and animated. Once we had settled down at our midday break, I asked Camisu what it was all about.

He was a serious man with a proud bearing and a lot of *gravitas*. Not the best tracker I had ever worked with, but on this expedition that wasn't much of a handicap because I was wandering more than hunting, and he was very good at maintaining authority around the camp and interfacing with any people we came across. He explained to me in his serious demeanor that they had been discussing the elder of the two girls whom Domingo, one of the bearers, was particularly enamored with. I was quite astonished that Domingo could be interested in such a young girl, but Camisu assured me that she was ready for matrimony.

A further reason for their lively discussions was then made known: A lion had, just a week earlier, caught a man traveling along this very path, and just a short distance from where we were. I could see that he was uncomfortable with the lion situation. Of course there were lions around all the time, and although I felt sad for the slain man's family, I did not think it all that unusual for people to be taken by predators in the remote African bush. When I said nothing, he blurted out, looking away from me: "They are saying that we must leave this area quickly. They are very scared of the lion."

"And you, Camisu, what do you think?" I asked, curious to know if he as the leading figure would admit to being scared too.

"Those people that we met, they are walking very fast so that they can be far from this place when it gets dark. The lion that eats the people is very bad in the night," he said.

"I understand this thing you are talking about. OK, we can also walk fast," and I nodded in a northeasterly direction, "but when it gets dark, we have to make camp, and if the lion is there, he is there. But I have a rifle, and if he comes, I can shoot him."

"Yes, Patrau, but they told us this lion, his medicine is very strong because they tried to kill him, but they could not," and now he looked at me imploringly.

"But Camisu, this medicine is stronger, and that is the truth," I said, patting the butt of my .375.

My calm self-assurance seemed to relax him a bit, and after he had spoken to the two bearers they also seemed calmer—up to the point where we found, in the damp sand on the edge of the perfect little stream for us to camp at, the fresh spoor of a large male lion.

My companions, especially the younger of the two bearers, were now worried to the point of being panicky. They first wanted to leave, but when I calmly pointed out that it was near sunset and that we were unlikely to find water again, they wanted to set the veld around us on fire to drive away the lion. That seemed far too drastic, and I refused that, too. I knew that one had to be very careful with lions at night, but I thought it somewhat less than likely that a lion would take on four humans if we were prepared. However, I knew I had to act quickly and decisively before the situation got out of hand.

I addressed Camisu in a forceful voice. "Camisu, stop talking like a young boy who is coming to the bush for the first time. This lion cannot kill us. If he even comes close, I will kill him," and I slammed my chest with my fist on the I. "Tell these men that we will build three fires here and here and here," I said as I firmly ground my heel into the ground to mark each spot, "and we will sleep between them. And I have this light that can see very far in the dark." I produced a remarkably powerful little flashlight I had with me. "If the lion comes, you put the light on him, and I will kill him with this rifle," and I thrust forward the .375 as if I was presenting arms to the chief of the army.

"Now take them and go and get some wood!" I turned away to show that it was absolutely the end of the conversation and that they had to get on with it.

Fortunately the combination of suggesting that he was acting less than manly and my adamant attitude hit the right chords, and he in turn had enough authority to get the other two into line. The strength they drew from the three fires that we kept going through the night might also have been a factor in deciding them to fall into line.

The first part of the night was quiet, but on Domingo's watch he heard rustling in the undergrowth. In seconds, he had us all on our feet and brandishing an assortment of weapons, but the flashlight revealed nothing. We eventually went back to our lairs, and while we were still awake we all heard the sound again but from a different direction. It was very clearly some small animal foraging. Camisu said he thought it was possibly a rat or a hare. Whatever it was, the rest of the night passed without event. I have to admit that for all my bravery I, too, was grateful for the three fires; if nothing else they afforded us a somewhat nervous, but reasonably calm night's rest.

++++++

This night turned out to be very similar. It was a lot quieter than the previous one. There were only the odd jackal and a hyena, probably because both the skin and the tusks had now dried a bit and gave off less smell. But they did not really present a danger. Hyenas are less bold when they are single. They only become really aggressive when they unite and form a cackle.

John woke us up at some point during his watch, though, asserting wide-eyed that there was a lion. That got our attention. We walked the perimeter of light with our rifles ready, keeping our eyes away from the glow of the three fires so that we would not be blinded, but we saw nothing. We then decided to sit up for a while, facing outward, to see if it would come back.

It was then that Gerhard confided in me about a previous lion experience. It was at a time when he had gone off hunting on his own in Zambia (I think), courtesy of a friend who was a safari operator there. Back home he had devised a contraption with which he wanted to play back tape-recorded sounds of lions roaring and feeding to see if he could attract other lions with it. A pride of lions at a kill is often extremely noisy, ferociously bickering and fighting among themselves. This, mixed with the background sounds of hyenas and jackals, makes for quite a bloodthirsty cacophony that could very likely get the attention of any lion within earshot, he reasoned.

One late afternoon when he was alone in camp, he drove out in his old Land Cruiser to shoot a warthog for camp meat, and also, he had quietly decided, to try out his idea. He got the warthog, loaded it onto the back, and then continued to an area near a water hole where he had previously seen some lion spoor. He parked the vehicle and mounted his device on the roof. Then he settled down on the back within easy reach of his device in a camp chair he had brought along. Also within easy reach was a spotlight he had connected to the battery of the Land Cruiser, his rifle—carefully cushioned and covered with his jacket in case of dew—and a beer or two. When it was quite dark, he activated his lion-luring machinery. He had a large speaker connected to the little battery-driven tape recorder, and it produced a good volume, no doubt resonating a bit in the tin cavities of the Land Cruiser.

He interrupted his production at appropriately spaced intervals to get a feel for the response from his audience, but they remained strangely aloof despite him turning up the volume a bit more. He was about to conclude that the lions in that area were not really appreciative of his talents when he heard a sound in the bush close-by. The spotlight revealed a lone hyena, uncertainly sniffing the air.

This was great encouragement from the lesser members of the audience! He decided that this popular demand clearly called for an extended season, and he settled down for some more broadcasting, checking from time to time with the spotlight, but finding only the hyena, dripping at the jowls from the smell of the warthog, but not brave enough to approach really close on its own.

The night wore on, and eventually even the unflinching loyalty of the hyena, with whom he was beginning to develop a personal bond, was not enough to compensate for the cold and the boredom and the torment of the mosquitoes. He decided that the hyena was not as reliable a source of the general enthusiasm for his production as he had first thought, and that he had best pack up.

In his usual meticulous fashion, he was busy disconnecting and rolling up when he heard a sound right next to the Land Cruiser. *Must be the hyena,* he thought. When he switched on the spotlight, he stared right into the eyes of a lioness!

Looking decidedly menacing, she was on the verge of jumping onto the back of the Land Cruiser. It was clear her intentions were dishonorable. During the broadcast, Gerhard had left his rifle lying on his jacket on the floor in the back of the vehicle; consequently, he wasn't at all ready to receive such a guest at such short notice. He decided that this was not the time for heroics, so in a most undignified manner, he dove into the cab of the vehicle on the opposite side, leaving all the show equipment on the top.

But this maneuver hardly solved the problem because he had taken off the Land Cruiser's doors for hunting, so he wasn't safe yet. It didn't help his peace of mind that his rifle was still on the floor in the back of the vehicle and that all his broadcasting equipment was chaotically strewn about on the roof. His immediate priority was to back away from the lioness as fast as possible. The retreat was, of course, affected with much desperate fumbling for the ignition in the dark and much trembling of the legs, which caused the Land Cruiser to stall and lurch and roar and crash over several trees and shrubs and through dongas in a most indecorous manner.

The copious revving of the engine probably served to have the lioness delay immediate action and to reconsider her options. By the time Gerhard had brought the Land Cruiser to a lurching halt at a point he considered safe, all his equipment had been swept off the roof (he saw some of it bounce off the bonnet), and heaven knew what had happened to his rifle!

To appreciate the effect this situation would have had on Gerhard, one needs to understand that he was always particularly organized and precise in all he did, but when it came to his guns he was a fanatic of rare obsession.

He was an avid collector of hand-built British sporting guns, and his care of them bordered on what some would call the absurd. I have to admit that I did not find it all that extreme, although I guess it was a bit strange that he at times insisted on carrying his gun in its bag in the bush, only removing it when he thought action was imminent.

That being the case, he was now almost more concerned about the fate of his gun than about mere survival. He left the engine running and unsteadily climbed out of the cab and onto the back to rescue it. Before trying to resuscitate the spotlight so that he could see what was going on, he took a moment to assess the general situation. Deadly quiet greeted him as he stood listening and checking for any sign of the lioness. He managed to fish the spotlight from the grass by pulling on its electric lead, which had thankfully survived the retreat, and switched it on. To his total consternation and amazement, the beam caught the lioness about twenty yards from the vehicle—she had actually followed him, and was approaching at a determined trot, ears pricked forward, looking extremely interested.

By now he had a bit of distance in his favor, and fortunately his rifle was still lying wrapped in his jacket on the floor. He was in a much better position to present a respectable front to her. He grabbed the rifle, but had to let go of the spotlight, which fell clanking onto the back and went out. In the pitch darkness that cloaked the spotlight's beam, he let off a hasty shot in the general direction of the lioness, painfully knocking the barrel against the cab, and then executed a second hasty retreat.

Fortunately his shot and the ensuing commotion of lurching off over the rough ground must have convinced the lioness that, after all, it might not be such a great idea to be so forward in her approach to this incomprehensibly behaving human. As he swung the vehicle around, now in forward gear, there was no sign of her in the headlamps.

He wasn't taking any more chances. He drove well away from the area before he stopped to compose himself and take stock of the situation. At least he had his rifle with him—he couldn't see in the dark, but he prayed that it had not been damaged by the inappropriate handling it had received.

The old Land Cruiser's engine was purring reassuringly as always, and he himself, apart from a few painful scuffs and a sore shoulder where he had hit it on the side of the door, was alive and well enough. But all his equipment was lying scattered in the bush, including the chair, which had been thrown off the back, and he seemed to have lost his pipe!

There was no way he was going to go back to look for all that right now. That would have to be done during the day at some time when he could sneak back to the area without anyone noticing. It was totally unnecessary to subject his ego to more bruising by having someone watch him hunt for all the equipment and being able to piece together some version of the events that was not likely to be flattering at all. As for the lioness, he did not care to see her soon again either.

✦✦✦✦✦✦

We finally convinced ourselves that it would take a really audacious and spoiled-rotten lion to come in between the three fires with someone awake and actively tending them. We went back to sleep, but John continued to complain about the lion. We took rather sleepy notice of this. I mumbled to him to let me know when the lion was nearly finished eating him because then there was a chance that it might want to start on the lion skin, and we still needed that—which didn't seem to do much for his sense of peace. The next morning we checked the area for tracks, but apart from those of a jackal and maybe two hyenas, there was nothing. This caused John to be on the receiving end of a lot of good-natured mockery. It was going to take some time for him to live it down.

The last day's stretch was easier because fairly early on we found a well-worn path, clearly used by the villagers, that we could follow—of course it ran only approximately in the right direction and required an indirect approach, but it was still less tiring, and, I suspect, faster. We had decided the previous evening that we should try to shoot something for the pot. The elephant meat that Elias and John had brought along was almost finished, and it would be good to arrive at the dwellings with some meat to offer the residents.

Gerhard and I hunted around the flanks when we were not carrying our loads, and we were lucky to get a warthog. I believe, together with reedbuck, it is the best game meat by far. In my opinion, game meat generally does not taste nice and is something to be eaten only when all other alternatives had been exhausted.

Once we had shot it, it had to be slaughtered and processed, but under Elias's expert guidance our three companions made short work of this. Elias and John quickly took off the skin and cut up the meat, while Lost Soul was directed to build a crude lattice structure from saplings and light a fire underneath it. They tossed the freshly cut meat onto this to be singed and smoked. Elias split open the heart like a butterfly and fried it over the open flame for immediate consumption. We had some of it, too—it was actually quite delicious. It took about an hour before the meat had formed a dry outer skin. Then they packed it into three equal bundles and tied it tightly with bark strips to carry on their heads. Almost nothing was left behind. At every rest they built a new lattice and fired the meat some more until it was partly cooked, dry, and almost black in color.

We finally reached the bush dwelling well after twelve. We walked into the clean-swept clearing between the huts and gratefully lowered our loads. There were five low-walled square huts, each about the size of a king-size double bed, with wide, overhanging roofs. Their crushed anthill-and-pole walls seemed sturdy, darkened and rubbed smooth in areas where the sun could be enjoyed on cold winter mornings, or its sting avoided on hot summer afternoons. I could see that the elephant-grass thatch on the roofs had thinned out in places, and the lattice skeleton underneath was drooping dejectedly over the sides.

More or less in the center of the small hamlet was a single, rather desperate-looking tree, bare except for some branches and foliage right at the top, and next to it was an open pole-and-thatch cooking structure a little larger than the huts. A log smoked thinly on the ash heap, and a few cooking utensils lay scattered around on the dust-trodden earth.

The cooking structure had a lattice platform about the height of a man, blackened by smoke and used for storing stuff and smoking meat, which, of course, would be a regular requirement because the residents supplemented their diet with game taken from the surrounding bush. The thatch roof was evidently meant to keep the whole effort dry, but it now only existed in swathes of its former glory.

Between two of the huts were twin maize-storage structures, circular, raised on poles to about hip height, and made out of slats with bark woven between them. Like two giant baskets, these had thatch lids. The place smelled faintly of stale wood smoke and rotting meat.

To the side was an area about the size of a tennis court where the trees had been cleared by chopping them off at knee-to-hip height, and then burning them once they had dried out, together with the other undergrowth. This area was in the process of being hand-planted with cassava.[1]

A number of people moved vaguely into the background as we entered the area, but two men, dressed in a combination of animal skin and tattered bits of Western clothing, stepped forward tentatively when they apparently recognized Elias. Greetings were exchanged, and another man, younger than the first two, joined us. He took the menial task of dragging up some sitting logs, smooth and shiny from use. Once everybody had taken a seat, the lead man got up and, followed by his fellow dwellers, solemnly went around, greeting each of us with both hands.

Some polite general conversation drifted and bobbed around aimlessly on a sea of questions and excited expectations. The grown women (above thirteen or so) each came up to greet the guests formally by kneeling down and bowing low. On the fringes of all this hovered a smattering of dirty, runny-nosed children, sometimes breaking into scuffles and self-conscious attempts at comedy, but mostly staring at us.

---

[1]Cassava is a tall plant with long, narrow leaves and roots somewhat like sweet potato, but not sweet. It remains, together with maize—and rice in the wetter parts—a staple food in the remote bush areas. It is grown in such small clearings, and more or less in enough quantities to sustain the owners to the next crop.

Eventually the lead man ventured a polite question. I deduced this because Elias, in the course of his lengthy answer, gestured in the direction from which we had come and the direction to Stephan's camp. He must have been asked about the elephant, too, because Elias succumbed to telling them the story, not in as much splendid detail, but sufficiently entertaining to awe and amuse. The lion skin came up for discussion next.

When I saw them turning their attention to it with suitably awed and respectful expressions and due recognition to Gerhard and me, I took the opportunity—Gerhard had a very limited command of either Zulu or Fanagalo, so most of the talking was left to me—to explain through John that we were hoping to leave the skin here and for them to keep it safe, on its frame, until either Elias or ourselves came to collect it. Lead Man and his two companions appeared to consider that for a moment, and then Junior started a new and quite lengthy conversation thread, the other two adding comments, all very serious and at times emotional.

At the end of it John very solemnly turned to me and said: "Patrau, it is like this. There is a buffalo in the bush. He is staying alone near a water hole where the people can get water when there is no rain, and sometimes they can fish there. One day some people came and they wanted to kill the buffalo for the meat, but they did not kill it, and that buffalo, he chased the one man into the tree, and he had to wait a long time to run away."

"Was it the same people that Elias and I found?"

"*Eh*, they were not the same, but they were the same like them."

"OK, carry on."

"Yes, now this buffalo, he is making a lot of trouble for the people. If he can see you, he will chase you and you have to run away. And one day he killed the wife of this man," he nodded toward Junior.

"What? He killed her?!"

"Yes, he killed her. He says she went to fetch water together with the other women and they did not see the buffalo and when it came out it was very close, and she could not run away fast because she had the child inside, and then he killed her."

"But why don't they go and kill this buffalo? It will hurt more people!"

"*Eh*, but they are very afraid. They cannot kill this buffalo. They say it is very strong and they are only three, and this buffalo . . ."

He became self-conscious and didn't finish the sentence, but I suspected that the buffalo had built up some superstitious currency for itself.

I translated all of this for Gerhard. "OK, but what now? Do they want us to kill it? What about the lion skin?" he replied, swatting impatiently at a tsetse with his hat. Sitting quietly through long, irrelevant discussions was never one of his strong points.

"I think that's where it is going. Let me make sure," I replied.

Turning to John, I said, "John, you must tell this man we are crying with him for his wife. What are they saying about the lion skin?"

"No, they say the lion skin, it can stay here. They will look after it very well."

"OK, tell them thank you."

After John had told them what I said, I asked him, "Now, what about the buffalo?"

"They are asking if maybe you can go and shoot the buffalo because they see you are a very great hunter and you are not afraid."

Looking for a way to inspire them to keep our lion skin safe, I said, "Hey, you know, I think we can try to shoot the buffalo, but I think if we shoot it and they do not look after the lion skin nicely, then the buffalo will wake up again and it will come right between the huts and it will make really big trouble."

While John was impressing this tale on them, I turned to Gerhard. "Well, it seems as if the gods are presenting us with yet another task before we can return. I am beginning to understand what poor old Hercules and Jason must have felt like."

"OK, John," I said. "We will try to shoot the buffalo for them. We will rest now and go this afternoon to see if we can find it. But we can't stay in this place too long."

The whole arrangement seemed to suit everybody down to the ground. They would get rid of their supernatural buffalo and gain an abundance of meat to boot while we get our lion skin well cared for—and the hunt didn't seem particularly unattractive, either. It did mean that we would have to spend at least one night (and maybe even a bit longer), but it didn't seem appropriate to leave immediately anyway.

Besides, the King of the Waters of the Heaven was again mustering his forces in the northwest to do battle with the Sun King, and if one kept quiet one could already hear the angry rattle of the assegais on the rawhide shields far to the northwest. It seemed sensible to be in a place where we could keep dry during the night.

These social procedures had taken more than an hour, and my attention was beginning to tune sleepily to the incessant buzzing of the flies and the soft crooning of the long-legged chickens wandering around the clearing, searching for scraps of food with tilted heads. It seemed like an appropriate time to excuse ourselves from the gathering and attend to the logistics of our situation.

"Where do you think we should nest tonight?" Gerhard asked once we had disentangled ourselves from the circle.

"I don't know. I've been wondering, too."

He lit his pipe. "It looks like rain. If we are going to build a shelter we'd better start now. One thing is for sure: You're not getting me into any of these huts. I can't think there would be one free if you look at all these people and children here anyway, and even if there was, I'd prefer to sleep out in the open."

"For sure. I've been wondering if we couldn't nest under these wide overhangs."

After inspection and a bit of scheming we were convinced that we would be able to sling our hammocks between two corner poles of the overhanging roof. They had been very sturdily fixed to the wall uprights with rawhide, and were further held in place by the latticework that held up the thatch.

I beckoned John and Elias out of the gathering. "John, what do you think? Should we stay here for the night? Should we sleep here, in the dwelling?"

"*Eh*, we can sleep here. The rain, it is coming."

"OK, but have you asked the people?"

"They said we must stay," he replied.

My experience with people like these in the remote bush has always been that they were friendly and hospitable and generous. We decided to try our hammock plan for a siesta. It was a bit difficult to get into the hammock, and one could not sit upright, but otherwise it was perfect—shaded and cool and well-protected from the rain, as long as one chose a side where the thatch was still in reasonable condition.

After the commotion that erupted when we first slung the hammocks had died down, we settled in for a short siesta. John came and lay down on the ground around the corner of my hut. Lying sleepless, I took the opportunity to ask him about some of the issues I was wondering about. "John, I see three men here. How many grown women are there?"

"They are five."

"Are they all the wives of the men?"

"No, the one, she is the mother of the big one." This was Lead Man. So at least one of them had two wives.

"OK, now tell me, John, these huts—their roofs are going bad. One of these days they will not keep out the rain anymore. But the people are not putting on new grass. Why are they not fixing them?"

He seemed not to have given the issue any thought, probably because he did not consider it to be important. He took a minute before he responded. "*Ah*, these people, maybe they cannot stay here long."

His answer confirmed my impressions of this set of dwellings and many others like it that we had come across in the remote bush. They were typically made by a group of one or two families. They would use the dwellings until the game in the surrounding bush, or the fish in the pools, had been depleted to the point that it could not support them any longer, and the patch of land they had cleared for planting was no longer producing enough to last them to the next season. Then they would simply pack up their stuff (not more than could be carried by the family), and leave to start again at some other place.

The structures they erected were neat, showing deft if rudimentary workmanship, but they never appeared to do any maintenance on them. They simply let them gradually deteriorate, with the result that they usually appeared dilapidated and sad. After the family had left for their new home, the bush would swallow the remains and within a few years there would be no sign of them having ever been there, except perhaps for a patch where the vegetation appeared smaller than the surrounding bush.

Their snaring activities, at least initially, mostly targeted the smaller, easier game species. It was only later they attempted to go after the larger, more formidable ones, usually starting with the grazers. The result was a skewing of the game populations, right up the predator and scavenger levels. The absence of the smaller game animals and their predators, and eventually the larger grazers, would gradually start affecting the nature of the vegetation, too, so that the whole habitat within the area of influence of the dwelling would change.

But the density of the dwellers and the frequency of resettlement and even the impacts of roaming hunting groups from larger settlements were low enough so that, over the longer term, this lifestyle did not affect the environment to the point where the vegetation and the game population could not recover. Of course, natural phenomena such as prolonged droughts or outbreaks of disease among animals also affected the whole balance, but the latter would still be accommodated within the powerful ebb and flow of nature as long as the other human impacts were of sufficiently low intensity.

Even in the relatively short period of around forty years that I have been wandering around the African bush, I have seen these seminomadic lifestyle patterns more or less disappear in all but the most remote areas that have been spared the "blessings" of Western civilization. With the relatively rapid introduction into Africa of modern civilization, the well-established and sustainable equilibrium of traditional rural African life was disturbed.

In its place came a migration away from rural lifestyles to larger settlements and towns where people went to look for a better life. Unfortunately, except for a tiny percentage (overwhelmingly the political elite and their cronies in business) who grew fabulously wealthy, the vast majority had to eke out an ignoble existence in squalor, often sustained only by foreign aid.

As for the rural areas, they did not escape the ravages of devastating wars that grew out of the creation of countries and borders and political parties and the meddling of great powers. With these came crude politicking and corruption, things that were alien to the populace before. Wars meant modern weapons in great quantities, and these stayed behind in the hands of "soldiers" turned commercial hunters, and the roaming hunter bands grew more deadly and reached ever farther to devastate the game in even the remotest parts.

The great tragedy is that this lifestyle, together with the (different) system of scattered larger settlements that relied more on agriculture and some commerce, and the societal order of more or less loosely organized local chieftainships that went with it, really represented a unique balance of humans within the ecosystem that had been sustained for eons.

On a larger scale, all of it was again kept in balance by natural meta-cycles of famine and plenty, and by diseases and (usually limited) tribal skirmishes. People living in rural Africa in this manner might have been considered poor, deprived of modern medical care and amenities, and generally backward by Western observers, but they were a happy and content people living in harmony with their environment. Yes, much is made of the extended life expectancy and reduced infant mortality that is often cited by analysts, as if those are the Holy Grail of peace and true happiness, but I wonder—and I cry for Africa.

I dozed off uneasily to the muted clucking of the scavenging chickens.

The Labors of Jason and Hercules

The sun had disappeared behind white cloud plumes when we set out northwest to the water hole to see if we could find the evil buffalo. Junior, now wearing only his loincloth and an ax, led the way, followed by Gerhard and me, with Elias and John (the latter for the sake of communication) bringing up the rear. The other two also wanted to come along, but Gerhard and I refused. It would simply make the party too large.

At a brisk pace along a fairly well-used path it was a walk of an hour and a bit. We had to skirt around the west to get downwind as we approached the area. The water hole was situated on the east side of a long, shallow depression, wet and dense with reeds and marsh vegetation, and labyrinthed with narrow tunnels and open patches made by elephants and buffaloes and pigs.

It might have been an ancient riverbed, or perhaps hollowed out over eons by game carrying away bits of mud on their feet and coats as they left the mud wallows, I mused as we skirted the marshy area toward a pool in a rock basin on the east side. It had beautifully clear water fed from a spring, and a slow seepage from it was nourishing the marshy area on the west side. The vegetation around the area was lush, with large trees and tall grass reaching up into the lower branches. Although the area was trodden down quite a lot by game this late in the dry season, it was still dense in places. *Absolutely the ideal haunt for an old* dagga[1] *boy, and a nasty area to run into one as notoriously aggressive as this one,* I thought.

---

[1]*Dagga* is an African slang word for mud. Buffalo bulls often become solitary when they get old and are pushed out of the breeding herds. They then tend to find a quiet spot with water, good grazing, and lots of mud—*dagga*—to wallow in, and they seldom wander far from it— hence "*dagga* boy." They are sometimes joined by other old bulls and even younger ones that have not yet made the grade to breeding bulls, and then they tend to be less area-bound.

Hunting buffalo is never something that can be taken lightly. I have found them, especially the bulls, self-assured and combative especially when in a group, and often just plain nasty when alone. I had heard many a tale of bush dwellers being chased into trees, even gored or killed by a charging buffalo—and one, sometimes told in hunting camps, of the poor fellow that got chased into a tree too small to get his feet out of reach of the buffalo, and then having the flesh literally licked off his bones by the animal's rough tongue!

There is usually no chance of just a mock charge like with a lion or elephant. A buffalo just keeps coming, like a black rhino, and because of its size and strength it is almost unstoppable and difficult to evade. Moreover, its big bulk belies its amazing speed and agility.

I had some personal experience with the buffalo's brazen aggressiveness once while wandering around alone in the bush between the Great and the Little Letaba Rivers on the border of Kruger Park where Gerhard and I operated a concession at one time. It was around midday and sweltering hot. As I rounded a raisin bush, I spotted a herd of about seven mature bulls resting in the shade of a lone marula tree in an open swath about a hundred paces from me. They were upwind and unaware of me, and I stood watching them for a bit through my binocular from behind the cover of the raisin bush, marveling at their powerful hulks and the sweep of their great horns. I didn't want to disturb their tranquility, so I decided just to skirt past them quietly.

I wasn't taking particular pains to remain hidden from them because they were quite far away and apparently very relaxed, and I didn't think they would really react even if they did spot me—except, perhaps, to move away. I had only gone a few paces, though, when one threw up his head and looked in my direction. The others immediately seemed to take his cue. They all moved to face me in a line, and stood staring, their heads lifted and noses thrust forward in their typical belligerent manner.

I stopped to watch them. One of the largest bulls shook his mighty head and took a few quick steps forward, then stopped. Another followed, stopping just short of him, and then another. Next the lead bull shook his head again and started walking forward in an intently focused manner. When he sensed the others following him, he broke into a trot. The others took off after him, and all the time they kept purposefully focused on me, eyes wide and alert.

It looked nasty, to put it mildly, but I was still a bit unsure if they were serious or perhaps just inquisitive or playful. Then I thought of the many times bush-dwelling Africans had told me that the one animal they were really scared of in the bush was the buffalo. It would charge you for no reason, and once it did it would focus on killing you. They were now about fifty paces away and the thud of their heavy hoofs had an ominous rumble, thundering like a passing train. I knew it was too late to turn and run—actually, not even a top sprinter could really run away from any of the dangerous animals in the African bush—so I let loose into the air with the .404. This stopped them, and they turned and trotted away at an angle, but with tails and heads held high in arrogant defiance.

✦✦✦✦✦✦

The individual we were looking for apparently had a particularly malicious attitude, and despite our two guns, encountering him in that kind of terrain could be dangerous work. Our biggest problem, however, would be to find him at all. Our chances looked rather slim. The clouds had spread across the skies, rumbling darkly, and the wind was strengthening. It was unlikely that he would be at his mud wallow at this time and in this weather. He could be some way off, or close-by in the fringe bush, quietly waiting out the storm, and unless we stumbled on him by chance, finding him was unlikely, we knew.

There were lots of tracks around the pool—buffalo, elephant, sable, kudu, zebra, and smaller game, as well as predators, but we didn't see any lion sign, which was significant—he would have been irresistible for a large pride or two or three full-grown males.

187

"John, ask this man if there are any other buffaloes that come here," I asked, staring at the profusion of tracks in a soft spot. It was really not clear that they were made by only one buffalo. Junior shook his head and replied in Sena, gesturing to the northwest.

"*Hmm.* That makes it a bit easier, but it's still going to take a lot of time to make some sense out of all these tracks and find him. I don't think we have much of a chance now. Let's do a three-sixty around the pool and maybe we get lucky," Gerhard suggested.

"Yep, I think we should, but looking at this I actually think our best bet is to come back after the rain. Then we have a good chance of finding one set of his most recent tracks, and if he really is the only buffalo. . . ."

Gerhard grunted his agreement as we set off to comb the area around the water hole and for three hundred paces from it.

We completed our round without finding anything except more tracks, and with too little time left before dark to do much else, Gerhard and I decided to take a bath in the pool, after making sure from Junior that there were no crocodiles in it. Although this pool appeared to be quite remote from any river or even seasonal stream, I have found crocodiles in pools very far from permanent streams, and it wasn't totally impossible that there could be a nasty surprise lurking in this pool!

The water was cool and soft on our skins, and there was something primitively exhilarating about lying back in the half-light and staring up at the angry black skies, slashed by brilliant streaks of lightning, and feeling the faint throb of the thunder and the sting of the first drops against one's face.

Afterward we walked back in silence through the lightning-torn evening, bent against the sting of the rain. By the time we arrived at the dwellings the storm had calmed into low breathing far off to the east and slow-sifting rain that silently wandered deep into the earth under the dripping trees. The only light was from a small fire the women had lit under the cooking structure roof when the worst of the storm had passed. Those of the dwellers that were not inside their dark huts were taking their chances with the leaking roof. They made way for us so we could dry out. John made us some rice with freeze-dried mince and warthog sloshed over it, and it actually tasted quite good. And then we went to bed.

I had devised a way to hang my little Coleman from the roof structure so that I could read, and it was very pleasant lying under the overhang with *War and Peace* with the even hiss of the Coleman and the whisper of the rain in the background.

++++++

The rain stopped around midnight and then it started clearing, and the morning broke clear and vibrant, making even the rain-soaked little village seem cheerful.

"You know what? I think we need to give that buffalo a bit of time to move around and make us some tracks to go by," Gerhard said from his hammock under the overhang of the next hut.

"Sure. Right now he's probably finding a nice sunny spot to get dry and get warm before he even starts thinking about a stroll. He most probably won't go to the wallow or the water till around twelve or so."

"That's exactly what I was thinking," Gerhard replied.

"*Ja*, but you know, I'm not sure how much it rained, but if there are lots of little pans that now have water out there, he might start wandering around because he can drink and wallow in any pool he likes in the veld," I said.

"Sure, but he has no reason to move fast. If we find his tracks we will catch up with him."

We moved to the smoky fire that John had going and gratefully accepted his mugs of coffee. It was pleasant to take a bit of leisure.

When we had each settled ourselves on a log, and Gerhard had his pipe going properly, he said: "Remember that old soothsayer that prayed for us to find an elephant on that expedition up the Save River?"

"Sure. In fact, the message came back that we would be shown two bull elephants that day, and we were," I said.

"Yeah. Anyway, that's the sort of man I think we need for this job," he said with a smile.

◆◆◆◆◆◆

Gerhard was referring to a somewhat unusual experience we had had one morning while on a part-reconnaissance, part-hunting expedition along the Save River in Mozambique. The area had been a well-known and rich safari area during the colonial years, and Robert Ruark is rumored to have written *The Honey Badger* in a hut somewhere there on the riverbank.

We had been working our way westward from the Indian Ocean for about four days. It was hard work, and slow. Although in places we encountered huge white syringa forests with a closed canopy overhead and no brush underneath, most of the way was through dense shrub acacia, which required a lot of chopping and clearing to get the vehicle through.

We had been lucky to find a wily old bush character called Mazenya to act as our guide and tracker. He had come highly recommended by the patrons of a *shebeen*, or drinking hall, several of whom boisterously testified to his impeccable credentials from the smoke-darkened interior of what was once the store room of the small shop next door, but had since been put to less reputable use.

The pragmatic owner hadn't thought it conducive to business to attend to the crumbling structure, which had lost part of one wall, but had instead invested in a counter made of two empty oil drums with some rough planks placed over them, and a few tree stumps to serve as seats for his patrons and the hostesses who kept them company. He had a stock of Mozambican beer (which was actually not bad-tasting at all, considering that one almost invariably had to have it at room temperature or above).

I suspected that the patrons' enthusiasm for Mazenya might have had something to do with his own frequenting of the *shebeen*, but by then we had already lost a day in fruitless inquiries in and around the ragged little village, and we decided we would throw in our lot with the famous man.

Mazenya did, in fact, think of himself as famous. We found him after quite a search where he was poaching in the bush some twelve miles west of the village, and once he had overcome his fears that he might be in some sort of trouble, he loudly informed us with much arm waving that he was the son of a chief, and that he had been widely recognized as the best tracker around "in the time of the Portuguese." He turned out to be quite a remarkable old character. He was very jovial and had a pleasant sense of humor, always ready for a joke or a prank. He certainly knew the area quite well, and although we didn't have much opportunity to test his skills as a tracker, we found no reason to doubt his knowledge and experience of the bush and the animals.

As we moved farther away from the coast with its threadbare remnants of colonial-era development, it became clear that people were only then slowly beginning to move into the area after the displacements that happened during the bush war years. In the sixty or so miles that we had gone upstream along the river, we only encountered two groups. One was a lone seminomadic family that had settled on the banks of the river, and the other was the heir to the chieftainship of a place called Zinave. Mazenya explained to us that Zinave had been a large village on a hill overlooking the river, and an important junction where a lot of roads (bush footpaths) met and where people used to meet and interface.

The new chief, descended from the original Zinave, was a young man of maybe eighteen, but clearly intelligent and of good breeding. His party of about twenty consisted of women, men, and some children, all related to him—the royal family, so to speak. Among them was also a grizzled old man whose long, tousled hair had gone completely white with age. He was small and frail, with a hunched back, and his deeply wrinkled skin was very dark, almost blue-black, which made me think that he might be from Malawi. He was quite an intimidating sight. His wrinkle-obscured eyes and toothless mouth gave him a mummylike appearance, and he never stopped mumbling to himself, shuffling his feet around, and stomping on the ground with his walking stick. He was not related to the royals, but was the official *sangoma*[2] of the young chief.

As he had done with the lone family we had come across a day or so earlier, Mazenya immediately introduced himself with enthusiastic aplomb, informing them that he was the great and well-known Mazenya, the son of a chief that they had so often heard of but had never had the good fortune to meet personally. The chief and his followers seemed a little nonplussed by these assertions, but they had just arrived in the area a few weeks earlier, and were still a bit uncertain of what to expect. They were probably also a bit overcome by Mazenya's means of transport and his party of two armed white men and the two additional men we had taken on as carriers and camp hands on Mazenya's recommendation. So they acquiesced to Mazenya's elevated claim, but I suspect that if the chief had been a little older or more settled in, he might have had some embarrassing questions for our tracker, despite the vehicle and escort of white men. Mazenya, of course, never for a moment appeared to even contemplate the possibility that his credentials might be questioned.

So for the moment we were accorded the status of visiting royalty (which Mazenya seemed to relish much more than we did), and the chief invited us to spend the night in the humble encampment. The camp was situated just below the hill where the original village had been, between three gargantuan baobab trees whose bastion-like trunks formed the corners of a triangle with sides about thirty yards long. The area between the trees had been cleared and swept clean, but the chief had not yet set up formal court. He and his followers simply slept on the ground on grass mats until the royal quarters could be completed up on the hill.

We accepted the invitation but made our camp just outside the triangle, and we spent a very pleasant evening with the royal family, especially after Gerhard was able to shoot an impala for them. Of course, the show

---

[2]Traditional healer, soothsayer, and sage, more or less.

was completely dominated by Mazenya, who spoke loudly and incessantly of his fame.

It was during these ramblings that I learned that Mazenya had sympathized with FRELIMO during the war, and had once been captured and badly tortured by RENAMO, whom he hated passionately. He also told me that, during the war, the area we were in was RENAMO–held, and that they would organize massive meat hunts where a few hundred men would string out in a long line, about fifty yards apart, and would move through the bush abreast, machine-gunning anything that moved, including sometimes their colleagues, I suspected. This explained the very low game population and total absence of any sign of elephants we had found on our expedition.

That evening in our hammocks, Gerhard and I decided that we had seen enough. We would turn back the next day. We would try to find the place Mazenya told us about at Massangena where one could cross the Save, and return along the southern bank through the Zinave National Park just for the sake of variety. We were now convinced there was simply no chance that we would find any large game anywhere in the area.

The next morning, however, held a surprise for us. It was only beginning to gray in the east, and we had just unwound from our hammocks when we were summoned to the chief's morning prayer session. The whole family had gathered around one of the baobabs, which we now noticed had a well-trodden path around it, with some animal parts hung on the trunk here and there. They were kneeling down in a circle around the tree, facing outward.

We dutifully each found ourselves a spot and waited. The old man was clearly in control. He started wailing in a thin voice. This went on for quite some time before we had to get up and shuffle around the tree along the path a few times. Then some more kneeling and bending down, accompanied by more eerie wailing. I have to admit that I found this solemn ceremony around the ancient tree trunk with the old man's reedy, sing-song voice that quivered through the quiet gray of the morning deeply moving. Although I couldn't understand what he was saying, and he probably focused his entreaties and ululations mainly on the people with him, to me it was like a sigh from the soul of Africa.

I felt strangely disturbed and contemplative when it had finally ended—to the point where I did not, as I would normally have, dismiss outright Mazenya's announcement that the old man had graciously asked in his prayers that we find some elephant, and the reply from "Nkhulunkhulu" had been that we should head in "that direction" (he indicated northeast with his arm) and that we would then be shown two bulls by midday.

Gerhard and I looked at each other uncertainly, not sure of how to interpret the situation, and reluctant to deviate from our firm conviction of the previous night. In the end we resolved to follow the old man's suggestion. There was always the possibility that some lost elephant or two might be wandering around to the northeast—in fact, the old man might even have been aware of some—and anyway, on this expedition we had had very little opportunity to walk, so it was not an unattractive option.

We set out about thirty minutes later. To our surprise, both the old man and the chief tagged along. We first wanted to object, but then thought better of it. It didn't really matter. The chances of actually coming across large game were extremely remote, and besides, this was the old man's show, we felt.

There was almost no sign of game as we walked, only the spoor of some impala and other small bucks here and there, and that of the odd jackal. After about an hour we had to slow down. It was increasingly difficult for the old man to keep up. He was barefoot, and although the soles of African bush men become thick and horny from walking without shoes, a large enough thorn will penetrate them. There were also extremely sharp, four-pronged burrs in some places.

It was a pleasant type of bushveld, not very dense, with a lot of acacias, but almost devoid of mammal life. Birds were abundant, though, and we amused ourselves by quizzing each other on their names and sounds, and we asked the old man (through Mazenya) questions about the names and uses of the different plants we came across.

After midday it had become searing hot, and although we had been taking frequent rests for the sake of the old man, the heat was tiring. We must have covered about six or seven miles, but the game situation had not changed; in fact, the farther we went from the river, the drier the veld became, and the fewer signs of game we saw. We had fallen into trudging along rather mechanically, not deeming it worthwhile to be particularly alert, and began to think of turning back.

Suddenly, as we walked into the soothing shade of a patch of white syringa, Mazenya, who was walking in front, stopped dead in his tracks and tilted his head to one side to listen. And then we heard it: The gentle rumbling of an elephant's intestines. It was to our front left, probably about a hundred yards or so away, and as yet invisible to us. The sudden excitement hammered inside our chests as we checked our rifles.

We made a slight detour in our approach to get the light breeze perfectly in our favor, but soon we saw them: two bulls, resting during the midday heat under the cool syringa canopy. One was ancient. The hollows above his eyes were deeply sunken, and his skin was almost completely black and deeply wrinkled, hanging in loose folds from his emaciated body. He was tuskless. The other was a young askari bull, his tusks barely fifty pounds a side, but promising to be a fine specimen. I looked back at the old man to give him thumbs-up of congratulation, but he and the chief were suddenly nowhere to be seen.

We stood looking at the elephants for quite a while as they stood, unaware of us, gently fanning themselves with their great ears. It didn't make any sense to shoot. They weren't trophy material. We were simply marveling at finding them and enjoying watching them.

"Pal, I think we must turn back now because we haven't got water or food to spend the night here, but we should come here tomorrow and spend a day or two in the area to see if there aren't any others around," Gerhard whispered close to my ear.

I nodded absently, searching the trees to our rear for a sign of the old man and the chief, but not seeing any.

We moved away quietly and started back. After about fifteen minutes I said to Gerhard, "Did you notice the old man and the chief are no longer with us?" Gerhard looked over his shoulder in surprise.

"What do you mean, they're 'no longer with us?'" The tone of his voice made me look back in surprise, and there, some twenty yards behind us, were the two of them.

"Never mind. For a moment, I just thought . . ." I said lamely.

We spent the next two days walking back to the area with Mazenya and thoroughly working through it. We didn't find a single elephant track, and neither could we find the spot where we had come across the two bulls. I didn't mention the old man and the chief again. Neither did I comment on Gerhard's outrage at not even finding a single elephant sign ". . . when we saw two just yesterday afternoon!"

++++++

We got going after nine. I love walking through the veld after the rain. The bush looks fresh and buoyant, and one gets a filtered picture of only the most recent wildlife activity—all that happened in the past few hours. The wind had changed and was in our favor as we set out, and we encountered some zebra and baboons, and saw tracks of kudu and small antelopes and bushpigs on the way.

Gerhard dropped to an easy squat beside the pig tracks, and pointing with a slightly bent finger as was his manner, he said pensively: " 'This here is quite a big boar."

Then, looking up at me, he said, "Do you remember that night we came back from the Zambezi Valley and that group ran in front of us and we hit the big boar? It was somewhere south of Bulawayo, I think. That was a big boar too. Remember, his tusk tore a gash of almost four inches in our front tire when we hit him."

"I remember. You were driving. You did damn well to bring us to a standstill without losing it. I still can't believe it didn't destroy the front suspension. Just shows you how hard those vehicles are. I mean, it was like running into a concrete block, at that speed. I remember that the tire was a complete write-off, and all our spares were flat, too, and we had to repair one, there, by the side of the road in the dark. We were quite angry with ourselves about deciding back there in the bush not to repair our flats because we were going to head out and we'd soon be mostly on tar. Little did we know!"

"*Hmm . . .*" Gerhard grunted, looking a bit wistful.

"You know there's a poem by Thomas Hardy called "The Convergence of the Twain" about the *Titanic* hitting the iceberg on that tempestuous night. It could just as well have been written about us hitting the boar and then standing there beside the Land Cruiser in the dark on that lonely roadside." I started reciting the last few lines I could remember:

> *Alien they seemed to be:*
> *No mortal eye could see*
> *The intimate welding of their later history.*
> *Or sign that they were bent*
> *By paths coincident*
> *On being anon twin halves of one August event,*
> *Till the Spinner of the Years*
> *Said "Now!" And each one hears,*
> *And consummation comes, and jars two hemispheres.*

Gerhard had remained squatting, listening with cocked head, and when I stopped he looked up, surprised, and said, "Jeez, where did you learn that?"

"I read it once and it reminded me so much of that night on the road that I read it again, and then it sort of got stuck in my head like sometimes a few lines from a song or a tune. But I'm not so good at reciting it. You should hear John Gielgud do it. *Sir* John Gielgud, I should say."

"I dunno, it sounded damn good to me. And besides, you are here, now, and you and me were there, then, and I've never heard of Sir John, but he was absent both times and somehow I think he's extremely unlikely to ever join us in these kinds of places or situations," Gerhard half-mumbled gruffly.

I kept quiet, thinking about the instinctive wisdom of his logic and about the concept of "the moment" and how to recognize it and live it.

He filled the silence thoughtfully. "You know, I shot one once, on a night hunt, but I have never seen one in daytime. Have you?"

"I suppose very few people have. I did once—well, almost in daylight, but by a complete coincidence."

I wasn't going to continue, but when he remained squatting as if the business wasn't finished I said half-absently, "It was an unlikely place. On the way to Masvingo, there where the road winds between those rocky hills. I had stopped to sleep over. I made camp about a half-mile from the road in the bush.

"Early the next morning before sunrise I was standing on a boulder having my coffee and sort of just enjoying the small hour and not at all expecting to see any living thing except perhaps some cattle or goats, and two of them came trotting round the base of the hill on their way, I guess, to their day lair. As you know that area is quite populated, but my impression is they are tolerant of human habitation. A bit like leopards and jackals.

"You know, my grandfather farmed in the southern foothills of the Soutpansberg. It was an area that had been farmed for many years, and there was almost no game left there. In fact, apart from bushpigs and the odd small antelope like a duiker or a steenbok, you wouldn't find any game before you were a good thirty miles farther north on the other side of the mountain. He used to complain a lot about bushpigs wrecking his maize fields," I continued, following the loose drift of my thoughts.

"He farmed with cattle, but he cultivated some maize on the riverbanks where it was a bit flat. It rains a lot there, and it's quite heavily wooded—mainly acacia, if I recall correctly, so they had lots of places to hide, especially along the river where it was even thicker. They would come in big drives just as the cobs were beginning to form, and sometimes even before, and they were apparently very destructive. They would knock over the plants and chew them up. Of course, in the process, they would knock down a lot of plants they didn't chew up, too."

"My grandfather always used to say that they were very cunning. They came only in the dead of night and not every night, never used the same entry point, and never grazed right on the edge of the field. They were always a bit inside, so it was difficult to know about them unless you spotted their tracks where they entered, or you went inside the field, which is not something normally done once the maize reaches flowering stage. So you could easily end up discovering at harvest time that you had large areas inside where the maize had been flattened."

"Quite an unpleasant surprise if you thought you had a full crop to harvest," Gerhard said reflectively.

"Sure. It got so bad he appointed a sort of a contractor to keep them out of the maize at night. He was recommended by a neighbor. A grizzled old character named Ben who came from Vendaland to the north. He had a battered side-by-side 12-gauge shotgun that was, of course, illegal, and my grandfather said he didn't inquire how it came into his possession.

"He gave him some buckshot, which was graciously accepted, but Ben preferred old bolts he had sawn the heads off of. They had to be roughly the same size as the inside of the shell, I assume, because I'm told he would take out the buckshot and work the sawn-off bolt into the cardboard casing. They had to be supplied by my grandfather as part of the arrangement."

"Can you imagine what those things must have done to the barrels?" Gerhard said, his face twisting in agony.

"Yeah, but somehow I don't think Ben really concerned himself with that. As long as something lethal came out the other end, he would have thought it was a great idea. And of course, if it stopped working and he survived the event, then ways would have to be found, however crude, to make it work again."

Gerhard gave a knowing nod.

"Anyway, Ben would apparently go to the fields around midnight, completely naked except for the shotgun and an ax, and creep through the maize on his hands and knees about twenty yards inside the field until he would hear them feeding. Of course, he made many fruitless circuits on many nights, but every now and again he would get lucky and pinpoint them. Then he would sneak up to them until he was just about among them and simply let loose with the 12-gauge into the darkness where he thought the biggest concentration was.

"My grandfather told me when he saw the state of the shotgun he made him demonstrate that it actually worked before he hired him. It worked, but Ben was apparently so scared of firing the thing that he would turn away his head and close his eyes tightly before pulling the trigger. So he didn't have more than just a general impression of where the shot was going to go.

"I guess most of the time he would hit absolutely nothing. Sometimes he would get lucky and kill one outright, and sometimes he would wound one. He was apparently a good tracker because the next morning he would follow the blood trail of a wounded one and he often got it, or it led him to the lair and he got another. The whole operation, as I remember, was apparently reasonably successful . . . if for nothing more than as a conversation piece!"

Gerhard chuckled and rose from his squat with the deliberate grace of a gymnast. "He was also either very brave or a bit stupid. Those things are damn dangerous. But why did he undress?"

"Not quite sure, but I suppose he was able to move more quietly through the maize without clothes on—or perhaps it was something Freudian."

Another chuckle from Gerhard.

We approached the water hole carefully from the upwind side, working our way to the edge of the marshy area. The water had pushed higher up the rain-washed edges and more swathes of bright silver gleamed among the reeds and elephant grass. At the pool end, the lazy trickle had grown into a rippling gurgle that busily worked its way through the flotsam that had accumulated against the lip of the rock. But it was as deserted and quiet as a restaurant abandoned by its regular patrons.

"Well, we have three choices: We call it a day, or we do another three-sixty, or we split up and each take a quarter and meet here again in an hour.

That should give us about a half-mile around the water hole," I suggested as we moved into a patch of shade, not sure of how good any of the ideas were.

"Well, pal, there is no way we can just go back now. I like the split-up idea because with the three-sixty there is always a chance that he is either inside or outside the circle, so we never cross his tracks," Gerhard grunted as he fiddled in his pipe stem with a piece of grass.

I explained our plan to John, and we split up. Elias, Junior, Gerhard, and I each took a quarter. John went with Elias.

Elias and John were the last to rejoin us under a leafy marula on the downwind side of the water hole about an hour and a half later. None of us had found the buffalo's tracks, but John and Elias came with the news that they had found the tracks of two large male lions just before they turned back, which had to be a bit more than half a mile from the water hole. They had followed them for a bit, which was why they took longer to get back.

It was almost midday, and out of the shade the sun stung with that fierce intensity it always has after a rainstorm. We decided to have some tea and take stock of our situation.

"OK, so we haven't found any sign. There's really one more thing to do, and that's go and sit at the water hole to see if he comes," Gerhard said with some finality.

"Yep, but I don't have much hope. The thing is, there are lots of shallow pools around now. They will probably dry out within a day or two, but for now he has lots of choices of where to drink and wallow. On the other hand it doesn't make much sense to do another three-sixty, or another fan search. And we are here now. We might as well sit for a while."

"OK. Let's have some tea and a rusk first, and then we go and check again. One can never be sure. As we know, old *dagga* boys like this are creatures of habit," Gerhard said, but we were both doubtful of our chances.

As we sat back with John's tea, I said, "Those lion tracks they saw. You know, they could have been made by two males patrolling the edge of their territory, or it could have been young nomads looking for a pride to take over, or just roaming around in no-man's land where they can hunt without being harassed by a local pride. From what they told us, this sounds most likely."

"*Ja*, could be. If they start hunting in this area and they find the old man, the chances are very good that they will take him—that is, if they are both grown."

"*Hmm*. John, those lion tracks you found, ask Elias if they were *madoda*[3] or *bafana*[4]."

"*Ah*, Elias says they are *madoda*," John said.

"OK, well, that means if they stay around, the chances are very good they will get him. They may have him already." Gerhard voiced both our thoughts with a hint of grimness.

"*Ja*. But you know, even if we find his tracks, getting him in this kind of bush might not turn out to be all that easy," I mused. "I remember once hunting buffalo in the *miombo* forest east of the Gorongoza. The bush there was of course quite different from here, but about as dense, maybe a bit denser. There were open, grassy spaces, a bit like on that plateau where I shot my elephant. The buffalo would come out at night to graze there, and during the day, especially when it was hot, they would go into the deep forest to drink and rest."

"*Hmm*. Interesting how animals have different habits in different places and how they adapt to their situation," Gerhard said between slurps of tea.

"Exactly. Now I don't know if they had taken on this behavior because they were being hunted, but I doubt it. The area was very remote. I mean, I had left the Land Cruiser about three days back when it simply became too difficult and slow to break through the bush with it.

"Anyway, I didn't have the greatest tracker. A youngish guy. Tall. Jacqui was his name. We could quite easily pick up the fresh tracks of the previous night in the open grassland, but it took Jacqui quite a bit of figuring out where they entered the forest again because they would wander around a lot along the edges and around the grassland while feeding. If I had had someone like Elias it would for sure have been a lot quicker.

---

[3] A grown man.
[4] A young man.

"Anyway, we tried for several days, but we simply couldn't get close enough to them in the thickets. It was quite frustrating. One had to crawl on all fours for most of the way. It was, fortunately, a soft type of bush. Not many thorns, but you could not see for more than about five yards."

"Sounds quite hairy. Had you wounded one in there, it would be real nasty," Gerhard remarked.

"*Ja*, very. And I was alone too. No backup gun. You should have been there. Anyway, it was damn tiring to crawl along like that. They were extremely alert. There was almost no wind in the thickets, but despite our best efforts they always seemed to smell us before we could see them. Once or twice we got to about ten or twelve yards from the closest ones. We could hear them but not see them, but then they would find us out and break, and all we would get was some deep tracks in the soft ground and a whiff of dust. This bush is as dense in places."

I stopped, because that was the point I was trying to make: That we could still have a difficult or impossible task, even if we were able to pick up his tracks.

Gerhard said, looking at me sideways, "So, did you get one?"

"Well, yes and no. One day—it was around eleven o'clock—we found a place where they had watered and wallowed. They hadn't been gone for more than half an hour. The mud that had dropped off their hides was still wet. And we could directly see where they went into the forest. I knew this was as good as it was going to get.

"The fact that they were so close gave us extra motivation, and we crawled in after them, sometimes even on our bellies. It was slow work. After about an hour we were very close. They were resting and we could hear them grunting and fiddling. I never prayed so hard for a good wind. We crawled forward so carefully that I became exhausted from the concentration—you know, sort of numbed.

Eventually we could start making them out, but just vaguely. Most of them were lying down, chewing their cud, so we could only see the bottom of their bodies. No horns, no heads. We moved around a bit to get a better position, but it didn't help much, and it took a long time to move just ten paces. We were very close; I guess not more than about eight or ten paces from the closest ones. I knew they were going to smell us very shortly. I was getting a bit desperate after so many tries.

"Then Jacqui pointed out one that was standing a bit away from the others to the side. It was very close, maybe only ten yards away, standing facing us, and I could see only its front legs up to the points of its shoulders. It looked huge. I couldn't see its head, but I thought it had to be a very substantial bull. I put my shot just next to where the throat joined the body, and the bush exploded. One second there was one hell of a commotion, and the next it went dead quiet.

"Jacqui and I went forward to check. There was so much blood there, it seemed as if someone had dumped it from buckets."

"*Hmm.* Hit in the engine room," Gerhard grunted.

"Yep, in the engine room. We found the bull about a hundred yards farther. Incredible, hey, that it could still go that far. It was dead, but it was a cow."

"What, no! Are you serious!?" Gerhard said, looking shocked and sorry at the same time.

"Yep, I'm afraid so. A bloody cow, after all that effort. The biggest damn buffalo cow I had ever seen. Something of a freak, I think. She was bigger than a bull in body. And fat. Very fat. She was probably infertile because she had almost no udder and very small teats. She had a good head too, for a cow, but she was still a cow.

"I was disgusted at my luck, but the locals were delighted with all the meat. They came from far and wide to carry it off after Jacqui sent out the word with one of the bearers. That was the end of the buffalo hunt. The next day I had a light bout of malaria or something, and I just lay under a bush for three days, and besides, the place was then crawling with people. I think those buffaloes must have permanently relocated to at least the north of Tanzania."

"*Ja*, that was real rotten luck," Gerhard chuckled. Then, becoming more businesslike, he said, "Shall we go and check again?"

We dutifully, but halfheartedly, trudged back to the water hole. Gerhard climbed into a large leadwood with his binocular, and I took a siesta, stretched out in its shade, having informed John that his life was in danger if he allowed as much as a single tsetse to sit on me. I had just drifted deliciously into non-awareness when Gerhard gave his low whistle and beckoned me up the tree.

"Look at that."

An elephant bull had emerged from the trees and was slowly ambling up to the water. He was huge and old, and his tusks must have been eighty pounds a side. We stared in absolute astonishment. He was one of those very rare prime trophies. Gerhard slowly breathed a string of low swear words. "What do we do now?"

"I dunno. We have already broken so many rules. I'm not even sure the outfitters have another elephant on their license," I whispered. "We took three, and probably the American partner guy took one. I can't think that they could have had more than four on their license."

"No. Very unlikely."

We watched as the bull took a leisurely drink and cooled himself with a shower, then wandered over to the mud wallows and proceeded to have a luxurious mud bath. He languished in the shade by the edge of the marshy area for quite a while before ambling off into the bush with the cooling of the afternoon.

No game came after that, and we knew that the buffalo wasn't going to come either, but it was enough for us to sit quietly in the tree through the limp hours of the afternoon, watching the sun die in crimson splendor above the purple of the tree line on the other side of the marshy area.

It felt like the end of a chapter. We had put a serious effort into ridding the little village of their buffalo, and we knew that tomorrow we would walk away from it to new adventures. It really would be the end of the elephant hunt, with Lost Soul and a helper heading for the camp with the tusks.

I felt a little uneasy about abandoning the village folk to the buffalo like that. To them, and especially to Junior, we must have seemed like a heaven-sent intervention, suddenly emerging into their isolated little world, powerful, unreachable, incomprehensible, sent to remove this menace that was really only affecting a part of their little world, but to them had acquired a much larger and darker significance.

But then again, the rainy season is about to start, and they won't really need to go to the water hole again until late in winter, and by then the buffalo could well be dead. I tried to swat away the guilt, but it still didn't feel much better. I could only imagine how disappointed, even disillusioned, they would be when we told them.

We were just about to get down from the tree when a movement on the other side of the clearing caught our eyes. It was a male leopard, probably the largest one I had ever seen. We watched him through our binoculars as he stood at the edge of the tree line for a few moments, regally looking over the clearing, then spontaneously lying down and rolling playfully in the loose sand. He slipped to his feet in a single movement of liquid feline grace and glided over to the water's edge, where he drank delicately and was gone— silent as the shadows on the ground.

If there is any animal in this bush one could feel superstitious about, it's a leopard, I thought as we clambered down, followed by showers of loose bark.

After taking another bath in the pool, we walked back in silence through the coolness of the early evening. We had told our three companions that we thought it was not really worth spending more time on trying to find the buffalo. They had not commented. They seemed to accept our decision with a sort of stolid resignation of something they had no power over, but I could sense the deep disappointment they felt, and the atmosphere had suddenly turned gloomy.

At the village the men (and Gerhard and me) gathered separate from the women and children. The flames flickered feebly on the somber faces gathered around the small fire,[5] their eyes pinched against the burn of the smoke. In the background the women hovered anxiously. They had heard

---

[5]Africans living in little villages like these usually make modest fires (just sufficient to serve the purpose of cooking or heating) because the wood has to be carried over a long distance, usually by the women.

that we had been unsuccessful in our search for the buffalo, and now Junior proceeded to tell them of our experiences.

When he had finished there was silence, until I asked gently, "John, what do they think we must do now? We have gone to the place of the buffalo twice, and we have not found him. Not even his tracks this morning after the rain. Maybe those lions got him?" I tried to sound optimistic.

John didn't look at me with the happy *aha* look I was somehow hoping for. "*Patrau*, the people, they are saying the buffalo is very strong. He has hidden his tracks from you. He will come out again when we leave."

I felt a deep compassion for those people, so caught up in the situation, partly real, partly imagined, apparently simple from one perspective, but actually immensely complex from another.

"OK, but what do they think we must do now?"

John's face was expressionless and he looked away when he answered, "*Ah*, I don't know," which really meant, *How can you ask me? You are the one who should know.*

We were interrupted by one of the women placing two bowls before us, one containing cooked chicken in gravy, and the other rice, and a calabash of water. Each of us rinsed our hands in a bit of water from the calabash, and then we proceeded to eat, taking turns to form a little ball of rice from one bowl, and then using it to scoop some chicken and gravy from the other. It was quite delicious, but there wasn't a lot, so Gerhard and I held back a bit. They didn't have much to offer, but they generously presented us with the best they had.

In the course of the meal I said to Gerhard, "Pal, this now seems to be a much bigger issue than we thought. These people are scared, and now that we are leaving without killing the buff, they are paranoid, it seems to me."

Gerhard swallowed his mouthful and said pragmatically, "Look, why don't we leave tomorrow, but we go via the water hole. And if necessary, we sleep there. It's a bit of a detour to the west, but at least we will have given it another bash. If we still don't find any sign of him, he's probably left the place."

"You know, I can't tell you how relieved I am that you also feel this way. I was even thinking that I'd stay behind if you wanted to carry on.

I was thinking, back there when we told them and they were looking so disappointed: *Where are we rushing to, anyway?* This is one of those moments in life that we so often pass by without noticing, but if you allow yourself to live it, it turns out to actually last as long as the rest of your life."

The expression on Gerhard's face as he nodded agreement was more eloquent than words.

I told John and he translated, and save for a few low *"ehhh"s* there was silence around the fire, but the moment was pregnant with feeling, and it was really special, simply being there in that remote part of the African bush, gathered closely around the little fire with those people, having chicken and rice with them, and thinking about walking back to the water hole in the morning to see if we could find the buffalo.

Later, out of the comfortable silence, Lead Man's voice rose deep and soft, then stronger in a sonorous song, and the others joined him with beautifully harmonized intonations as only African men can do. It was a spontaneous song about hunters who had come to kill an evil buffalo. It was followed by other songs that drifted away into the African night with the glow of the fire and the smell of wood smoke until the Southern Cross hung low in the south. When the singing died down and we pushed the kettle onto the coals for a last cup of tea, I told Gerhard a story that I had been reminded of by the situation.

++++++

"I must tell you of a situation I was in that was very similar to this one. It was the time I wandered into the area to the south of the Zambezi Delta on my own. I passed the Gorongoza along the way, and I spent one night and a day wandering around its fringes, but it was in a sorry state with probably only a few terrified animals doing their best to avoid being killed off for meat. Remember I told you I had heard from a bush pilot who had flown over the area to the northeast in the direction of the Zambezi mouth and the Indian Ocean, and he said that it seemed to be totally untouched—most probably because it was so damn remote, with almost no roads into it.

"It was remote. To the west and south RENAMO and FRELIMO were still snapping at each other, even though a peace deal of sorts had been agreed on, but out there it was so distant with so few people that it wasn't really territory that anybody thought worth dominating. So there was still quite a bit of game left—eland, zebra, sable, elephant, though not many, but lion, buffalo, even blue wildebeest . . . and very few people. I could walk for five days on end without any sign of humans."

"Damn, I knew I should have gone with you. Can't think now why I didn't," Gerhard lamented.

"Can't remember, either. I know I did tell you."

"*Ja*, sure. Damn shame I didn't go," Gerhard said as he knocked out his pipe and proceeded to clean it meticulously with a grass stalk he had plucked from the roof thatch.

"*Ja*. Anyway, one afternoon I was walking along an old elephant path with my little group when we met up with some Africans. They turned out to be two junior headmen from the area and their followers, heading for the local chief's house to discuss some issues with him. Having met up with them, old Kalemba felt that we should join them and introduce ourselves to the chief, whom he knew, because we were wandering around in his territory and it was good manners. It was also important for the *chefe* who was with us to meet him.

"But now I need to first tell you what happened on my way into the area. I traveled up that road heading north from Dondo, which took me more than five hours to do sixty miles. I passed through one of those little villages with a few broken-down ex-Portuguese buildings around an open space and mud huts and little shops right up to the road edge—you know, it was almost like a crowd constantly edging forward closer to a popular attraction. A youngster came running up trying to sell me some maize buns, fresh from the open fire. I stopped and sent him to fetch me more because they're wonderful to chew on, and I was quite hungry. It also breaks the monotony a bit. Of course, a crowd gathered because a vehicle passing through and stopping with a white man in it was apparently a bit of an event.

"While I was waiting for the buns I noticed an important-looking guy standing toward the back of the crowd. He looked like an official because he was wearing a white shirt—well, more or less—with insignia on, and a wide-brimmed hat. When he saw me looking at him, he came up and introduced himself. I was hoping he could speak a bit of English because I needed information about the area and a guide and bearers. It turned out his English was little better than my Portuguese, which is nonexistent.

It also turned out he was the local *chefe do posto* and that the little village was no less than his regional headquarters! He had real, well, I guess actually just about absolute authority there, and when he realized we had a language problem, he sent for someone. This was probably the single biggest stroke of good luck I had had for the whole trip because emerging from one of the mud huts was Kalemba. He looked like a scarecrow set up for an April Fools' joke—all tattered and almost weathered away, and clearly well-oiled by the predecessors of the half-empty bottle of Manica beer in his hand."

A chuckle from Gerhard.

"But I wish you could have seen how he pulled himself together when he got a whiff of what was going on! He snapped up straight as a ramrod and said, '*Gut aftanun, Senōr!*'

"He had been summoned because he laid claim in the village to being able to speak English, but that little sentence was about the sum total of the Queen's language he had mastered. Of course, no one in the village was able to dispute his claimed fluency! Anyway, we ended up speaking Fanagalo, which he had learned on his wanderings in South Africa, mostly working in the mines, I guess."

There was more chuckling through a blue cloud of pipe smoke. "*Ja*," Gerhard agreed. "What would we have done without the South African mines?"

"Well, they have been a great help to us on many occasions. Anyway, with Kalemba's help we were able to communicate reasonably well but, of course, very slowly. First I had to explain where I was going and what I was going to do there, which was quite difficult to explain because all I wanted to do was wander around in the bush south of the Zambezi between the Gorongoza and the sea. This was an area of almost 14,000 square miles, so how do you explain a white man—*with a serviceable vehicle!*—wanting to do something as completely absurd as that?"

A knowing smile from Gerhard.

"However, after a painfully slow explanation I managed to get to the bottom line: I needed a guide and two or three bearers. When Kalemba heard this he really turned on the charm. He insisted he had hunted in the area with the Portuguese and he knew it well; moreover, he proclaimed himself to be the best tracker in Mozambique. I was in a difficult position. On the face of it Kalemba didn't seem anywhere near capable of what I needed, but I could hardly back out of the situation."

Gerhard grunted.

"It helped when the *chefe* confirmed at least the Portuguese hunting part, and that he was a 'good hunter.' *He is probably the main poacher in town with whom the chefe shared the spoils of the bush on the quiet,* is what I thought."

"*Hmm*, very likely," Gerhard said.

"Anyway, I took him on, and he actually turned out to be as tough as rawhide and quite good in the bush. I also hired three bearers whom Kalemba and the *chefe* recommended and who were quickly summoned with a lot of shouting and arm-waving and frantic running around 'because the *patrau* is going far and he is in a hurry.' Of course all of this suited me perfectly, and you know how lucky it actually was. I mean, all from the same village, in one stroke. So no more endless inquiries and searching around. It saved a lot of time.

"There's always a twist, however, isn't there? While my new recruits went off to collect their *simpahla*,[6] the *chefe* confided in me in a badly broken up explanation that he had never been out of the village because he didn't have a vehicle, and he didn't think he could travel his domain alone by bicycle or

---

[6] Zulu word for personal belongings, tools, and equipment.

on foot, and could he come with me so that he could at least see what the area looked like?"

"What!? Are you joking? What did you say?" Gerhard exploded in disbelief.

"Well, what *could* I say? I knew this was dead wrong. I also knew that he didn't actually understand that I was not going for an afternoon drive in my Land Cruiser—we were actually going to cover most of the ground on foot. No doubt he thought it would simply be great arriving at all the remote little villages in grand style, all doffed out in his cleanest dirty uniform, and driven by a white man in a Land Cruiser!"

I cringed in disgust thinking back on the situation, and Gerhard's pained expression was one of no less than absolute revulsion.

"But it really seemed even less possible to get out of this than it had been with Kalemba's generous offer to join me. It was probably the single biggest stroke of bad luck I had had for the whole trip. He turned out to be a real pain in the arse. He was unfit, scared all the time, talked too much, turned official every now and then, expected to be served by the rest of the party, and he nagged us constantly to use the vehicle to drive. Heaven knows how we would have done this because there were no roads at all. It took us more than half a day to break eighteen miles into the bush eastward from the Dondo track, where I left the vehicle."

Gerhard snorted indignantly. "Serves you right. I would have told him straight to bugger off, lazy bastard!"

"*Ja*, maybe, but believe me, it was a difficult situation, and I ended up with the chap in my party. Anyway, back to the encounter on the bush path, we now set off with the two headmen for the chief's home—took us a day and a half, about. Of course, when the newcomers saw that my guys had fresh meat, they wanted some too, so I had to do some more hunting for the pot, which took a bit of time. I had to repeat that when we got closer to the chief's village because the assembled council of headmen and *chefe* under the secretaryship of Kalemba felt that we could not, with an armed white man in the party, arrive without an offering of meat. Of course they were right there—good manners, you know."

"Of course. So you had your gun with you. How did you get it in?"

"Oh, remember that guy—Pedro, I think it was—in Maputo that got us the rifle permits the time we went to reconnoitre the area north of the Save? He organized it for me. Not sure how. Cost me a few dollars."

"OK, clever. *Ja*, that was also a great trip, hey?"

"Yes. Great trip."

"Anyway, keep going with the story," Gerhard urged as the moon's thin sliver cleared the roofs of the huts. It was quiet in the little village—just the flutter and hiss of the flames and our low voices.

"OK," I continued. "Well, the chief lived in a small village—about six to ten families, I guess. His house was a little to the side. Not mud, but poles planted close to each other, with narrow gaps between them, and with two stories, and a pole fence around it. It was interesting and would be cool, I think, in that climate. Of course, when we got close to the house we had to stop for the *chefe* to put on his official shirt with the insignia. He was to be there *ex officio*."

Gerhard gave a gleeful "you poor sod, I could have told you so" chuckle, which I ignored.

"The chief's adjutant came to greet us at the gate and inquire about our business. The old fellow saw us immediately. He was a fine old gentleman; friendly, mild-mannered, courteous. A real aristocrat. Wish I could have taken him along rather than the damn *chefe* we had in tow. I bet he had a few nice stories to tell. Anyway, the adjutant had us sit in a circle with the chief, the two headmen, the adjutant, the *chefe*, and me. The others sat around the edge, with Kalemba behind me for translation."

"The chief patiently listened to each one's story, asking a question now and then. At one point his wife came up. She did not prostrate herself like the women usually did. She simply came and stood behind him with her hand on his shoulder. He put his hand on hers and explained each of our stories to her. She listened graciously, smiling at each, then she went off (to organize food for us, I later realized, and I was then very grateful that I had shot a warthog for them)."

213

"The food was pot-fried chicken in gravy with a bowl of rice like we had tonight, and we ate the same way, taking turns to roll a ball of rice and dip it into the chicken pot—delicious, but not a lot to go round. When we had finished eating, the chief called Kalemba aside and had quite a long conversation with him. We sat awkwardly in our little circle, not able to converse, like people waiting in a doctor's waiting room, but with none of those tattered magazines to flip through. With the chief gone, it suddenly didn't seem to make sense sitting there in the circle.

"When they rejoined us, Kalemba spoke to me in Fanagalo. Apparently the one headman was from the area to the northeast 'where there are many rivers and the sea,' and he quickly added, 'and many *njamazane.*' [7] (I think he threw in the last bit just because he thought I might not want to go there otherwise.) The people there were mainly fishermen living off catches they made in the 'many rivers,' he explained to me. It sounded like it could be the Zambezi Delta, or close to it.

"Anyway, a lone bull hippo living in one of the rivers had become rogue and was attacking their canoes when they passed. He had already overturned several, causing a total loss of the catch and scaring the fishermen, and a few days ago he had actually bitten into a canoe and badly damaged it, nearly killing one of the occupants. It was then that the people sent their headman to come to put the case to the chief for help."

"*But what on earth was the old man supposed to do?* I wondered. Unless he could find some ex-soldier-turned-poacher with an illegal AK-47 to kill it, probably at a considerable fee, he was as powerless to deal effectively with the situation as were his subjects. For traditional fishermen to go after a rogue hippo in dense marshland was of course, well, hard to imagine. So now, with me suddenly turning up as if sent from heaven, the chief wanted to know if I would kill the hippo for them. Now I'm sure you must see that I really couldn't say no, and besides, I was planning to go in that direction anyway."

"Of course, of course," Gerhard replied, nodding solemnly.

---

[7]Wild animals.

"Well, that's what I thought, too, and I told Kalemba so, and he told the chief. This is the part you're going to love: The *chefe*, who had been more or less left out of all of these discussions, now realized that something was going on, and he asked Kalemba what it was all about. Even before Kalemba had quite finished explaining, he donned his most official pose and announced that the hippo could not be shot without permission from Maputo!"

At this point we both exploded in convulsive laughter, Gerhard almost falling off his log, and me, gasping between bouts of laughter, feeding his mirth with images of the situation.

"Now, can you imagine the looks on the faces of those people? It went dead quiet around the circle, but one of those silences that screamed at you. I mean, think of it. They knew only vaguely where Maputo was, let alone imagine that someone there might have anything to say about what they thought was best here, about eight days' walk from the nearest little track and then at least three more days driving over those terrible roads. To them, 'Maputo' might just as well have been on the moon, and as far as they were concerned, the *chefe*, the official ostensibly in charge of them, was about as relevant as Goethe!

"Their reaction was a mixture of utter amazement, exasperation, and indignation all rolled into one. I think the poor *chefe* might actually have been in serious physical danger. Then the chief said in a very quiet voice, almost a whisper, but it was like a clap of thunder: 'Will the hippo ask for permission from Maputo before he kills one of my people?'

"If possible, at that point, it went even quieter—even the children and the chickens were silent. Everybody, including the chickens, stared at the poor *chefe*. He went all gray and unofficial and tried to fabricate an explanation, to which the chief listened with pointed politeness. It was all absolutely delicious."

When we had overcome our amusement, I continued.

"But the thing is, I was in a difficult position. I had a humiliated *chefe* on my hands who took himself quite seriously. If I shot the hippo, he could make all sorts of trouble for me when we got back. Getting charged by a hippo or any other animal was one thing, but a gun-toting militia with an ego-stressed small town official behind them was another matter. I thought I'd better apply a bit of 'if you can't beat them, join them' technique.

"So I told Kalemba to tell him that he simply had to go there to make a report to Maputo about the situation, and this, I think, pleased him immensely because he was suddenly very important again. While he was loudly explaining to all around why he absolutely had to go to 'investigate' the situation without delay, I whispered to Kalemba to tell the chief on the side that we would go there and I would shoot the hippo for him if I possibly could without falling foul of our dear *chefe*."

"*Ja*, what a mess," Gerhard said, thoughtfully scratching his tilted head, as he often did when contemplative.

I added a snort of disgust. "Anyway, we set out the next morning with the headman and his following, due northeast. The old lady came up and handed me a bag of wild rice to take along—it was delicious. We walked hard for two days, but it was wonderful because it was beautiful country. It's *miombo* forest in that area. The soil is sandy, and the bush is softer and a lot taller because of the rain. The *miombo* is beautiful. Some trees, like the *msasa*, are as thick as the Land Cruiser and two, three, four stories high, almost like tropical forest in some places. The farther east we went, the more it opened up into flat grassland with beautiful forest islands in it. There was elephant and buffalo and zebra and waterbuck and blue wildebeest. Oh yes, and sable, really good sable.

"But what made the situation even nicer is that we lost the *chefe* along the way. We had been walking fast, and after about a day he got very tired. Then we met a little group of people on one of those footpaths who were living in a little bush settlement (like this one) fairly close-by, and I got Kalemba and the headman to suggest to him that he go with them and rest up in their village. The poor chap didn't have much of a choice. He was footsore and chafed raw between his legs, and I think it was clear to him that we weren't going to wait for him if he fell behind, no matter which flippin' shirt he put on."

Gerhard chortled maliciously.

"I positioned us as his special emissaries who would report back on the situation, and this made him feel really important."

"What a pain in the arse!" Gerhard snorted. "You should have shot him in the foot earlier and saved yourself all the trouble."

I chuckled. "Of course, I'm sure that's what you would have done, except you wouldn't have wasted a bullet—you would have used a big rock!"

"Not a chance. If I had been there, he wouldn't have been on the trip!" Gerhard exclaimed.

"Anyway, we got to the area during the morning of the third day. Beautiful country. Flat grassland all the way to the horizon. It had become gradually more open as we went east, until there were almost no trees, just the open grassland, cropped short by the grazers—buffalo and eland and waterbuck and zebra, mainly, and some blue wildebeest and the odd elephant. The hippo were also doing a lot of grass-cropping, of course. The headman (they said his name was Vasco) took us to a little village with just a few huts made of plaited palm leaves on the bank of a small river. That's where we spent the night.

"That afternoon we went to the area where the hippo had last been seen. The river was about twenty paces wide at the point where the villagers always left their dugout canoes, but the whole area was really marshland with bigger open stretches of water, connected by streams and canals, some wider, some narrow. There were no trees, but the banks were thick with reeds as tall as a house. You couldn't see more than two or three paces into it.

"We went out into the stream with one of the canoes—Kalemba, Vasco, and I. Vasco poled us along with a long thin bamboo, moving up and down the canoe as if he was on a shopping stroll. The stream—actually more like a canal—had tall reeds on either side that almost touched at the top in places and were as dense as a haystack. It was like walking along a deep ravine with water below and the reed walls and a strip of blue sky above. I could see lots of hippo tunnels along the banks, and you could peer down them as far as the next bend, but that was it. A hippo could get within three or four yards of you without you having a clue it was there!"

217

"Sounds real nasty," Gerhard said.

"It was. You know those dugouts. They are wonders of crude craftsmanship, but they are usually not quite straight and often very uneven and unstable. Actually they had two types there. The usual dugout type we know, and a few of another type, made out of bark only."

"Yeah? I haven't seen any like that," Gerhard replied.

"*Ja*. I saw that type there for the first time, and again some years later on the Lugenda River near the Tanzania border. I have never seen anyone making this type of canoe, but I have come across trees from which bark had been taken. The people making the canoe would strip the bark off a thick tree that had a long enough and straight enough trunk. They would take if off by splitting it along a single straight line from top to bottom and, of course, around the trunk at the top and the bottom. Then they would somehow peel it off, probably using a machete. Must be a tedious task.

"Anyway, then, I think while it's still wet, they would put it over some sort of a mold, I would guess probably fashioned from a tree trunk. They would cut two narrow triangles out at each end, and they would first fold in the two side pieces and then the center one so that the ends of the canoe are closed, lifted, and a bit pointed. They use wooden pegs to keep it all together, and I think they fill up the gaps with an animal-fat concoction.

"As I said, I've never seen them making one, but I guess they would tie it down tightly on the mold with grass ropes till the bark had dried out and was fixed in position. The ones I have seen were typically a bit more uneven than the dugout ones, but, of course, they are a lot lighter. I imagine that is probably why some of the guys there used that technique because the nearest large-enough trees were far off, and they would have to carry the finished product a long way. Naturally the bark ones are not nearly as sturdy as the solid wood ones, but they are hell of a lot lighter and not at all flimsy."

"*Hmm*, interesting," Gerhard said, and then he added thoughtfully, "Actually, thinking of it, one could make quite a neat canoe like that if you went to some trouble."

"Sure, you could. Of course, the trees do the same kind of dying irrespective of which type of canoe they are asked to produce. The tragedy is, it always has to be a very large, very old, and probably a very beautiful tree," I said.

"Anyway, whatever the kind of canoe involved, I realized I would be in the same kind of serious trouble if the hippo charged us in the water. I'd have very little chance of killing him from such a platform before he got to us. I certainly couldn't stand up and swing around—Vasco, of course, walked up and down the damn thing as if he was on a wide concrete slab cast on compacted earth."

From the look of incredulity, almost pity, on Gerhard's face, I could see that he couldn't believe that I didn't feel as comfortable in an unstable canoe as in an easy chair watching TV. He'd been a champion gymnast, canoeist, and navy diver, which made it difficult for him to imagine the situation of mere mortals like me.

"OK, OK, I know you don't appreciate my situation, but on the day we have to run away I won't appreciate yours," I said.

"Anyway," I continued, "I thought if the brute charged us, especially from the right (because I shoot from my right shoulder), it would all be over before I even got a front bead on him. Maybe I'd be able to stick the barrel in his mouth from the hip and get off a token shot, but at that point it would probably be rather irrelevant. Since we were already on the water, I thought we might as well see through the day.

"We cruised up and down, trying to entice him to charge us from wherever he was, and I can tell you, I was more than just nervous all the time. We did come across a herd of hippos, which Vasco discreetly skirted, but there was not a sign of the rogue.

"In the course of the day I decided that it was stupid to create a situation that was almost certain to end in disaster. By then I was a lot wiser than the time we set off into Botswana in your little Land Rover and almost got eaten by those lions because we were so damn brave we couldn't see how damn stupid we were."

Gerhard chuckled knowingly.

"So that afternoon when we got back, I had them lash two canoes of the dugout type together—they used plaited grass ropes—with a crude platform made of driftwood between them. I could then position myself on the platform. It was a bit difficult to maneuver in the water, so Vasco had to get an assistant pole man. That made four of us on the contraption—Kalemba, Vasco, the assistant, and I—but it was nice and stable and it worked well. At least I was more confident that I would be able to deal with the hippo.

"We cruised around in our man-of-war for two days each morning and each afternoon, and in between I watched them fish with their nets and hand lines. It was all very interesting, and I ate a lot of fish and rice. Of course, I had to kill some meat for them, so I shot a zebra. Fortunately there were enough fish to eat, so I didn't have to have any of the damn zebra. Anyway, I was treated like a king. It was a bit embarrassing. Although it was quite tense when we were out hunting the bull, it was also very boring. I told Kalemba we would try for one more day, but then we had to leave. I was running out of time."

"*Hmm,* tricky situation. One can't really set a bait or something," Gerhard reflected.

"Exactly. It was a question of waiting for him to make a move, and it was highly frustrating. Late in the afternoon of the second day when we were already back in the village and preparing for the journey back the next day, two scared men came running in to tell us that the hippo had suddenly appeared and attacked their canoe as they were returning to the mooring. The hippo had overturned the canoe and tried to bite it, but fortunately no one was hurt. We immediately rushed to the area and started cruising around.

"The overturned canoe and the rowing pole and some dead fish were still drifting around, but there was no sign of the beast. It was eerie. It was dead quiet, with the soft splashing of the poles in the water the only noise. The surface was as smooth as a mirror, and black. It was already getting a bit dark and I was uncomfortable that I wouldn't be able to shoot accurately. I can tell you it wasn't very soothing for the nerves. After a few passes of some hundred yards up and down the canal, I was beginning to think that it was going to be more of the same. I said to Kalemba we would do one more run and then call it a day."

"Then, just as we got to a place where the canal became a bit wider, probably about seventy yards or so, a hippo broke the surface close to the shore and about fifty yards from us. The villagers immediately screamed that it was him!

"It looked like a big bull to me, but he almost immediately went under again. The two locals were half hysterical and I must admit I was not feeling particularly comfortable, either. If it was the rogue and he charged, it was going to be one of those moments of truth. I was on my knees facing in his direction and waiting . . . but then nothing."

"*Ja-nee*, you were in for it!

What gun did you have?" Gerhard asked, appearing unusually spellbound.

"I had my .404, and I had a 400-grain soft up the spout."

"*Hmm*. Good," he said gruffly.

"Sure, the gun could do the job; it was just the question of whether I could get off a good shot before he hit us. Anyway, for a few seconds there was no sign of him. Then I noticed the water sort of bulging up in a smooth wave about twenty yards away. It was him, the bastard, coming at us below the surface!

"I still couldn't see him, only the moving wave. Now try to imagine this: The light is failing, you know the damn thing is coming for you and bloody fast, but you can't see it, or at least, you got nothing to shoot at!"

"That's hairy. What did your companions do?" Gerhard asked, fumbling for his pipe without taking his eyes off me.

"Well, the two locals simply abandoned ship, without even asking for permission! Kalemba, well, he was sitting in the canoe to my left and a little in front, and I shouted at him to lie down in case he got in the field of fire. I realized he wasn't in the mood for a conversation of any sort, for he had his eyes tightly closed and was muttering to himself and gripping the sides of the canoe so hard that not even a ton of dynamite would have gotten him out. I think he couldn't swim and that was the only thing he could think of doing at the moment.

"Now look, let me admit that I seriously considered taking my chances in the water, too, but I thought it had to be about nine feet deep there, and I knew that I'd lose my gun, so I stayed. Anyway, as you know, in such situations I become a bit fatalistic."

"I know," Gerhard said with a grin that was more like a grimace.

"*Ja*, so there wasn't a lot of time to think and plan. It was more like you get overtaken by the sequence. I remember thinking that he'd probably break the surface at some point, and that it would hopefully be far enough away so that I could get off a shot. The wave was coming on fast, and I knew it was going to be a very short chance, and the *only* chance!

"Then he literally exploded out of the water about ten yards away! I still couldn't see him in the spray, but when he opened his mouth, I saw this huge pink shape and the incisors, and I let go roughly at the center of it! I actually hit the brain. He dropped his head and hit the raft like a truck out of control on a downhill!

"I saw it coming, so the moment I fired I dropped flat onto the platform with my gun underneath me and held on for dear life, literally. Fortunately the contraption held together just enough to keep me and Kalemba out of the water. Of course we were drenched. I mean, the wave washed over the raft with such force that it would have taken us off if we hadn't had a good grip.

"When I got the water out of my eyes, I looked around but I couldn't see the bull at all. I wasn't sure if I had killed him or wounded him or had completely missed him. I had no idea if he was coming back for round two. So I waited for a few minutes, and when nothing happened, I told Kalemba to call the two locals to their posts so that we could get out of there. They were quite a way off on the bank by then, and they absolutely refused to get back into the water."

"For reasons completely unclear to you, of course," Gerhard interjected mischievously.

"Absolutely. Well, by now it was dark. Kalemba and I rowed ourselves back to the mooring with our hands. It took a long time and it wasn't so easy on my nerves because I kept wondering about the crocs and those semi-freshwater Zambezi sharks they keep around there.

"We met up with our erstwhile guardians at the mooring place and headed back to the village. They were very subdued during the half-hour walk, but when we got there they had a lot to say about the whole thing to the assembled audience, who had heard the shot and had gathered to hear the news. I didn't understand any of it, but Kalemba explained that they said the hippo was dead, and that I was a great hunter. I asked if they had mentioned anything about their hasty departure from the scene, but he said no.

"Anyway, I wasn't sure about the hippo. Nobody actually saw exactly what happened once I had fired. Kalemba and I were trying to survive an earthquake and a tsunami and the two locals were having a competition to keep ahead of the other so the hippo wouldn't get him first."

"Yeah, but I'd say if he was in any reasonable state he would have come back at you, so maybe it was a fair assumption that he was either badly wounded or dead," Gerhard said.

"Sure. Anyway, we went back the next day to have a look, and we searched more than, well, I'd say a half-mile either way of the spot, but we found nothing. We went back the village, and I was busy preparing to leave for the return journey when three men came running up shouting at the top of their voices. There was a hell of a commotion.

"It turned out they had found the bull on their fishing rounds much farther downstream, almost at the sea. The bull was dead. I couldn't resist going to have a look even though it would mean that the rest of the day would be a write-off. That's when I saw I had hit the brain through the roof of his mouth. More luck and intervention by the Universe than skill, I can assure you! Of course as the carcass began to bloat it became buoyant and drifted along with the current."

"Quite a story. But tell me, why is it the first time I've heard it? Why hadn't you told me before?" Gerhard asked half-accusingly.

"You know, it's the first time I have ever told this story to anyone. The thing is, I was in a bit of a difficult situation. I had decided I was going to take a different direction back with a loop to the north, which was where I was heading before I got sidetracked by the hippo business.

"Also, I just felt I couldn't face the *chefe's* company for the five or so days he would be with us on the way back. He would slow me down too much anyway. I also wasn't sure at that point if he had gone back to his headquarters with someone else. Then there was the problem of how fast the news would travel and if he might get to hear of the hippo before I got past the place where I had left him. What would he do about it if he had heard the news and saw me? I didn't want any surprises when I got back to the civilized parts of Mozambique, and also, I didn't want any incriminating notes made against my name in the Mozambican authorities' books that would revisit me on later trips.

"So that evening I called the whole lot together, and I had Kalemba explain to them that nobody must know about the hippo because the government would come and punish them with the fires of Hell and put them out of their village. Fortunately Vasco and his fellow emissaries confirmed all of this from the conversation at the chief's village. So it was sort of buried there. Vasco would go back and report to the chief that the hippo had disappeared when I got there and was no longer a menace, and I myself preferred to not think of it.

"As you know, a secret is only a secret as long as you are the only one that knows it. Once you confide in someone. . . . That person might confide in someone he absolutely trusted, and so the secret would spread. As it was, I was very nervous the next time I entered Mozambique. But besides all of that, each story has its time. There is nothing worse than a good story told at a bad time. And now was the time for this story."

"It's almost scary how similar the two situations are," Gerhard mused as he got up and stood facing me with his back warming to the low flames. "Of course, as in this case, it would only be a matter of time before another hippo or an elephant or a lion turned rogue, and they would have the same situation."

"True, but I tried at least to offer them some advice before we left. I had become quite convinced that the hippo was intimidated by the double canoe, at least while it was daylight. So I thought that they would be a lot safer if they always traveled in two or more canoes through the dangerous areas. It would require a bit of coordination and planning, but having watched them over the three days, I didn't think it would be difficult to arrange—besides, they had time.

"I told them that if they also always had a "hippo-watch" posted on at least one of the canoes, armed with something like a piece of flat wood on a handle that he could beat on the water, they would most likely be able to convince the hippo that he had to find alternative forms of amusement. I delivered the plan with a bit of ceremony, like an instructive session, with drawings in the sand and demonstrations, and it seemed to reassure them a bit."

"So, did you leave the next morning?"

"I did . . . and I think it's now time for us to leave for our hammocks."

Buffalo Hunts

That morning we got a slow start. The previous night's late storytelling kept us holding onto the last delicious snooze a bit later than usual. We had to get Lost Soul and his new companion going on their way to the camp on the Zambezi with the tusks and then pack all our gear and the extra food our hosts had given us. The sun had climbed above the treetops by the time we were finally ready to set out on our quest to exorcise the buffalo spirit. This time every able man left in the village volunteered his service in a way that we simply could not refuse.

We were almost ready to march out when we thought we should take a final look at the lion skin and make sure it was properly stored. It was more than just a bit smelly, so we had leaned it against the back of the farthest hut under the roof overhang and had more or less forgotten about it. To our consternation, when we went to retrieve it, it was gone!

Our immediate thought was that someone had stolen it. A lion skin is a great prize. Not only does it have monetary value, but it is considered strong *muti* [1] and as such it could be sold in little bits—the nails, the mane, bits of skin, with a cumulative value even higher than the complete skin. As longtime traders in animal products, our hosts would be well aware of this.

But I could not bring myself to believe that any one of them would steal it. "Do you think any one of them . . ." I began as we stood, flabbergasted.

"*Naaa*, pal, I doubt it. And what's more, none of them seems to be the *sangoma* [2] type that might want it for himself," said Gerhard.

---

[1] Medicine used by traditional healers and psychics.

"Sure, but what, then? There's not even a mark here," I said.

We started looking a bit closer. There were certainly no marks or any evidence on the hard-trodden ground behind the hut that could give a clue of how the heavy frame had been removed. Besides, many feet must have passed over any signs there might have been. About ten yards away in the loose soil of the cassava field we found some drag marks.

"Look, there's no way this frame could have been removed without at least somebody noticing," I said. "I think it is time for a little heart-to-heart. Let's call John and Elias."

"I agree. I don't know what the real explanation is, but someone could have told us," Gerhard fumed.

It was clear that Elias and John were as astounded and indignant as we were.

"The thing is, John, they promised to look after the skin, and now it's gone even before we have even left!" I seethed.

By now Lead Man had become aware that something was going on. As he turned the corner of the hut and saw the empty space, he let out an involuntary gasp and clapped his hand over his mouth.

"Well, he doesn't seem to be part of the scheme, or he's a damn good actor," I said to Gerhard when I saw his reaction.

"Look, pal, I think you can tell John it's the end of the buffalo hunt unless we find out exactly what happened to the skin," he growled through furious clouds of pipe smoke.

By now the whole village had gathered around anxiously. Typical of Africans in this kind of situation, there was suddenly an impenetrable veil of collaborative "I don't know" drawn over the eyes of everyone. They just went completely blank.

"John, you can tell them they must remember what I said would happen with the buffalo if they did not look after the skin well. You can tell them that if we don't find out what happened to the skin, we will be walking away

[2]Medicine man or psychic.

from here. The buffalo will be their problem, and it will not be the same problem as before. It will be a really big problem for them, even if they go to another place." I blatantly abused their superstition.

There was a long silence following on John's translation, with everyone looking down. Just as the silence seemed to become unbearable, Lead Man said he'd like to speak to his people alone.

We withdrew to where the stuff for the buffalo expedition had been left lying on the ground next to the cooking structure. It took about half an hour, with a lot of talking, even shouting, emanating from behind the hut before Lead Man emerged and approached us.

John translated Lead Man's synopsis. He said an *umfaan* [3] had noticed the skin was gone on the morning after our arrival. He was very scared and went to tell his mother. She, in turn, told the matriarch. The women and children followed the drag marks, dead scared, and found the frame about two hundred paces away. It was broken, and the few scraps of skin left were chewed into soft pulp. They were now terrified that we would leave without killing the buffalo if we found out. They were also terrified that they might be blamed for it, so they agreed to keep quiet and swore the children to silence in the hope we would not discover the missing skin.

"*Patrau*, he says he is very sorry. The women have made a big mistake. They did not know."

Then he told John of the old hyena, almost on its last legs, that had been scavenging for scraps of food around the village for some time.

I translated all of this back to Gerhard. "You know, the thing I find amazing is that they, knowing of the hyena, did not think of putting the skin somewhere safe, or at the very least of telling us of the danger."

Gerhard could only shake his head in disbelief. "Look, that's now water under the bridge. The point is, what do we do now? I think you are right that they should have done something, but they didn't, and that should not be too much of a surprise either. Perhaps we should have done something."

---

[3] Young boy.

"Sure. Look, I think the women have had punishment enough, and they probably have more coming their way. The men apparently really did not know. Should we not just carry on with the hunt? Let's face it, even if we could get the damn skin processed by Elias in reasonable shape, the chances of getting it out of here and all the way home without also getting into serious trouble are slim."

"Yep, you're probably right," Gerhard said.

"Look, John, it's OK. You can tell them we are cross, but we forgive them. They knew about the hyena, and they should have put the skin in a better place, or they should have told you and Elias. I ask them to promise one thing: When the men come back from the buffalo hunt, they must find the hyena and kill it; otherwise, it will make big problems for them. I mean it could take one of the children! I cannot understand why they have not killed it already. Surely they can see it's dangerous!"

It took some time to get the whole procession organized again, but we set out *en masse* about half an hour later, all armed to the teeth, each with his weapons of preference, from hunting knives, axes, machetes, and spears to big-game hunting rifles. A knobkerrie or two was thrown in for authenticity. We marched through the bush with all the confidence and élan of an untested army on a major campaign—Elias and Junior at the head, followed by Gerhard and me, and then John, Lead Man, and their remaining comrade. Lost Soul and his carrying companion were in the rear with their load of tusks.

We got to the water hole just before midday. John was left some way off with all the impedimenta and instructions to brew some tea, while the rest went forward to scout. It was a bit chaotic, with so many eager soldiers and no real commander. Gerhard and I resolved with a sideways glance at each other that we would have to impose some order among our troops if there was going to be a serious intent to hunt.

The sun had baked the bare fringes around the water hole into a dense heat that seemed to push against our bodies as we approached from the coolness of the tree line. It was tempting to plunge into the rock pool and let the generous abundance of the water dissolve the caked dust and sweat from us, or if that would be too indulgent in the face of what the situation demanded, then to at least remain there in shadows where the air was soft and smooth against our skin, and wait until the buffalo appeared.

Elias and Junior, however, had already walked out into the mirage glare and the rest spilled out after them. They seemed as eager to arrive at the destination, the water's edge, as they were for evidence of the quarry. They found the bull's tracks almost immediately, leading out from its favorite mud wallow. They saw where it had lowered itself into the coolness of the ooze and had moved its great body so that the mud bubbled luxuriously up its sides, seeped into the folds of its skin, and balsamed the patches left bare by old wounds or the ravages of years of buffalo bull life.

It hadn't been gone for long. "Less than two hours," I grunted to Gerhard as we looked down at the heavy hoof prints.

The edges were still dark from the water that had run down its legs as it walked from the watery slush, and the little bits of mud that had dropped from its body were still damp. We knew it was close, and if we were careful and just a little lucky, we would find it quickly.

The tea was forgotten for the moment. Elias and I exchanged glances, and without the need for words we settled on the spoor, Gerhard and I slightly back on either side, about five paces apart, and Lead Man and the rest of the mighty cohort firmly waved a good distance farther back. The wind was a mere breath, but hot, on the left sides of our faces.

The spoor was easy to follow, but the bush was dense. In dense vegetation the buffalo could be very close and we wouldn't see it. We went forward carefully, senses quivering for a sound, the hint of movement, perhaps even that sweet-musty smell. I have heard hunters say that buffaloes have poor eyesight and hearing, and this may be true when they are in a noisy herd, but in my experience they can hear pretty well when they pay attention. They don't see so badly either, especially when they charge you!

The bull had moved along leisurely, stopping here and there to rub against a tree trunk or spar the bark from some young trees, or pluck from a tuft of grass, and the odd blades that had fallen from its mouth were still wet with saliva.

As we dropped down into a shallow depression, we saw it, slightly below us, some fifty paces away. It was almost impossible to spot where it lay with its back toward us under some sickle bush, but the flick of its ear had given it away. We could only see bits of its broad, black back, its shape patchy through the sickle bush trunks and mottled shadows; its right ear; and the sweep of the mighty right horn, worn blunt at the tip.

A quick glance and a nod between Gerhard and me, and we moved a few paces to the right to get a clear line of sight. Then, involuntarily, we both hesitated. It somehow seemed wrong to shoot the bull lying down. Mighty warriors should be afforded the dignity to go down fighting, sword in hand!

We looked at each other uncomfortably. I considered for a moment whistling to it so it could get up and face us, but we knew that if it jumped up it could well be obscured from our view. If it then ran, it would be lost in a split second in the thick bush, and, the wind could shift any moment. We both knew we were here to do a job.

Another nod, and we fired. My bullet broke its neck just behind the skull, and Gerhard's broke its spine just behind the shoulder blades. It never even knew what had hit it. It simply rolled over and died with a few feeble kicks.

As we stood for a moment, rifles ready, to make sure it wasn't going to get up, Junior suddenly rushed past us, and before we could stop him, ran up to the bull and hacked his machete deep into the neck muscle, again and again, his face contorted with rage and pain, until he finally stood bloodied, with head bowed, hands on his knees, panting hoarsely through his open mouth. We stood back, silently watching, our hearts going out to him.

"I think we should go and have some tea. They don't need us here anymore," I mumbled through a tight throat, and turned away quickly.

It was a job done and a moment to be remembered, but not fondly, and probably one impossible to really share with anybody who had not stood there on that hot morning and saw Junior staring down at his bloody machete lying between his feet.

We slurped at the tea without talking. The buffalo was no longer our problem. Lead Man and his companions were probably already at work, reducing the bull to flame-dried bits. I felt as if we had worked hard to arrive at a destination, and we had, but somehow it wasn't a destination. It was just a point from which to depart again.

It struck me that life really is like that—a frantic pursuit of one destination after another, only to discover each time that arriving was not really arriving; it was more like departing for the next destination. It made death seem almost attractive. My musings were interrupted by Gerhard.

Ever impatient, he cleared his throat and asked, "Pal, what do you think we do now?"

He really meant, "Let's get going. There's no point in hanging around here any longer."

I had to stretch above the loose jumble in my mind to answer him and I heard myself saying: "Yes. As they say, the die has been cast; *jacta est alea*. Well, I was thinking, we have already moved around quite a bit in the area to the west of Stephan's camp, and we know it a bit, but not in the area to the east. So maybe we could head northeast and hit the river downstream from the camp, then work back westward and see what we come across. It will take us four days, maybe a bit longer, I'd say. Of course, we could also just head straight for camp. We could be there in two and a half days if we moved," I added, not very enthusiastically.

"*Hmm.* You know, since we met back there at that other water hole, we haven't really been doing any serious hunting of our own choice: We went to the elephant, we carried the trophies to the village, we looked for their buffalo. So I think we should go northeast and see where fate leads us," Gerhard replied with an edge of excitement in his voice that pricked my own sense of adventure.

"Right. I agree. I just hope we don't bump into any poachers—or should I say, 'hunting parties.' If we do, we just have to take it as it comes. But it's already a bit late in the day. We have maximum two hours of walking left, probably less, before we have to start making camp for the night anyway. I think we should stay here for tonight. We have really nice water, we can swim, and we can go and sit in that tree again to see if anything interesting comes to the water hole to flavor our sunset."

"*Ja*, good idea," he said, and as our eyes met, the quiet companionship between us was almost tangible.

We stirred early the next morning, packing gear and filling the water canisters in the half light. Then we headed back to the kill to say good-bye to Lead Man and his companions before setting out. Lead Man and Junior had made good progress on the carcass, their companion having been sent back to the village to fetch extra help for carrying. John and Elias helped themselves to some good cuts of buffalo meat, and we said our good-byes, a warm and slightly sad affair. Then we moved on unhurriedly northeast into our new adventure, and once again, anything was possible.

✦✦✦✦✦✦

The day was uneventful and burning hot, and the afternoon had again donned a dark menace of cloud on its northwestern brow. Soon the white cloud-heads frothed, blocking out the sun, making it a bit cooler, but threatening an evening storm. It took its time, finally breaking over us around eleven o'clock with earth-trembling crashes and hammering rain.

We had our usual small sheets stretched over our hammocks, but that wasn't up to this kind of storm, and we ended up sitting in my hammock under a poncho, feet on a log to keep them out of the water, watching the lightning tear rain-streaked gashes into the night and reminiscing about how we regularly seemed to get rain and buffalo hunting together. It had happened in the mopane and marula veld of the Zambezi valley; in the tall elephant grass on the Limpopo flood plains near Chikwarakwara where we got chased off the trail of a herd by a belting thunderstorm; and in the teak forests of Naivasha the day that I missed a chance to shoot the biggest buffalo bull either of us had ever seen. Missing that bull was something for which I think Gerhard never quite forgave me.

++++++

We had picked up the spoor of a bull herd of about six just after dawn at the place where they had spent the night in an open patch next to the track where we were driving. The morning was gray and woolly with cloud but dry, with a nice, brisk breeze to aid us in our hunt. There were two big bulls in the group, but one seemed to be really enormous, with front hoof tracks the size of soup bowls.

We had one of those rare, really excellent trackers with us—an old man from the Nuanetsi Valley to the south, Techu, who was as good as Elias any day. The buffalo moving more or less in a specific direction in a group made tracking relatively easy, and we could move fast, the spoor freshening steadily as we gained on them.

As the morning progressed, the clouds dropped lower until their undersides were almost touching the treetops and weeping a steady drizzle over the bush. We were soon completely soaked and cold, but we could see that the buffalo were close, and we were thinking that they would not be moving a lot in such weather, so we soldiered on.

It was my turn to shoot—Gerhard had shot an elephant the previous day—but we were hoping that we'd be able to take both the big bulls. I had a borrowed a .375 H&H (the manufacturer shall remain unnamed) but the gun was really poorly constructed and badly finished. I loathed it. We were still young at the time, and it would be only my second buffalo—Gerhard had already shot a few.

Despite the rain, the tracks remained relatively easy to follow in the soft sand below the teak canopy, but the wind was not in our favor, and soon, when he thought they were fairly close, Techu left the spoor and made a huge semicircle to the left to try to get downwind of them. It had now started raining quite strongly, and one could see no farther than fifty paces, but Techu was a consummate master and his intuition of where he was likely to find the bulls seemingly infallible.

He suddenly stopped and pointed. At first we couldn't even see them, but eventually we were able to make out the blurred dark blotches on the ground. They were lying among some shrubs under the trees. We tried through our scopes and binoculars to make out which was which, and where the big bull was, but it was extremely difficult in the rain, with water getting onto the lenses and streaming into our eyes.

Then, suddenly, the big bull rose from among the others and stood staring at us through the veil of rain, nose thrust forward defiantly, huge and black. My single most vivid memory of the moment was his enormous pair of horns, sweeping down and up and back, as wide as a small car. They seemed to fill the scope aperture as I raised the rifle.

He was standing almost facing me, and I lined up the cross hairs just where his neck joined the body and in line with the point of his shoulder. I squeezed the trigger and . . . nothing happened!

In my haste, I had not taken off the safety! I was vaguely aware of Gerhard throwing an incredulous glance in my direction and then whipping up his rifle and leaning forward into it to shoot. I was aware of the bull breaking away, the safety slipping forward, and the bull (or some bull) briefly blurring through the scope aperture as I threw up the rifle. Our shots burst almost as one. I noticed the magazine of the .375 coming out and spilling its contents onto the wet sand. We heard the sound of the bulls crashing away from us through the bush and then the sad sift of the rain on the leaves.

We started following through the rain, but there was nothing. Not even the tiniest smear of blood on a leaf. We had both missed cleanly. We eventually stopped, miserable and wet, when the rain became so heavy that we could no longer distinguish their tracks from older ones.

"What happened?"

"I don't know—the safety . . ."

"Well, it was the biggest damn buffalo I have ever seen."

And that was it.

++++++

It was three days before our slow northwestward drift brought us our first glimpses of the misty-blue slopes on the north side of the Zambezi. It had been a pleasant walk. There was quite a bit of game around, but we weren't hunting—shooting anything bigger than for the pot would have created a huge logistical problem.

We just wandered along, enjoying the bush, allowing ourselves to be led off course by a bird or something interesting, stopping for honey, checking tracks, quizzing each other, arguing about trees and birds and tracks and animal habits, listening to our black companions' endless talking at rests, and reading. At least I did; Gerhard hadn't brought a book, so he would sit for long periods, staring into the distance, puffing at his pipe, fiddling with his gun or some other piece of gear, or borrowing a page from my diary in order to draw something.

He was an incurable schemer and would constantly chisel away at ideas for business ventures or devices that he could manufacture, often coming up with amazingly innovative ones. I remember one day when he arrived on my farm with an idea sketched on a piece of paper. It was for a special high-lift vehicle jack—an indispensable piece of bush equipment, commonly used by bush people in a variety of emergency situations, and by wannabes in the display mode, mounted as conspicuously as possible on their shiny 4x4s together with a pick and shovel that had never seen serious use.

Gerhard's jack was different, for he had devised an elegant lift-and-lower mechanism. He wanted my advice as an engineer, but apart from some minor suggestions, there was very little in the way of improvement on his design that I could offer. It was very cleverly thought out. He manufactured the jack and had done reasonably well with it as far as I was aware, but it never quite got the appreciation from the market that the elegance of the design deserved—good craftsmanship is often poorly appreciated.

Of course we talked a lot, too, about characters we had known, business, politics, our lives in general, about the bush, and our own experiences.

Often these were stories we had listened to a few times before, but somehow they always seemed special when told by the low flutter of the flames under the gallery of stars gazing down on us in the echoing vastness of the African night.

We had both been blessed with exceptionally interesting fathers. One evening, as Gerhard reminisced about game fishing with his dad during the pre-bush-war years in the Mozambique Channel off Bazaruto Island, I was reminded of a story my own father once told me.

++++++

"My dad never did game fishing as far as I know, but he also used to wander around in Mozambique quite a bit during the fifties. He said I was too young to go with him, but years later he told me this amazing story about a trip he had made to Barra.

"We were living in the Kruger Park at the time. He did various odd jobs there, including being a game ranger for a while, and acting as the official park artist. Of course in those days Kruger Park was nothing like the slick commercial tourist operation it is now. It was a lot less developed, a bit like a frontier situation with huge tracts that really were quite remote and unvisited even by conservation staff—no real roads, only tracks here and there.

"Dad became friendly with the local police sergeant at Skukuza, quite a salty old character himself, believe me. They both had a passion for exploring and for fishing, and I think that's what made them click because thinking back, I can't imagine they had much else in common.

"As you know, my dad was a fine craftsman. He built himself a beautiful little wooden skiff in his garage, and the two of them set off for Mozambique in our little blue 1953 Peugeot 203, loaded with supplies for their safari and with the skiff precariously tied upside down to the roof."

"That was quite a brave enterprise," Gerhard interjected as he got up to shift the logs a bit deeper into the flames. "Most of Mozambique must have still been quite wild in those days even though the Portuguese may have done a bit of civilizing. Those little Peugeots were a little underpowered and had narrow wheels like Marie biscuits, if I recall correctly?"

"Exactly. Very tough and reliable, though. My dad had taken to doing quite a bit of exploring inside Kruger Park with it. You know, I think it only had a 1300cc engine, but he often commented that it could knock out most other vehicles used by the conservation staff, including some 4x4s! It was apparently quite remarkable over bad terrain. The wheels were thin but quite big, and that was helpful.

"The French built some really good vehicles between the 1950s and 1970s. Remember the Citroën, and the Renault? And remember all the ancient Peugeot 404 pickups still running in Botswana when we went there in the 1970s?"

"Sure," Gerhard responded. "Every young guy dreamed of having a Renault Gordini, and the Citroëns were ahead of their time with their adjustable air suspension. Peugeots were the Toyotas of today. Only maybe a lot tougher."

"*Ja.* Anyway, the two of them drifted up the coast from one remote little beach to another, and eventually they ended up at Barra. They decided to stay there for a while, and one morning as they were rowing out along the lagoon, they came across a strange ceremony.

"There was a rowboat anchored in shallow water on the lagoon's edge. Suddenly a detachment of five black men came marching down toward it. They were dressed in a sort of uniform with khaki shorts and navy blue roll-neck jerseys, but no shoes or hats. They halted at the water edge, and stood smartly to attention in two lines about a yard apart, waiting.

"And then a splendid apparition happened. A weathered-looking old Portuguese guy came marching out toward them. He was short and thin with a heavy beard, and tanned almost black, and my dad said he reminded him of a piece of rusted wire.

"Listen to this: He was dressed in a spotless white ceremonial naval uniform, all braided in gold and full of regalia, finished off with a pair of crude homemade sandals. He was marching very proudly, stiff as a rod, swinging his arms to shoulder height. Very serious."

I continued the story between our chuckles. "He marched between the two rows of the contingent and when he got to the last two men he halted smartly and threw out his arms sideways at shoulder height. They first thought it was some special sort of salute, but then the two men at his sides stepped one step towards him. As they did, they sort of bent slightly so that they took his outstretched arms on their shoulders. All this was done with military precision to counts of three from the fifth guy, who seemed to be something of a corporal or such."

"What on earth? Are you serious? You're not making this up to pull my leg here?" Gerhard asked suspiciously.

"No, no. This is the exact story he told me. Or at least as well as I can remember it. It was all quite serious and extraordinary for a remote Mozambique beach, he said. He and the sergeant were completely mystified. They couldn't make out what it was all about. They sat staring, forgetting to row, and they drifted slowly along on the outgoing tide.

"Once the old man hung suspended between the two, the corporal guy gave a command, and the whole procession marched forward into the water toward the boat. They straddled the boat, two men on either side, and once they were in line with a raised bench, they lowered their load on it, and the old guy sat down. All the time he was stiffly staring straight ahead and ignoring his detail, which now proceeded to clamber into the boat in a somewhat less elegant manner. On the command from the 'corporal' they took up the oars, and in time with his pace keeping, they started rowing straight across the lagoon.

"On the other side of the lagoon, drawn up on a short slipway, lay a motor launch, about forty-five feet long. It was an old design, military-looking, and painted brilliant white. The procession headed straight for that. When they arrived at the slipway, the porting procedure was repeated. The esteemed naval officer remained where he had been deposited on the land, while his detail marched onto the launch along a wooden gangway, which was rather crudely constructed from local materials.

"Nevertheless, they marched on and proceeded to hoist the Portuguese flag on a short mast on the vessel while the officer and the corporal saluted.

Then they came and stood smartly to attention on either side of the gangway on the vessel, and the officer marched forward. He saluted the ship as he stepped onto the gangway, and he got duly saluted by his detail as he moved through their ranks, and the corporal turned and followed him around the boat—evidently on some sort of inspection.

"By now my dad and the police sergeant had drifted more or less out of sight of the vessel and its crew, and they couldn't see what other solemn ceremonies were conducted, but they later found out that the Portuguese guy was the local *chefe do poste*. Because Barra is close to Inhambane, at some point it must have been declared an important point, so it obviously had official government representation."

"Amazing that they kept up that ceremony and with nobody even looking," Gerhard said.

"Well, at least that once, they had a spellbound audience. That's not the most interesting part of the story. There were, of course, no other Europeans around, so it was sort of inevitable that they eventually got to know the *chefe* over a few glasses of brandy. He took them on a special tour of the launch. My dad said it was completely rusted through—irreparably, he thought. You could see the concrete slipway through its bottom. It would sink like a stone if it ever got into water. Nevertheless, they dutifully kept on painting and polishing it as they had been told the last time anybody bothered to pay attention, and he kept on formally inspecting it once a week, dressed in his full ceremonial uniform."

When our laughter had subsided into quiet chuckles, I continued, "Even more amazing was the *chefe*. He was originally from Madeira. He and his brother had set out from there in a little rowing boat somewhere during the course of the Second World War. They gradually rowed their way along the West Coast of Africa, going ashore when they felt like it, spending time here and there."

"What!? That's absolutely astonishing," Gerhard interjected. "Now that's what I call adventuring. Just drifting off into the unknown, not even knowing where you're going to end up."

"Absolutely. They rowed all the way round the Cape of Good Hope, and up the East Coast as far as Mombasa. They apparently didn't like it much there, so they turned around and rowed all the way back to Barra. They settled there on the lagoon, but the brother died after a while, probably from malaria, and when time came to appoint a *chefe do poste*, he probably seemed to be the best choice, or more likely the only option.

"The old chap turned out to be a very ordinary Madeira Portuguese. At the end of the inspection tour, he would take off his uniform and revert back to being one, keeping himself busy with fishing and so forth. I can only wonder what became of other official duties he might have had, like keeping records and sending reports. He very likely couldn't read or write. He had apparently been in the Portuguese navy at some point, but nowhere near an officer of rank. That must have been where he got his taste for military ceremony. Where and why he got the elaborate uniform was a mystery. My dad said they didn't think it was appropriate to ask him about it."

"Just shows what being in the right place at the right time can do for you," Gerhard chuckled.

++++++

The next morning we turned west, following the Zambezi upstream toward camp, but keeping back from the edge of the flood plain. It was narrower in that area, with low, rocky ridges pushing out gnarled black fingers from the higher ground toward the river. The vegetation was mainly scrawny-looking mopane, half bare and black as the rocks they were attempting to survive on. Where we glimpsed the flood plain, we could see game dotted here and there—waterbucks, a few warthogs, zebras, the occasional elephant, even single or small herds of buffaloes. We decided we were still too far from the camp to shoot one, so we simply enjoyed watching them through our binoculars.

Late in the afternoon we came upon a place where a dry ravine from the uplands opened wide onto the flood plain. Some huge Ana trees grew there, and we decided it was an excellent spot to make camp. While we were preparing the camp, I noticed Elias and John get all excited, apparently about a plant—a smallish, sparsely growing shrub, with fine light green composite leaves arranged in perfectly symmetrical rows on either side of their stems and forming a very delicate plume at the end.

They were enthusiastically digging up the roots, talking excitedly. I walked over and asked John what it was. He explained that it "made a woman like you when she sees you after you had put some of the root in her drink."

He also showed me how the fine branch tips would curl up instantly when touched. This was quite intriguing. A love-potion plant that reacted instantly and visibly to touch! Of course, we had to have some of the roots too, mischievously contemplating using it on some hapless woman, but never actually getting round to it.

++++++

This peculiar plant reminded me of an experience I once had on the way back from one of my expeditions into the northern reaches of Mozambique. I had decided that I wanted to use my return journey to explore the stretch of land between the Beira–Mutare road (known as the Beira Corridor) and the Save River. There were almost no roads through the area indicated on my map, but I thought I'd leave the Mutare–Beira road at Bandula and try to work southward, more or less hugging the line of the mountains to the west and aiming for a place called Massangena, where I knew from a previous expedition I would be able to ford the Save River. From there it should be fairly easy to continue southwest to Mapai, where I could ford the Limpopo, and then turn northwest to cross into South Africa at the new Pafuri border post.

It turned out to be quite an enterprise. There were several minor roads and tracks, but none consistently heading south, and it was a rather nerve-testing process of trial and error to follow the tracks, while at the same time trying to conserve fuel so that I would have enough to make it through.

One evening, about halfway between the Corridor and the Save, I was driving along a track through some dense forest that grew on the lower slopes of the Bvumba Mountains to the west. The sun was setting, and I was urgently looking for a place to make camp for the night. Trying to find a camp while *en route* was always a bit stressful.

It inevitably ended up in a forced trade-off between the darkness and the quality of the spot—I wanted to delay it as late as possible so that I wouldn't unnecessarily lose traveling time, but I also wanted a pleasant spot with nice trees away from the road and from people. I have always much preferred sleeping among wild animals to sleeping among people, and I always look for a spot where I am sure people are at least three miles (preferably much farther) away.

There weren't many people there, but the forest was so dense that I couldn't find an opening to drive away from the road. Eventually I came across a faint hint of a track leading off into the forest. It was a bit risky to take untraveled tracks in Mozambique because of the danger from land mines, but I was desperate and frustrated enough at that point to ignore the stern voice of my judgment.

Unfortunately, after about thirty yards, my way was blocked by a large tree that had fallen across the track. I got out to investigate whether I might be able to drag it out of the way with the Land Cruiser, but it was too big and wedged against other trees. I would have to search on.

As I got back into the cab, the skin over all of my body suddenly started burning—under my clothes, in my hair, even my feet. At first it was only slightly, but within less than a minute it became so intense that I could hardly bear it.

Now, just for some perspective, I don't think I could be called squeamish, and more than one doctor that had had the misfortune of having to stitch up some wound I had contracted in the course of my rather reckless lifestyle had remarked that I had an unusually high tolerance for pain, but this burning was so severe that I felt I was being overwhelmed by it.

I had often been burned by noxious nettles in the veld, but it was always local, with some swelling where the nettles had come into contact with the skin, and while it was certainly unpleasant, it was nowhere near this intense burning. There was no evidence of skin irritation either.

I was soon in a state of near-panic. I could not understand what was happening to me, and I was beginning to fear that I had contracted some exotic African disease in the bush that was now manifesting itself and that I might be about to suffer a lonely and painful death.

I kept driving, more out of desperation than considered action, and when I came to a little stream I stopped in the middle of it and literally fell into the water. It seemed to have little effect. I tore off my clothes and stood naked in the cool evening breeze, and this provided some relief, but only while the cooling effect of the water evaporating from my skin lasted. I repeated the dip-and-cool routine a number of times, and during the short respites I got from the burning, I could feel that the rest of my body seemed to be functioning normally.

This gave me some comfort that total organ failure was not imminent, and the state of near panic subsided a little so that I could at least think clearly. I still had no idea of what the cause of the burning was and how long it would last, but I was beginning to allow myself the probability that it was some external irritation and that there was a reasonable chance of life after the burning.

So, back to the original problem: where to spend the night. I took a double dose of antihistamine from my medical kit and continued along the track. Still burning fiercely, but at least able to put it into a reasonable perspective and concentrate on the search, I eventually spotted a clump of trees that seemed (from their sky-etched silhouettes) to have a nice dense canopy that would give protection against the dew and provide some coziness.

I drove off the road but to my disappointment they were mango trees—huge, and probably once the property of some hapless Portuguese family now living in poverty in Madeira or Portugal, or possibly even killed during the terrible war.

Whatever the fate of the original owners, the trees would now most likely have been taken over by new African owners. Sure enough, investigation revealed a footpath leading farther into the bush. I followed it on foot, and it led to a small cluster of huts, their pointed silhouettes black against the star-strewn sky. I could make out people moving around a small fire, but when I approached they all ran away, screaming in terror.

I stood waiting on the edge of the fire's glow, uncertain of what to do. Mercifully, the burning had at least subsided quite a bit, but I was fearful that it might return. After about ten minutes a woman emerged timidly out of the darkness, stopping about ten paces away. She said nothing, simply looked at the ground in a way that I interpreted as asking about my business, but it was soon clear she did not understand a word of my best explanations in English, Zulu, or Fanagalo.

Suddenly she let out a long wailing scream, and within a few minutes people came running, clearly from other clusters of huts farther away in the dark. Soon I was surrounded by a circle of wildly shouting and gesturing people. They were highly excited but didn't seem particularly aggressive, so I wasn't worried, just puzzled. There was no way I could speak to them. Even if there was one that could understand me, I would simply not be heard above the din.

I was at a loss of how to handle the situation, wondering how the strange stalemate would play out, and what on earth I was going to do about a place to sleep when an old man I had noticed standing quietly on the outside of the circle pushed through the people and approached me. It immediately went quiet.

He greeted me in Fanagalo and inquired about my business. I explained to him that I was traveling through the area and wanted to sleep under the mango trees and I had to get the consent of the owner. He immediately agreed and said that I would be safe there. He turned out to be a local headman of sorts, and seemed a really pleasant old chap, so I invited him to dinner.

He came after I had had a shower and had started with the best meal I could put together with the few bits of food I had left. I wasn't able to make a fire because the locals had long since carried off any available scrap of wood to keep their fires burning and, as happens in areas where larger groups of people congregate, had even started eating away at the forest around them for wood. I had to rely on my gas stove. My affliction had by then completely gone away, and I was feeling normal.

After we had finished eating and I had cleaned the utensils, I turned off the little Coleman. It was suddenly quiet. A slow mist was creeping up from the slopes and the African night was soft and cool around us. There was something poignant about me and the old headman sitting there, him in my chair, me on the food box with my back against the mango trunk, talking late into the night.

He told me about working in South Africa and how he, as a bush person, experienced Johannesburg and the mines; he discussed the "time of the Portuguese"; he talked of the game situation in the area (it was nonexistent—too many people); and he explained how people there survived. The area produced quite a bit of fruit, which the inhabitants traded, and they would make charcoal from the surrounding forest to trade as well, mainly to intrepid merchants sojourning south from the Beira Corridor in search of merchandise.

I was surprised that they produced charcoal that far from the main road to Beira. The practice of charcoal production to fuel the insatiable energy needs of its sprawling shanty cities is one of the ironies of Africa. People living along roads near cities (and apparently others living farther afield) produce the charcoal by burning forest trees. Some cart it to the cities on their bicycles in large sacks and sell it there directly. The sight of them, the riders often grotesquely dwarfed by the size of their loads, precariously wobbling their way toward the city, is something to behold.

Others bring their sacks to the roadside and line them up on the shoulder in neat rows like soldiers on parade. There they are purchased by either merchants or by truck drivers on their way to the city wanting to make a bit of extra money.

Still others bring them to railway lines where they are bought by railway personnel and stacked onto trains to sell in the city. I have seen locomotives with the driver's "booty" free-riding along, stacked two high all along the sides of the engine!

The result of this trade is, on the one hand, negative, in that huge areas along the roads (and ever farther away) are being stripped of trees that are not being replaced. This is not only environmentally undesirable but also makes for a rather scruffy-looking and unattractive roadside environment. It also means that, as the tree line recedes from the road, people lose their livelihood.

On the other hand, there is a positive side to it, as this process of deforestation clears fertile land, which becomes attractive to entrepreneurs for investing in agricultural projects. Of course, a host of factors need to be reasonably aligned before an investor would be convinced to put large sums into an agricultural venture. These include such arcane issues as government policies, local customs and laws, population density, amenability of the local people to the project, the availability and quality of infrastructure, the availability and effectiveness of export facilities, and the availability of inputs and enterprise support functions. This means that realization of the benefits becomes rather remote and dubious.

As the old man was leaving, I asked him about the burning. He listened carefully to my explanation, and then said he thought it was caused by a kind of plant in the area that he described as *"lo moya ka hena hena chisa"*—literally, "the breath of him it burns." To my relief, he confirmed that once past it would not return, as long as I did not get within range of the devilish breath again. I have often thought that if some repressive regime ever found out about this plant they would have little trouble dispersing protesting crowds of their citizens.

✦✦✦✦✦✦

The next night we decided to make camp right on the edge of the flood plain. We found a grove of acacia in a slight depression, leafy and generous from the extra moisture that must have been preserved there. John and Elias set off on a trek across the flood plain to fetch us water for a shower, and Gerhard and I settled down facing the river across the plain with our backs against a huge, bleached-white tree trunk that the river had once tossed there in anger.

As the sun dropped into the water to the east, it flamed the river into angry red, but the fierceness of the day's heat was broken and the coolness of the evening air seeped in deliciously. Soon the fading light started stealing away the known shapes into mysterious haziness, but strings of geese and egrets and other birds remained etched like black ink spots across the pink-gray canvas of the sky. We lingered against the tree trunk until the gathering darkness forced us to be practical about preparing our camp for the night.

Later, when we had just settled back with John's bedtime tea, a roaring tumult suddenly tore open the tranquil hum of the night and brought us to our feet in a chaotic stumble for guns and machetes. It took us a minute of tense bewilderment before we concluded that it was a pride of lions taking on some large prey a few hundred yards from us.

We stood listening to the desperate life-and-death drama for about half an hour, a few desperate bellows audible through the fierce growling leading us to conclude that the prey was a buffalo. When it finally subsided to occasional snarls and short roars, we settled down again, Gerhard remarking that at least we could be assured that we wouldn't be bothered by lions that night.

But he was wrong because somewhere in the small hours, sated, they started roaring, mighty, full-throated roars that seemed to roll out from deep in their stomachs. It made our bodies tremble where we lay in our hammocks and finally drove us out to sit by the fire, feeling that most primal of African sounds crash over us like mighty waves, touching the very bones in our bodies, and making our African souls reverberate, thrilling us with awe and delicious fear-pricked wonderment. Would that such could be the content of one's last hours.

When it got light, we went to check. We approached carefully, not wanting to be surprised by the lions, but they had left, probably to drink and seek shade. Two hyenas and a few jackals retreated reluctantly from the kill as we approached. It was a buffalo cow. The carcass had the choicest parts already eaten, so it had to be a pride of at least six or so lions; of course, the scavengers had also done some eating.

Her left rear leg was still untouched, and it was deformed and grotesquely swollen—the legacy of an old wound. It hinted at the sad drama of the last weeks: the fateful day of the injury, perhaps a horn butt from one of her own, a crocodile bite, or even a snare. Then the slow creep of the infection set in and with it a gradual weakening and the struggle to keep up with the herd. The cow fell farther and farther behind, and then the lions caught the scent of decay and followed her for those desperate last hours of charges and parries until she was tired to death and knew her fate was sealed. Finally, there was the suffocated agony of those last moments. . . .

That afternoon, as we topped one of the low ridges pushing out toward the river, we spotted a large herd of buffaloes some five hundred paces away on a grassy plain—possibly the herd the cow had been part of, we surmised as we sat watching them through our binoculars. They were just beginning to string out toward the tree line.

The herd seemed about a hundred and fifty or so strong, and there were several good bulls, including some really nice ones. We thought we were close enough to camp to be able to fetch a vehicle to collect the meat and the trophies, so we quickly decided that it would be a good option to try to take the two bulls we had left on our agreement. The trick would be to get close and select one from the moving herd on the open plain. We decided to try to intercept them when the bulk of the herd reached the small, shrubby mopane at the edge of the plain.

We lost sight of them as we dropped from the crest and got into the mopane. We tried to keep a line to where we thought the interception point had to be, but it felt a bit like swimming through thick soup toward a moving object. Fortunately buffaloes are self-assured and noisy creatures, especially in a herd, and, as we got closer, we could hear the muffled snorts and the breaking branches as they lumbered through the vegetation. Then, suddenly, a young heifer pushed through the foliage right in front of us, about ten paces away. She spotted us, and with a snort of alarm she swung around and was off at a gallop. In a flash, the whole bush exploded around us. Breaking branches and hurled stones catapulted through the air as the herd thundered away!

Gerhard shouted, "Let's run after them!" as he took off at a run.

I was for a moment taken aback by the audacity of his reaction and a bit skeptical, but as I fell in with him I realized he was right. With only one heifer having raised the alarm, the herd's reaction would likely be uncertain, and they would probably not run far before stopping. It takes a lot of energy for such a big body to run, and buffaloes don't run unnecessarily—in fact, no animal does. A buffalo typically will only run a short distance when spooked before stopping and turning around; the big bulls will then move back to face the danger.

We weaved and crashed through the trees in the drifting dust, with branches tugging at our clothes and whipping and tearing at our bare skin. Our own noise made it impossible to know how far ahead the buffalo were, so we had to stop every now and again to try to get a rough sound-bearing on them. After a while Gerhard and I got separated from each other as I took a slightly wider arc to the left, thinking that the herd might tend to head deeper into the trees as they ran.

Suddenly, the trees opened up a bit, and there they were, not more than fifty paces away. Some were still trotting through the trees, but a few big bulls had stopped and had turned around to face the danger. They stood there in the drifting dust like a fortress wall, their mighty heads raised high, noses thrust forward, defiant, formidable. They were intimidating despite the heavy .404 in my hands. For a moment I wanted to just stand there and watch them, so keenly enjoyable was the sight.

The Spirit of the Hunt, however, was fast and fiery in my veins, and as I dropped to one knee, I scanned the line of bulls for a good one. I squeezed off on a big brute near the center, and, almost simultaneously, I heard Gerhard's .450 explode somewhere to my right. The mopane was swept back in their mighty surge away from our shots, and then there was nothing—just the drifting dust against the wall of trees and the fading thunder of their flight.

"Did you get one?" Gerhard shouted as we both moved forward, surprised at how close we had been.

"I think so. I had to shoot fast, but they were close. You?"

"Yes, I think so. He turned a bit when your shot went, but I think it was good. Let's go and see."

There wasn't any blood on the spot where my bull had stood, but within twenty paces it was as if huge scoops had been splashed on the ground from a bucket. I had aimed just above the base of his throat, and had probably severed a main neck artery or hit the heart. It was definitely a fatal shot.

I left the spoor and walked across to see how Gerhard had done. He had found pink frothy blood after about fifty yards. It was clearly a lung shot, but there was also some darker blood.

"A lung shot on the left, I think, and just behind the shoulder but at a very small angle as he turned away. I think I probably hit some of the organs, too."

"He probably won't go very far," I nodded.

"No, but how was yours?"

"It looks like into the engine room. Buckets of blood. He probably won't go more than a hundred yards or so."

"OK, well, we are a bit more uncertain about mine, so let's give it a chance to settle down while we go and find yours," Gerhard suggested.

We found him quickly. He lay dead on his side, the last remnants of life spilled in a crimson pool in front of him. He was a fine trophy, but as we stood looking down at the mighty head, its eyes now glazed and unseeing, I felt the fierce flame of the hunt fade.

I suddenly felt drained and tired and even vulnerable. I knew well by now the cunning manipulations, the powerful alchemy, of the Spirit of the Hunt that subtly mixes the primitive craving for excitement, the lure of deadly danger, and the primal instinct to hunt and kill. Many times I've felt this combination of emotions racing through my veins—only to slink away when the deed is done, leaving me with a feeling of sadness and regret. I felt very alone at that moment because this was something I knew I could not talk to Gerhard about. He was too pure, too singular, too heedless in his conviction of the absolute supremacy of the Hunt to be able to hear, and so I just smiled and nodded at his compliments and the ululations from John and Elias.

Practical matters forced themselves forward. The sun's fiery red belly was already touching the treetops, and out there was a buffalo that could possibly still be alive. We went to look for the blood spoor, but despite how clear it was when we first saw it, it took some time for us to find it again. We followed it, finding a place where the bull had lain down, gotten up again, and then moved on. He was clearly very badly wounded and was probably not far away, but it was getting too dark to track effectively. It is also very dangerous to pursue a wounded buffalo in the half-light. We decided to withdraw a little and make camp for the night.

That evening, as we were slurping at our scalding tea after a sparse dinner, I said, "I must admit that your running after the buffalo was quite a surprise to me. I didn't think it could work."

"It was more intuition than anything else. I thought, *look, they usually seem to stop and turn after a while*," Gerhard said.

"*Hmm.* Makes sense. That's their habit—with predators, too," I mused.

"I'd say if they get too spooked, like when they are hunted heavily, then maybe they'd run harder and farther, or at least carry on walking for a longer distance once they had stopped running, and maybe then one wouldn't get another chance," Gerhard opined.

"*Ja*, I would think it would not work for just a few or even a small herd, either. For a larger herd like this one, well, not all the animals in the herd would have the same sense of danger, just as we had this afternoon when we bumped into that single heifer. So some would soon stop running because they wouldn't really feel all that threatened, and then more and more would stop until they just came to a standstill. It's a bit harder to run seriously if there's a lot of guys ahead of you standing in the way."

"Exactly. They're basically too lazy to run, and on top of that they're very arrogant and aggressive. They easily square up for a fight, because they have this self-confidence."

I chuckled. "Yeah. They're also inquisitive. A bit like cattle. You got me wondering. If you had to hunt a lot of meat for, say, commercial reasons, and you were really fit, or had a good horse, would you not be able to keep chasing after them, shooting one or two every time you caught up with them? They'd get tired quite quickly."

Gerhard chuckled thoughtfully. "I'd say it depends on how dense the bush is. I think that unless they are a big herd they would tend to disperse quickly, and you might end up having to run down one or two individuals."

"*Hmm*, I think you're right. When I was a little boy, my grandfather ran a cattle ranch north of the Soutpansberg. It was some way from a little siding called Mopani, a tiny place clinging desperately to the main north road. It had an oily little garage with a hammer-wielding bush mechanic and two faded petrol pumps in front, and a general store where you could buy anything from groceries to tires. It was also the place where the mailbag got dropped by the railway bus. It was the center of the local community, the place where the local legends got told and retold by the storytellers."

"Nice," Gerhard chuckled wistfully.

"*Ja.* Very quaint. Anyway, my grandfather's ranch was even named after Mopani—'Mopani Ranch.' It was a huge tract of land—I guess twenty-five thousand acres or more. He didn't live on the ranch; he had another farm near Louis Trichardt on the southern side of the mountain and that is where he lived.

"The cattle he kept there were Afrikaner—you know, the red ones with the hump on the neck and the long horns. There were a few hundred head of them and they would get herded together about once a year or so to select the ones to be marketed, but for the rest they would more or less roam around in the bush and hardly ever see humans. They actually became almost feral, and, in general, Afrikaners by nature have a tendency to be a little wild and aggressive.

"The rounding up once a year was a major operation of a few days for several horsemen. It was dangerous work because the cattle were really wild and often aggressive, too . . . and they had formidable horns. The cows had to defend their calves against leopards and hyenas, and they did so very effectively, but they were also quite effective against humans as well!

"Anyway, most of the farmers practiced a kind of extensive cattle farming. It's really a semidesert, that area, with severe droughts quite regularly, so the cattle need to be able to roam freely over large areas in order to find food. They are like game in that sense. Those cattle became semibrowsers and would live off mopane leaves when the grass ran out."

"Sounds like my kind of farming," Gerhard sighed wistfully.

"*Ja*, I've often told you, we were born thirty years too late. We missed all the fun. Anyway, once, when I was visiting my grandfather, I went with him to another ranch that was owned by people by the name of Nel, if I recall correctly. The Nels lived some fifteen miles or so farther west, deeper into the *gramadoelas*,[4] and we went there so my grandfather could buy some cattle.

"Now, the farther one went away from the main north road, the more primitive and remote things became. Most of the folks there were very simple people. Although they had possessions, they had very little money, so they lived quite simply. Some were real *takhare*,[5] I guess, but good people.

"The Nel home was a very basic little house built of raw bricks and plastered white with lime, with, I guess, no more than four rooms and, of course, a veranda in front. The father and mother and their son and daughter lived there. The daughter seemed to be in her early twenties and the son probably close to that.

"We arrived around ten o'clock in my grandfather's Ford F100 pickup. It was quite an event, and they all came out for the occasion; they didn't have a vehicle, and few ever came to their place. They used a donkey cart to get to the nearest little shop, which was at Mopani, some thirty miles or so to the east along a winding sand track."

"Splendid, absolutely splendid!" Gerhard exclaimed, delighted.

---

[4] Afrikaans word for remote outback.
[5] Afrikaans word for a rough, uncouth person.

"Yes. Poignant. We were offered coffee, which was ground in a little hand grinder and brewed in a bag in a pot of water on the wood stove. Strong and nice. Very real.

"We were invited onto the *stoep*.[6] The dad took his place in what was clearly his usual seat. It was the only chair on the *stoep*—an ancient chrome and melamine kitchen chair propped against the wall. I sat on the edge of the *stoep*, and the son, who was called Boetie, carried out a chair from the living room for my grandfather, and then he came and sat next to me.

"All the family members were enormous, and overweight, too. The dad was bald as an egg and dressed in oversize rugby shorts, with no shirt and no shoes. His body spilled and drooped over his shorts. It was a weekday, and these must have been his normal working clothes, it seemed to me— probably also his normal place of work.

"He had an enamel jug of water next to him on the floor with a tin mug next to it. Every now and again he would pour some water into the mug and take a swig, and then pour the rest over his head so that it ran down his body and onto the floor to cool him down."

"Sounds quite effective to me," Gerhard said.

"Sure. Now Boetie, he was also enormous. He, too, was wearing oversize rugby shorts and a shirt that had long since lost its sleeves in order to make room for his arms. It hung down over his shorts from his tummy like a curtain. He had an old sports cap on his head, which never seemed to come off. It was a bit small for him and the visor had come loose, leaving a gap where his hair stuck out like an auxiliary visor. He had a pair of tennis shoes on his feet, but the sole of one had come loose, and he had fixed it by simply winding elastoplast around the whole shoe a number of times."

"What a pair," Gerhard chuckled.

"*Ja*, but Sussie, who was the daughter, was even more noteworthy. While we were sitting on the *stoep* discussing the cattle transaction, she wondered off down the track toward the marshy area we had passed on our way up to

---

[6] Afrikaans word for veranda.

the little house. Actually she more like stumbled down because she walked leaning forward, in small jerks, almost stumbling with each step."

"Sounds a bit Frankensteinish," Gerhard said.

"*Ja*, but fortunately she seemed quite good-natured, which was a good thing, because we found out she was enormously strong. After a while she emerged from the reeds pulling a tree-fork sled like the ones we saw in the Save. On top of it was a twenty-gallon drum full of water!" I said, leaning forward to emphasize the incredibility of the sight.

"What!?" Gerhard exclaimed as he sat up abruptly and spilled hot tea on his bare leg. This triggered a disgusted exclamation best not recorded.

"Sure. I'm not joking, pal. She was a strong as a bull. The two of us would hardly have been able to move the damn thing, let alone drag it up the hill. The house was built on a slight rise overlooking the marshy area that had a small natural spring where they got their water."

"You had certainly run into the 'terrible family.' "

"*Ja*, extraordinary. When the dad saw me staring at her, he said, 'She's bringing the water because this afternoon her mother wants to scrub the kitchen floor,' as if he was referring to his jug being refilled!

Anyway, we finally set off for the *kraal* [7] to take a look at the cattle. It was about a quarter-mile away and we went in the Ford, my grandfather and I in front, the dad and Boetie on the back. The dad didn't bother to put on shoes or a shirt in that sun—and the burrs around the kraal didn't even seem to bother him much.

"There were twenty-five young oxen, which the dad had selected for my grandfather. All were about a year old, thin as grass snakes, and mean as caracals. They had been lying down, but they all got to their feet as we approached, and several pawed the ground and tossed their heads at us. They weren't picnic companions. They had learned the hard way that if you're not quick and nasty, you're dead.

---

[7] Afrikaans word for a relatively small and sturdily constructed enclosure where cattle could be kept.

"My grandpa looked them over from the kraal fence. He said sideways to me, 'They've got a lot of potential to put on weight,' and then said to the dad, '"OK, Herklaas, I'll take them. If you could keep them here in the kraal, I'll send over some horsemen to fetch them.'

" 'Nooo, Oom Danie, that won't be necessary. Boetie will quickly bring them through for you.'

"He then turned to the young man and said, 'Boetie, take these over to Oom Danie at Mopani Ranch, my son.'

"Boetie simply said, '*Ja, Pa*,' in a peculiar, high, thin voice, like a boy in puberty, and straightaway he opened the gate and went in to chase them out.

"Of course, they stormed out like a troop of scared bushpigs, nearly running us into the ground, and headed for the trees with Boetie in hot pursuit, whistling and shouting wildly in his thin voice. I didn't think we were ever going to set eyes on that particular group of cattle again, and from the look on my grandfather's face, neither did he.

"When we were alone in the cab of the Ford, he indignantly said to me past the stem of his pipe, 'This is a mess. I'll send over some horsemen, but it will probably be a waste of time. I don't think we'll see these again. Going to have to repeat the whole exercise. Damn Herklaas.'

"We set off bumping along the sand track back to Mopani Ranch, my grandfather every now and then muttering huffily to himself about how stupid Herklaas was.

"To our astonishment, about three miles from the Nel residence, there was Boetie in the road, trotting along at a good clip, with the cattle obediently bunched in front of him—all twenty-five of them. We had hardly arrived at the little bush cottage my grandfather kept at the ranch for his occasional visits and hunting trips when Boetie trotted up with the cattle. They were by then completely exhausted and prepared to go anywhere and do anything he wanted, as long as they could stop running!

"We helped Boetie put them into the kraal because they had to be branded. Then my grandpa offered to take him back home, but, listen to this," I said as I paused for effect.

"He refused! He said in his wheezy voice that he'd just take a drink of water and then he'd trot back quickly. Pal, he had just run fifteen miles through the midday heat, and it was then a bit after three. I mean . . . bloody astonishing, isn't it?

"Look here, you know I'm no slouch when it comes to running. I mean, I can run with the best in the country, but this guy was amazing. Given his awkward build, he was astonishingly mobile. He had kept right up with the cattle, and they hadn't just been trotting along docilely, especially not when they first came out of that kraal and, I can assure you, for quite a distance after that. To have kept them in a bunch, and through all the trees too—it was no mean feat. Then he ran back, as if he were taking a walk around the house!"

Gerhard was shaking his head. "Amazing," he said. "All that from a little house in the *gramadoelas*."

"Yep. As Julius Caesar realized more than two thousand years ago, *Ex Africa semper aliquid novi*. So if you were a man like Boetie, then maybe you could herd a few hundred buffalo like cattle," I continued.

"Sounds to me as if he and his sister could simply run them down and throttle one each," Gerhard snorted.

When we had finished chuckling about the Nels, we decided that I would leave very early the next morning to fetch the vehicle. Gerhard, meanwhile, would go after his buffalo with John and Elias and then would start cutting up the carcasses. We felt that it was a bit more than half a day's walk to the camp. It did not leave us with much of a chance to save any of the buffalo capes, which would degenerate rapidly in the heat without being salted, but, if I went at a good run and could make the return trip in, say, two hours with the vehicle and a lot of salt . . . it was uncertain, but it was worth a try.

I left when the dawn was still a gray smear in the east. I had drunk as much water and tea as I could hold before I left, and carrying only my rifle, ammunition pouch, hunting knife, and a water bottle, I set out at a trot. I had to make the most of the coolness while it lasted. I kept up a steady run, sticking to the edge of the flood plain where the tough elephant grass had mostly been trodden flat by game moving between the forest and the plain, and I had to stop only once, when the sun was just beginning to throw a shadow in front of me, for a small breeding herd of elephant crossing into the bush from the plain.

It was not much after nine when I spotted the camp, already twisting in the dance of the heat waves over the plain—*the wind of the sun*, as I once heard an old African man call it. I trotted in fifteen minutes later, thirsty, hungry, and dead tired, and found the camp almost deserted.

I was somehow disappointed. In a way I felt that I deserved at least a welcome back with a bit of a fuss from Stephan and Mack and Vic after having been out in the bush for so long. Stephan had taken Vic and Mack back up the river in his motorized dugout canoe, and most of the camp hands had been sent out to collect wood, which they had to carry all the way across the flood plain because there was no vehicle other than ours in camp.

I did find Nelson the cook and the kitchen hands fiddling around, and got them to make me some sandwiches from the fresh pot bread Nelson had baked just the previous day to eat along the way and give to the guys in the bush. Nelson was one of those delightful old-style Zimbabwean men—past his forties, well educated, intelligent, and respectful, but comfortable with who he was.

While I stood chewing on my first sandwich, waiting for him to finish the rest, I got all the news and gossip from him. Lost Soul and his companion had arrived with the tusks and had told them fantastical stories of our escapades in the bush. Vic had shot a good buffalo with Mack. They had waited for us to arrive for two days, but finally had to go back—Mack had to meet family members who were coming to visit him in Zimbabwe, and Vic had to get back to work. Mack and Vic were going to fly out with Frank. Stephan had spent most of the time while we were away writing in his hut. Jo'burg had been paid by Vic, and had left for home when we did not turn up. They had had rain three times already and were busy packing up to move out before they got rained in. Danny had already started breaking his camp and moving back to civilization.

I took three 110-pound bags of salt and two men from the kitchen and started back with the Land Cruiser, hoping to collect some of the others, especially an experienced skinner, on the way. I got back to my bush companions before midday, having been fortunate enough to run into two of Stephan's crew who both claimed they were skinners, and by early afternoon we were back in camp with the two buffalo still in salvageable shape.

So Far Away, But Sometimes So Near

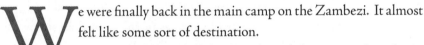

CHAPTER 12

W e were finally back in the main camp on the Zambezi. It almost felt like some sort of destination.

There was something extravagantly luxurious about being surrounded by such a profusion of conveniences after living at "ground zero" for so long. We had a slow, warm shower with enormous quantities of water that Nelson warmed on his cooking fire to just the right temperature, which we let soak into the thorn cuts and the cracked skin. Then a clean towel, and the crisp feel of a clean shirt and shorts—my clothes had become stiff and shiny from accumulated dirt and sweat, and they were so tattered from the ravages of the African thorn veld that I simply discarded them—to the delight of Lost Soul, who happened to be closest to my hut when I undressed.

We took up positions (in chairs) at the fire, each with a (reasonably cool) beer we felt we were justified in pinching from Stephan's precious stock, to watch the sun die in vast crimson and orange and purple over the upstream reaches of the Zambezi. Stephan had not arrived back from delivering Mack and Vic, and we assumed that he would be spending the night at Danny's outfit.

Nelson didn't even bother to call us to the table. He simply brought us a tray each (just a crude plank) with our food, and we ate at the fire—a buffalo stew with some vegetables that he had miraculously brought to reasonable palpability.

Afterward we sat quietly in the pale light of the half moon listening to the African night and reflecting back on those moments over the past days that, although experienced in common, burned differently in each of our minds. Tomorrow we would have to start packing and thinking of the real world, but tonight we could still drift along in the dream. We lingered late, watching the stars slowly shift across the blue-tinged black and reminiscing about our many wanderings together and the people that had shared bits of it with us.

There was Piet Meiring, our close mutual friend, always the cool-headed peacemaker and moderator of our fiery souls; Johan, Gerhard's brother, older than us, always rising above our reckless impetuousness, and sometimes our ridicule, with serene poise; Tom Orford, seasoned old bush veteran, mentor, often guiding our wild energies in the right direction; Gordon Cormack, respected bush companion; Don Price and Clive and Ian Lennox, teachers and bush companions; and Quintus, hunting companion, plucky, and a fine sportsman.

There were our parents, wives, and children, ever fearful and worried and (I suspected) a bit bemused about our escapades, but grateful and warm at our return.

There were our trackers, the sharers of our days and our campfires on our many hunts and wanderings, our teachers, our confidants, our close companions: Techu, Njani, Mazenya, Jo'burg, Elias, and Kalemba.

Finally, there were those who we had not both personally met but who had come vividly to life through the stories told around the campfires, or during the midday breaks, or during the long bumpy rides in the Land Cruiser: Rudolf Ross, Jackie, Vastudu, Ferdie Smith, old Johannes, old Daiel, and both our fathers and grandfathers.

++++++

The thin sickle of the moon was already past its zenith when we drifted to our huts with the bedding clean and cool and smelling of the sun. That night I dreamed about a great herd of buffaloes we were stalking. We saw them moving among the trees, but they were churning up so much dust that we could not see which one to shoot. Then suddenly there was a young bull, black and shiny, charging us through the haze. He tossed Gerhard over his back, and Gerhard sailed through the air slowly, his back arched and his arms thrown out gracefully as if in a fantastic gymnastic move. He somersaulted and landed on his feet and went on his haunches to break the impact, but he did not get up.

The buffalo slunk away, laughing, now suddenly with a human face, and I ran to Gerhard to ask him if he was all right. He said "Yes," but a thin trickle of blood was running down his chin and he did not get up. He said softly I must run after the buffalo and kill it, but I was overcome by him sitting there so still, talking to me but not looking at me, and I did not see the point of running after the buffalo with the human face because that would not make Gerhard get up.

I tried to explain to Gerhard that I would not be able to skin the buffalo alone, and that I would need help to break open a road for the Land Cruiser, but he still didn't get up, and it was getting dark, and suddenly there were lots of people shouting that we had to look for the buffalo. They moved around with vehicles and lights looking for it, but I knew there was nothing, absolutely nothing, I could do to make Gerhard get up again, and all the commotion seemed futile to me. So I sat next to him against the tree trunk in the night and he disappeared, but as I waited for the dawn I could sometimes feel that he was next to me against the tree trunk.

++++++

The early morning was mercifully kept at bay for a little longer by the closed lattice door, but eventually the day of preparing for the journey back had to be faced: cleaning and checking our guns and our the vehicle, sorting out the equipment and remaining supplies, and packing, doing our best for the trophies under the circumstances, making final arrangements with Stephan, who arrived around midday, and a lot more such necessary but mundane tasks.

It was as if we had somehow become detached from the bush, almost like it was just something we walked past in the street. Our senses had refocused on lists and tasks and equipment and money for Elias and John and the others, and plans for the next day's journey, and time. We and Elias and John became like objects to each other. It was as if the bush was standing back, anciently gazing upon us as we scurried around in our important little world of preparation.

There was a sad detachment, a lack of intimacy and passion, in the matter-of-fact evening that followed, and in the departure in the uncertain gray of the morning. The fond and lingering farewell it was supposed to be got lost in the immediacy of the start on the journey back, and I recognized this from previous return journeys. The magic of adventure seemed to dissolve in preparatory activities and in the focus on the next problem in the routine existence of all concerned. Gerhard and I would both start the journey back into our own separate worlds, withdrawing into long silences filled with the drone of the Land Cruiser's engine and the noise of the wind through the cab, broken only by utility talk.

We dropped Elias at the elephant path and said our good-byes, and I looked back at him standing so slender next to his enormous load of buffalo meat, holding his ax and his knobkerrie and his loose possessions in his impala skin, so alone, so near, but suddenly so far away, almost ephemeral. I felt a deep sense of sadness and loss, and I had to keep my head turned away and swallow hard. As I waved to him and he lifted his ax in response, I thought he looked like Gerhard for a second. Did I leave behind the wrong one, or was he still there, at the wheel of the Land Cruiser? Then Elias was gone behind the trees, and the rest of the lonely journey into the future lay ahead.